250 *Favourite*
CURRIES
& ACCOMPANIMENTS

Other books by Pat Chapman published by Piatkus

The Curry Club Indian Restaurant Cookbook

The Curry Club Favourite Restaurant Curries

The Curry Club Indian Vegetarian Cookbook

The Curry Club Favourite Middle Eastern Recipes

The Curry Club Chinese Restaurant Cookbook

The Curry Club Balti Curry Cookbook

Curry Club Tandoori and Tikka Dishes

Curry Club Vindaloo and Other Hot Curries

The Good Curry Guide

The Little Curry Book

250 *Favourite* CURRIES

& ACCOMPANIMENTS

PAT CHAPMAN

PIATKUS

Acknowledgements

The author and publisher would like to thank the following shops for their very generous loan of items for use in the photographs:

Global Village for ceramics, copper and brassware, textiles, Indian artefacts and carvings

David Mellor for baskets and cookware

Thanks also to the **Indian Tourist Office** for the use of the photographs on pages 151, 186, 219 and 243

First published in 1992 by
Judy Piatkus (Publishers) Ltd
5 Windmill Street, London W1P 1HF
First paperback edition 1993
Reprinted 1996

The moral right of the author has been asserted

*A catalogue record for this book is available
from the British Library*

ISBN 0-7499-1185-9
ISBN 0-7499-1293-6 (pbk)

Edited by Heather Rocklin and Susan Fleming
Designed by Paul Saunders
Photography by James Murphy
Food for photography prepared by Dominique Chapman
Illustrations by Hanife Hassan O'Keeffe

Repro by Hilo Offset Ltd, Colchester
Typeset in Linotron Sabon by
Computerset Ltd, Harmondsworth
Printed and bound in Great Britain by
Bath Press Colourbooks, Blantyre

Contents

Foreword

I was born in 1940 in Ealing, London, and from very early on I developed a passion for spicy food which you could say was practically inherited.

One branch of my family, the wealthy upper-class Lawrences, had been living in India for at least three generations when, in 1857, the great mutiny occurred. Nearly all the British were wiped out. Suddenly, my great grandmother, Alice Henrietta, became a three-year-old orphan, without family, wealth or status.

Another branch of my family, the humble working-class Lemmons, had also been in India for several generations. In 1872 Alexander Lemmon, a Government telegraph clerk, went in search of a wife and found Alice. That year they were married.

Their daughter, my grandmother, came to live in England in 1930, ending my family's 170-year relationship with the country, but bringing back with her a love and understanding of Indian food. Not only did I regularly enjoy granny's home-made curries, but at the age of six I was taken to an Indian restaurant in London (there were only three at that time). The restaurant was Shafi's in Gerrard Street, sadly long-since closed. I loved it. Visits became twice-yearly treats and the old Punjabi proprietor would make a terrific fuss of me, taking me into the kitchen, and cooking special goodies for me that didn't appear on the menu.

Not surprisingly, I was soon well on the road to becoming a curryholic! As soon as I could I was experimenting with Indian cooking. I bought the few Indian cookbooks there were, and tried to recreate the style of the Indian curry house at home. My friends began to regard me as something of an 'expert'. But curry house ingredients and information were hard to find. Garlic had to be ordered specially and ginger was unobtainable. Some spices such as cloves had to be ordered from the chemist! Occasionally a special trip had to be taken to buy ingredients from London's only specialist store, the Bombay Emporium (also long since closed).

This is almost impossible to conceive of now, in the 1990s, when we have supermarkets on every corner bulging with exotic vegetables and over 7,000 Indian restaurants dotted all over the UK. But as a boy in Ealing I remember the opening of the first Asian grocer in Southall, and the first Indian restaurant in West London (mid-fifties), and the subsequent remarkable growth of both the ethnic population and the Indian restaurant in the UK. The first UK supermarkets had yet to open.

Over the years, I built up a huge pool of information about spicy food and curry, which I felt could be usefully passed on to others. So I decided to form an organisation for this purpose and founded the Curry Club in January 1982, since when it has built up a membership of several thousands. It has a marchioness, some lords and ladies, a captain or two of industry, generals, admirals, and air marshals (not to mention a sprinkling of ex-colonels), and it has celebrity names — actresses, politicians, rock stars and sportsmen. It also counts among its members an airline (Air India), a former RN warship (HMS *Hermes*) and a hotel chain (the Taj group). It has 15 members whose name is Curry or Currie, 20 called Rice, and several with the name Spice or Spicer, Cook, Fry, Frier, or Fryer, and one Boiling. It has a Puri (a restaurant owner), a Paratha and a Nan, a good many Mills and Millers, one Dal and a Lentil, an Oiler, a Gee (but no Ghee), and a Butter but no Marj (several Majories though, and a Majoram and a Minty). It also has several Longs and Shorts, Thins and Broads, one Fatt and one Wide, and a Chilley and a Coole.

It has members on every continent, including a good number of Asian members, but by and large the membership is a typical cross-section of the Great British Public, ranging in age from teenage to dotage, and in occupation from refuse collectors to receivers, high-street traders to high-court judges, tax inspectors to taxi drivers. There are students and pensioners, millionaires and unemployed . . . thousands of people who have just one thing in common — a love of curry and spicy foods.

Members receive a bright and colourful magazine four times a year, which has regular features on curry and the curry lands. It includes news items, recipes, reports on restaurants, picture features and contributions from members and professionals alike. The information is largely concerned with curry, but by popular demand it now includes regular input on other exotic and spicy cuisines such as those of the Middle East and China. We have produced a wide selection of publications, including the books listed on page 288, all published by Piatkus. There is also a cookery video.

Obtaining the ingredients required for Indian, Oriental and Middle Eastern cooking can be difficult, but The Curry Club makes it easy, with a comprehensive range of Curry Club products, including spice mixes, chutneys, pickles, papadoms, sauces and curry pastes. These are available from major food stores and specialist delicatessens up and down the country. If they are not stocked near you, there is the Club's well-established and efficient mail-order service. Hundreds of items are stocked, including spices, pickles, pastes, dry foods, tinned foods, gift items, publications and specialist kitchen and tableware.

On the social side, the Club holds residential weekend cookery courses and gourmet nights to selected restaurants.

Top of the list is our regular Curry Club Gourmet trip to India and other spicy countries. We take a small group of curry enthusiasts to the chosen country and tour the incredible sights, in between sampling the delicious foods of each region.

If you would like more information about The Curry Club, write (enclosing a SAE) to: **The Curry Club, PO Box 7, Haslemere, Surrey GU27 1EP.**

Introduction

The phone rang one wet and windy afternoon in March 1989. On the line was a representative from the Government of India telling me about a forthcoming event in India – The Spice Fair. At first I thought she was trying to sell me something. Finally I realised I was being invited to join a small party of journalists to attend what promised to be a most colourful and exciting event. Our five-day stay was programmed to be packed full of fascinating activities centred on the Spice Fair itself and around the beautiful state of Kerala.

I am lucky enough to visit India once or twice a year. I go there to work, of course, if you can call swanning around as a VIP guest 'work', or on other occasions, escorting groups of gourmets around India as part of our Curry Club activities. I have been to India 15 times in the last ten years. Added end to end, so to speak, the time spent there would total over 18 months. Part of my self-imposed 'work' involves culinary observation – I'm a kind of kitchen spy. In the world of cooking there is always so much to learn. Wherever I go I scour the alimentary landscape for something 'new'. It might be in a shop window, at a street kiosk, in the market, at a restaurant, in a hotel or at somebody's home. Utensils, produce, raw ingredients and cooked items – all are studied with equal intensity.

One of the most exciting recent culinary developments in India is the establishment of two astonishingly good restaurants, by the Welcomgroup Sheraton Hotel chain, at their Delhi and Bombay flagship hotels. Both restaurants are called 'Dum Pukht' and their select menus are based on the food of Lucknow in northern India. Lucknow is the culinary capital of India. It was once the seat of the extraordinary royal Nawabs of Oudh, whose exploits and wealth 200 years ago matched, then surpassed, their one-time rulers, the Moghul emperors, who were by then in decline. The Nawabs' pursuit of the good life was legendary, especially at the dinner table. One learned work of the time, the *Guzashta Lucknow*,

by philosopher Abdul Halim Sharar, says 'the most important activity in human life is eating. As any community or nation progresses, its diet is the most salient guide to its refinement'! Whereas the Moghuls delighted in rich creamy dishes such as Korma and Roghan Gosht, the Nawabs preferred subtler, aromatic slow-cooked dishes. Many unique dishes were invented at the Lucknow court by teams of highly prized chefs. Dum Pukht cuisine was one such invention. Literally it means 'finishing off a partly cooked dish under a head of steam'. Nawabi chefs par-cooked an aromatic dish then sealed the pot's lid with a ring of pastry, allowing the dish to slow cook to its conclusion (see pages 125 and 234).

The modern day revival of this style of cooking is equally interesting. The President of the Indian Sheraton group was on a visit to a local Lucknow restaurant a few years ago. The story goes that he was so amazed by the lightness and inventiveness of the food that he asked to meet the chef, the 50-year-old Mohammed Imtiaz Qureshi, who comes from a long line of master chefs going right back to those royal chefs of the Nawabs. The President was so impressed that he offered Qureshi, who had never felt the need to learn to read and write, not only a job at the group's flagship hotel, but a complete restaurant and total control over its staffing, the menu and the food buying. His Dum Pukht restaurant duly opened at the Searock Sheraton hotel in Bombay and Qureshi was suddenly thrust into fame and the acclaim of the most critical of Indians – Bombay society. Before long his restaurant was duplicated at Delhi's Maurya Sheraton hotel to equal acclaim.

The point I am making is two-fold. Firstly it is really thrilling to find new culinary delights in India. But there is a more important point. Until half a century ago, it was the Indian royals who pioneered and financed their nation's cultural and culinary development. Abdul Halim Sharar might well have said it in his tome. Art, music, dance, costume, crafts, literature, philosophy, architecture: all benefited from royal patronage and encouragement. Most important of all, and given equal status to the arts, were the activities of the kitchen. The royal head chef was a man of immense power and influence, almost as great as the warriors and politicians of the day.

India's independent democracy has seen to it that their royals have had their powers cut to size. The days of the lavish courts are long since gone. The ex-maharajas still live well in their palaces, with more servants than they can count, but no longer are they willing or able to finance and pioneer new things. The story was the same world wide, and it could have meant the end of the great chef and culinary innovation.

Fortunately a new form of grandiose establishment was already gaining its place in India – the luxury hotel. In the last decade India's hotel industry has been transformed. Her great hotel chains vie with each other for culinary excellence, each operating rigorous chef-apprentice schemes and each encouraging initiative and innovation from the brighter ones. From where else today does the great chef emerge? And with what better reward? Their restaurants are jewels in the culinary crown – their chefs the true masters. Qureshi and his Dum Pukht restaurants are the proof, and they were the major discovery of my last visit to India.

But it was not the only one. For example, I discovered Bombay's favourite fast food – *Pao Bhajee*. It's a quick vegetable curry served with a bun, a kind of Indian 'baked beans on toast'. I was in good company when I found it and the story and its recipe appears on pages 176 and 248. I can't imagine how I hadn't come across it before.

Another wonderful discovery was the Goan sausage used in a cooking demonstration specially staged for my Curry Club gourmet group. We were at the then new and sumptuous Ramada Renaissance hotel, and were privileged to have Alice, the hotel's Goan-speciality chef, demonstrate for us.

Her Goan Sausage Pullao Rice really captivated me, so much so in fact, that one of the young waiters helping at the demonstration could not fail to notice my interest. In a scene reminiscent of an early James Bond movie, he whisked me aside and into a dark corner. Then, in an entrepreneurial whisper, asked if I would like a roll of Goan sausage to take home with me. Apparently his grandmother made them. He could bring it over next day. Accepting his offer, I advised him that, as we were leaving next morning, the transaction would have to take place early. Sure enough at 8 am, as we checked out of the hotel, the young man sidled up, trying to appear invisible, presumably to avoid being noticed by the management. A scruffy, oily brown paper parcel was proffered. The young man also suggested (for the first time) that a rather startling sum of rupees was expected (obviously far in excess of the value of the sausages) – my fault for not establishing the value of the transaction at the outset. Anyway an outburst from me would have certainly blown James Bond's cover. The rupees changed hands and deftly disappeared into the crutch area of his tunic, then off he sidled. A more attention-drawing or comical routine could not have been better scripted for a TV sit-com.

The suspicious package was duly carried as hand baggage from Goa to Bombay, and ultimately to my freezer in Haslemere, fortunately without attracting the attention of Bombay or Heathrow customs. Such incidents leave indelible memories, which in this case I can share with you, for indeed the very same sausages appear in the photograph and recipe on page 230.

So many of the recipes in my collection trigger off some association or a story surrounding them. On another occasion, for example, I well remember visiting Tippu Sultan's summer palace near Mysore. Tippu Sultan was the 18th-century ruler of Southern India, as powerful in the South as the Nawabs were in the North. Tippu's palace is an intriguing place surrounded by well-manicured lawns and regimental rows of colourful flower beds. I was 'working' again, this time leading a different Curry Club group of about 20. We had brought a picnic with us, prepared by the local hotel, and we spread this out under the shady trees. All around us were hundreds of other picnickers, all Indian tourists. Among them was a large party of Indian schoolgirls, all identically and immaculately dressed in straw boaters, crisp white shirts, navy ties and crimson dresses. It was a stunning sight on the green velvety sun-drenched lawns. But suddenly we became aware that we, as the only white faces, were ourselves the focus of attention. Dozens of Indians came over and politely requested that we pose for them, while they clicked away with camera after camera. It was most memorable. So was that picnic. One of the dishes we enjoyed under the trees that day can be found on page 75.

Then again, whilst I was leafing through my records I came across a visiting card belonging to the owner of Delhi's foremost *paan* shop. He is known simply as 'Prince Pan', but his simple kiosk turns over thousands of transactions daily in one of India's major industries (see pages 270-74). We know little of that industry in the west, apart, that is, from the nibbling of a few colourful tit-bits after the curry meal. I hope my final chapter on Après Curry explains and makes paan more interesting.

Cooking is a combination of skill and techniques honed and perfected and handed down over generations. Very little is new and original, especially in India, where traditional methods and tastes are greatly respected. But there is scope for innovations, and I am delighted to include new ideas from Chef Qureshi whom we met earlier (see page 8), and another master chef, Satish Arora, whose work is always inspirational. I have been privileged enough to have been invited into Satish's kitchen at the unique Taj Mahal Intercontinental hotel on several occasions. It is here that I learn the most, and it is always a thrill to find something new, and ultimately to pass it on in the pages of my books.

Such chefs have always inspired me to try innovative ideas of my own and it is an equal pleasure to pass them on too. Maybe you will feel inspired enough to have a try at inventing your own dishes. My Sag Paneer Charminar (Spinach and Cheese Pie) on page 196 was inspired by a visit to Hyderabad, but is in fact a modification of the Greek spanokopita filo pastry pie, and has an egg on top. It is not strictly an Indian dish – yet the paneer cheese and the spicing could not be found elsewhere. The combinations work well and taste good. The story behind it may amuse you. It was March again, but this time in 1985. I was on a business trip to Hyderabad in Central South India. It was midday, by which time it was almost violently hot. I was on my own, quietly admiring the *Char-minar,* a gorgeous, compact, white monumental gate, known as the 'Arc de Triomphe' of the East, built by one of the Nizams (more major Indian royals) in 1591. I soon became aware of the fact that I was not alone: a wiry old Indian with long white matted hair and wearing an orange *dhoti* (long Indian loin-cloth) was beckoning to me in a compelling and urgent manner. Surely he was a fakir, a holy man? I turned towards him and with a deft shove he pushed me into the adjacent mosque. He had evidently appointed himself as my guide – and I had fallen for it. There were at least three problems: he didn't speak English, the sun was becoming unbearable and you take your shoes off in a mosque. Immediately I found that the open marble courtyard floor was too hot for my now bare feet. My 'guide', also barefooted, seemed totally unperturbed. Then, in a surprise move, he produced a whole egg from his *dhoti* and broke it on the floor. At once it began to fry. So did my feet.

He then skilfully positioned himself to obstruct my exit, and with palm outstretched croaked, '*bakshish, bakshish*' (money, money). Hopping from foot to foot I couldn't pay him fast enough for my freedom. Having done so I fled past him to the nearest patch of shade. When I got there and turned to look back, he and his egg had vanished as if by magic. After a more careful look I realised this wasn't even the mosque – that was next door. I had been had for 100 rupees – just £3 at the time, but two days' wages for a labourer. And the guide – a fake of course – was certainly no fakir!

The story doesn't quite end there. Two days later I was 1,500 miles further north in Kashmir, negotiating with travel agents. Following my sizzling experience, I decided to leave my suitcase in Delhi and travel light in just sandals, slacks and a short sleeved shirt. I could not have got it more wrong! At 8,500 feet above sea level, Gulmarg was just beginning its post-winter thaw. It's a ski resort and as such was in full swing. Indian skiers in full gear – boots, gloves, anoraks and woolly hats – stared at me in disbelief. It was midday again and the sun was shining, but that same egg broken on the ground here would have frozen solid. My sandalled feet were still sore with blisters from the con trick and now there was a real chance of frostbite!

Mad dogs and Englishmen!

The last ten years have produced so many memories I could fill a book with them! But that's enough for now – after all this is a book of recipes not my memoirs, and I have no shortage of recipes to share with you either.

Someone asked me the other day what I was working on. When I explained about this book he was incredulous. How was it possible to find 250 more Indian recipes? The fact is that curry and spicy food are the staple foods of over one billion people, one-fifth of the world's population. Cooking with spices has been practised for nearly 5,000 years, with the only major refinements taking place during the courts of the Indian royals of the 16th and 17th centuries. And, as I've already said, there is no shortage of recipes to choose from. Here are over 250 of my favourite, previously unpublished recipes. Amongst them I hope you'll find many agreeable things, many old favourites and many new discoveries. I have included a few recipes from other 'curry' countries outside India, including Afghanistan, Pakistan, Nepal, Bangladesh, Burma, Thailand, Malaysia and Indonesia. But most of my recipes are a combination of delicious authentic recipes from India itself, popular restaurant dishes and some exciting innovations.

And, as with my previous curry books, this one is suitable for the newcomer to Indian cooking and the veteran alike and it may be used in conjunction with any of my other books, or it may be used on its own. It is completely self contained and will enable the reader to produce anything from a crispy nibble to a banquet, a snack to a supper, a starter to a dessert. I hope you'll enjoy them all.

But I have to confess that as I write this at my desk in Haslemere, a wind is howling and icy hail is slamming against my window. I cannot help but dream of fried eggs and frostbite, of picnics and spicy sausages, and of chefs, sultans and nawabs, nizams and fakirs, and of palm trees and Spice Fairs and sun and more sun.

You see, it's March again, and I must confess, I'm hoping for the phone to ring . . .

Pat Chapman

Pat Chapman
The Curry Club
Haslemere

Culinary Information

Cooking Indian food is a great adventure, as I hope the later chapters of this book will prove, but first some basics. I have gathered together information in this chapter which will be of use to new and existing curry cooks alike.

We look first at the equipment needed in the kitchen, from mixing bowls to microwaves. We then look at cooking terms and methods, including stir-frying and the casserole. With growing concern about the safety of food we next look at the keeping of curries, freezing and colourings.

Most people who cook frequently develop skills which use all their senses of sight, sound, smell, touch and taste, to bring a particular dish to completion. Temperatures and measures are almost ignored, things being done by instinct. I hope you will use my recipes as a spur or guide ultimately, but for the first few times you'll probably follow them word for word. So please read the paragraphs about cooking methods, measures and portions.

The Indian meal can be served and consumed exactly in the same manner as a European meal. The section on serving and dining will give you a lot of ideas, especially about entertaining. The chapter concludes with advice about alcoholic beverages. (For other beverages see pages 264-9.)

EQUIPMENT

Indian cuisine has been around for centuries and, traditionally, its preparation is a devoted and time-consuming job. Even today the old methods are the only methods in the villages and smaller towns in the curry lands, where electricity and running water are unknown, and time is unlimited. Fortunately the meal we get using modern appliances is indistinguishable from one prepared the old way and all my recipes use the simplest and most effective method to obtain the final result. Perhaps there is one area where traditional methods are best, and that is the tandoor or clay oven, usually dug several feet into the ground and fired by charcoal. Gas or electric ovens just do not match the flavour of tandoori-style cooking (but that's not to say the results we get are poor).

You should possess the following items to cook the recipes in this book:

- knives
- chopping board
- mixing bowls: large, medium, small
- large sieve
- large slotted spoon for use in deep-frier
- deep-frier (a pan with a basket, or electric deep-friers are wonderful)
- *karahi* or wok or large frying pan. (The *karahi* is the Indian equivalent of a wok.)
- *tava* or griddle pan or large frying pan. (The *tava* is a flat griddle pan.)
- casserole dish(es): 4-5 pint (2.25-2.75 litre)
- saucepans with lids: 6 pint (3.5 litre), 4 pint (2.25 litre), 2¼ pint (1.4 litre)
- oven tray(s)
- grill tray with wire rack
- bamboo steamer, 8 inch (20cm), or a metal steamer, a large pan, with a perforated inner pan, and a tight-fitting lid. (A colander over a pan with a lid can substitute.)
- the sprung-type mechanical vegetable choppers save work and are very much cheaper than the electric equivalents
- a barbecue is a great asset in the summer

Electrical Tools

It is with these tools that we can save time.

Blender
The device for making soups and purées requiring some liquid but which achieves the correct texture for curries.

Food Processor
An expensive but immensely useful kitchen tool. Its standard blade can be used to make purées,

although even with added water these are not of as fine a texture as those made in a blender. Other blades include vegetable shredders and slicers.

Coffee Grinder
An effective way to grind spices. It can handle most spices and grind them reasonably finely. Best results are obtained when the spices are 'roasted' (see page 28) and cooled first and the machine is not loaded past the half-way mark. A damp wipe leaves the machine ready to handle coffee beans without tainting them.

Spice Mill
A new attachment for 'Chef' units which grinds all spices, raw or roasted, to any degree of fineness you want.

Dough Hook Attachment
A great time and effort saver.

Rice Cooker
In my view, a total extravagance. But if you want one or have one, then use it and you'll get good results.

Warming Drawer
In the rice chapter I mention the use of a warming drawer. Some ovens have these, but if yours doesn't, use the oven itself on its lowest setting.

Microwave
A much maligned kitchen tool, the microwave seems to be regarded by some as the enemy of real cooking. I've heard people say that 'real' restaurants or cooks would not use a microwave. This is rubbish, of course. It gets its poor reputation as the purveyor of soggy pub pies, a role in which it performs at its worst. The microwave is a high-speed cooker with limitations.

Like the food processor, it is invaluable in some roles and useless in others. It is great for fast thawing of frozen foods, for casseroling and for reheating wet dishes. It boils water fast and is excellent for blanching vegetables, and it cooks papadoms. But in my experience, it does not handle the initial frying (bargar) of spices and purées effectively, and it is hopeless for cooking or reheating pastry.

Microwaves vary in power from 350 watts to 2,000 watts (the latter being ultra-powerful, very fast catering units), the average being 650 watts. Cooking times depend on the power of your particular machine, so again your own experience is your best guide. I'm not absolutely sold on the theory that microwaving detracts from flavours. There seems to be no scientific reason for it.

Pressure Cookers
These will indeed cook many things very fast. But I'm old-fashioned and find they make things mushy and rather tasteless. I thought I'd found the perfect use for my pressure cooker when cooking lentils, which it does 150 per cent faster than the conventional method, until a lentil got stuck in the relief valve one time. It was lucky that I noticed it early on, when the hissy jingling stopped. Even so, it had built up a dangerous pressure, and I've heard stories of exploding cookers. So I went off the whole idea. New pressure cookers, however, should be fine.

COOKING TERMS

This is a short guide to Indian and English cooking terms used in this book.

Bake	— cooking by dry heat in an oven
Barbecue	— open-air cooker, usually a pan containing charcoal with a cooking rack over it
Bargar	— frying, specifically of whole spices
Bhoona	— stir-frying, specifically of the spice paste
Boil	— cooking food in water in excess of 212°F (100°C)
Braise	— slow cooking in a pot with minimal liquid
Broil	— grilling
Casserole	— slow oven cooking in a covered pot
Deep-fry	— fast cooking by immersing ingredients in ample hot oil
Dum	— pot-roasting in a tightly enclosed pot
Fry	— cooking in shallow fat

Grill	–	cooking by radiant heat from top or bottom
Griddle	–	flat pan or heavy cast-iron plate with or without ribs, ideal for steak cooking
Hob	–	cooking surface with heat sources
Hot plate	–	flat heavy steel plate heated from underneath upon which food is cooked
Kalia	–	stewing
Korma	–	initially frying food then slow cooking (casseroling) until the water content completely evaporates
Oven	–	enclosed chamber with heat source
Pot-roast	–	casseroling but with more liquid
Reduce	–	boiling a liquid or sauce to achieve evaporation and to concentrate flavours and texture
Roast	–	originally cooking by naked flame over a spit. Now baking in an oven
Salamander	–	type of grill used in the professional kitchen
Sauté	–	frying
Simmer	–	cooking in a liquid maintained at just below boiling point
Spit-roast	–	cooking ingredients on a rotating skewer over an open flame or in the oven
Steam	–	cooking food above boiling water
Stew	–	cooking main ingredient(s) from start to finish in a liquid base
Stir-fry	–	cooking food in a flat frying pan or *karahi* or wok with minimal oil or water, stirring almost continuously until cooked.

COOKING METHODS

The success of cooking curry depends on properly blending and cooking out the rawness of ingredients. This is especially important with meat and poultry curries, which need sustained, fairly hot temperatures for up to 1 hour. Traditionally in India they would be cooked in a container on a stove with much stirring, or in a clay pot with lid, left on a wood or charcoal fire to look after itself, simmering away for hours. That's the way it has been done for centuries and that's the way it's done to this day in all but the wealthier Indian houses. But with modern temperature-controlled ovens, we can dispense with tradition and use technology. I find **casseroling** (braising) gives the best results for most meat curries. The heat from the oven is non-directional – i.e. it heats the dish up from all directions – and although I use a moderately hot temperature, the contents will not burn nor stick provided you follow the following method.

You need a casserole pot of 4-5 pint (2.25-2.75 litre) capacity, with a good lid. Preheat the oven to 375°F/190°C/Gas 5. Pre-fry the garlic, ginger and onion to help cook out raw tastes. (Each recipe which uses this method details the pre-frying stages.) Place the meat into the casserole pot along with the pre-fried items, and mix well. Put the lid on and the pot on to a rack in the centre of the oven. Total timing in the oven will vary according to what type of meat is being used. I find lamb takes longer than stewing steak, for example, and one lamb may be more tender than another, so a little testing is wise. But the range is 45 minutes to 1¼ hours.

After 20 minutes or so take the pot out, inspect and stir. Add a little water if the contents look dry and add further ingredients if the recipe requires it. Return the pot to the oven.

Inspect and stir again after around 40 minutes. Again add water if necessary. Taste and add salt at this stage.

If tender turn off the oven and hold the casserole in the oven until you wish to serve (it will be all right for up to 30 minutes). Or continue cooking as dictated by the tenderness of the meat. Once you use this method, common sense will show you what to do.

The alternative to the casserole method is to simmer in a karahi or heavy 4-5 pint (2.25-2.75 litre) saucepan on top of the stove, on the hob. The heat must be very low, and you should stir frequently. Add a little water if it looks like sticking. The cooking time will be longer.

COOKING VEGETABLES

Until well into this century, vegetables were regarded with considerable dislike. This was probably due to the cooking method.

They were invariably overcooked – not by the odd minute or two, but by hours. I have in my granny's old cookery book, dated 1898, a number of vegetable recipes. To cook carrots, it states (and I quote verbatim), 'put them in boiling water with some salt, and boil them from two to three hours. Very young carrots will require one hour.' I don't need to test that recipe to picture the results. Little wonder vegetables were detested.

The concept of minimal cooking to retain the crunch and goodness of vegetables is relatively new. I should make the point that this is the way I prefer my vegetables so you'll find that my cooking times in the recipes that follow are very brief. If you prefer a softer texture, cook for longer.

These are the three stove-top cooking techniques for vegetables.

Boiling

Bring an ample quantity of stock or water to the boil. Add the prepared raw vegetables and simmer until you have the texture you require. Keep the liquid for subsequent stock.

Steaming

This technique retains the most flavour. Water is boiled in the steamer base. The vegetables are placed in the steamer tray which fits snugly above and clear of the boiling water. Put the lid on and steam until you get the texture you require. It is well worth buying a proper steamer if you don't already have one, but a pan with a suitably sized colander and a good-fitting lid will do. Chinese bamboo steamers are good too, for use on a rack in the wok or karahi.

Stir-frying

Some vegetables can be cooked from raw without water, by stir-frying in oil. Best results are obtained by using flat thin items (such as mangetout and green beans) or by cutting larger vegetables into thin strips or slices. Do not have the heat too high. Medium heat will cook the vegetables in a few minutes without burning them, so long as you keep stirring them. (See Chef's Tip on page 160.)

Other techniques include baking, casseroling, microwaving and pressure cooking. In some of the following recipes I have used the former two techniques and have discussed the general principles of the latter two on page 13.

KEEPING CURRIES

Some people say that the historical origin of using spices in food was to mask the unpleasant taste of ingredients which were prone to 'going off' very quickly in hot countries. I don't know how true this is, but no amount of spicing will disguise bad ingredients. Equally, whilst currying may be one way to use up leftovers, you cannot expect your 'leftover' curry to be as good as one made with fresh ingredients. Only absolutely fresh and top-quality ingredients, prepared and cooked as soon as possible, will produce top quality curries.

What happens next produces two schools of thought about curry. One is that it should be cooked and served 'fresh', the other that it is better left for a day or two to marinate. Neither restaurants nor cooks in the Indian home would leave a completely cooked curry overnight. In the restaurant it could lead to quality-control and health problems, and it's not the way they cook the dishes anyway. In India, without adequate refrigeration, the ambient temperature would cause the food to go off within hours.

But given a refrigerator and sensible quality control, keeping a fresh curry overnight is safe enough. Provided that the raw ingredients are absolutely fresh, not frozen, and are cooked immediately, and provided that the dish is cooled rapidly after cooking, then covered and placed in the fridge at once, it will be safe for up to 48 hours.

As a general rule, any meat or poultry curry can be served immediately after cooking, or a few hours later, or even a day or two later. The taste and texture of the dish will change as marination takes place. This usually means the spices will become blander and the principal ingredient softer, and it's up to you which you prefer. Vegetables, in my opinion, taste better served straight after cooking, but they too will keep. Lentils improve with keeping after cooking, but rice does not, although you will get away with keeping rice for a day or maybe more. Fresh chutneys should always be served fresh.

Common sense must prevail when keeping any food. If you prefer this method of preparation, I would suggest you observe the following points:

1. Do not keep fish or shellfish curries in this way.

2. If you intend to keep a curry for a day or two, undercook it slightly, i.e. cut back the timings by 10 minutes. You will obtain a better texture when reheating – simply simmer until ready.

3. Use common sense about which vegetables will keep.

4. Keep away from warmth, preferably in a fridge.

5. Use a cover or clingfilm.

6. Inspect meat or chicken after 24 hours. Smell and taste it. It should look firm and good.

7. Ensure that the curry is reheated – simmered – for at least 10 minutes.

8. During reheating, taste, and if it needs a boost of a little more spicing, add early so that they cook in well.

9. Do not use if you even suspect it may be going off. Forty eight hours is a long time for any dish to sit around, and freezing is a much safer method of storing.

FREEZING

The freezer is one of the West's wonder tools. It is not available in India and the curry lands, except for an elite wealthy few (even the fridge is rare over there). But to the western householder, it is a mandatory item on the inventory. Like the fridge, it too has its uses and drawbacks.

The main point about home freezing is to preserve seasonal items for use out of season. I like to do this with some things and not with others. I prefer to freeze my own sweetcorn – it tastes so much better than the commercial versions. On the other hand I think bought frozen peas are in many cases better than home-frozen ones. You can freeze fruit and vegetables raw, exactly as they are when picked or purchased (cleaning and discarding unwanted matter first). I often do this, but the textbooks advise that you should cook the subject matter first, at least blanch it, to remove bacteria and gases. It's up to you.

Freezing comes into its own with the preservation of cooked foods and it is ideal for curry bases and sauces, and for some complete dishes. Freezing will change the taste of a curry – it's like a long marination. It will soften meats and vegetables and tends to intensify certain whole aromatic spices, though the overall taste will become blander.

Here are a few common sense freezer observations:

1. Use only fresh ingredients, not items that have come from the freezer.

2. Choose your subject carefully. Some ingredients are not suitable for freezing. Items with a high water content change markedly in structure when they thaw, their texture becoming unpleasant.

   Meat and poultry are excellent, as are all lentil dishes. Some vegetables work well – aubergines, peas, beans, carrots and mashed potatoes for example. Most soft fruit and vegetables are not as successful.

   Fish and seafood work well. Rice is satisfactory but I can never see the point – it takes so little time to make fresh rice (and it has better taste and texture).

3. Always undercook a dish destined for the freezer by about 10 minutes to allow for 'tenderising' in the freezing process and reheating.

4. Take out any large whole spices before freezing, especially cassia, cardamoms and cloves as they tend to become a bit astringent.

5. Get the dish into the freezer as soon as it is cold. Do not freeze if the food has been kept

warm for a long time or reheated, especially chicken. There is a risk of bacterial contamination.

6. Be aware that spicy food can 'taint' other foods, so preferably pack in a plastic container with an airtight lid.

7. Label contents with description and date.

8. Use within 3 months.

9. When reheating ensure that the dish is thoroughly hot and cooked through.

10. You may find the spicing has gone a little bland, so taste and cook in more spices as needed.

11. Finally, *never ever* freeze, thaw and refreeze an item.

COLOURING CHEMICALS

Spices are used in Indian cookery primarily to enhance the taste of the principal ingredients. They also affect the colour of the dish. Turmeric is used to give yellows; coriander, cummin, clove, etc for shades of brown; paprika and chilli powder for red; fresh coriander and chilli for green. Saffron, the world's most expensive spice, gives a bright orangey-gold colour, and deep crimson is obtained by use of *ratin jot* (similar to alkanet root). Natural colours such as these have been used in the sub-continent for as long as anyone can remember, and are used in this book.

It took the latter half of the twentieth century and food factories to forget the old ways. In the interests of time- and cost-saving, chemicals have crept into so many Western food products that I haven't space to mention them. Not surprisingly, chemical technology has crept into Indian food as well.

Nowhere is this more apparent than in the tandoori/tikka department. Those bright orangey-red chunks of chicken and lamb look so attractive on their beds of lettuce, onion rings and lemon wedges, but it's all, quite frankly, baloney. The authentic dish in the Punjab, from where this style of cooking originated, looks pale and anaemic in its natural un-dyed state but is, of course, just as tasty, for these chemicals are quite tasteless.

I am not emotive about the use of chemical colourants in food. I am not allergic to them, but like everyone else, including the manufacturers, I don't know what, if any, their cumulative effect is. I listen to the contemporary debate and I feel the manufacturers should listen too. My conclusion is that when I cook for the public I must do without chemicals, so I set about looking for alternatives. I found a substitute for that deep red colour in beetroot powder and for yellow in anatto seed powder. Combinations of these work well for tandoori. The colourful pullao rice at the restaurants makes use of a sunset yellow chemical. What should be used is saffron, which gives its delightful orange-yellow colour *plus* the bonus of fragrance, but its cost prohibits most restaurants from using it. Other chemicals used on rice include red, orange and green. Restaurant rice is particularly attractive and for those who wish to copy it I give the colouring method on page 229.

MEASURES

One of the great problems about writing down recipes is precision. Measures must be stated, yet most cooks with any proficiency rarely bother with scales – they just do things by sight, sound and appearance. In this book I have used teaspoon and tablespoon measures, particularly for spices. If analysed this is really very inaccurate. The European and British standard measure for a teaspoon is 5ml, 15ml for a tablespoon. The dessertspoon is not recognised but seems to hold 10ml. The American standard tablespoon is 14.2ml. The old Imperial British standard is 17.3ml and the Australian is 20ml.

I emptied my drawer the other day of spoons and lined them all up. There were nineteen teaspoons, ten tablespoons and fifteen dessertspoons. Using salt I measured level spoonfuls and weighed them on an extremely accurate set of electronic postal scales (accurate to a half gram) and discovered I had fourteen different salt weights from 44 spoons.

I then started to weigh my different spices to find that a teaspoon of white cummin weighs, let us say, 5g whilst black cummin weighs 4g. Ground clove was 3.5g. The density of every spice varies quite markedly. I have assumed that for most spices a heaped teaspoon (whatever that is) averages 5g and a tablespoon 15g.

PORTIONS

Most of the recipes in this book serve four people (except where stated) with average appetites. I normally allow 1½lb (675g) nett of the principal ingredients of a main course, i.e. after it is shorn of anything inedible, for four servings. Usually there is about ½lb (225g) of extra items in a dish, to give about 8oz (225g) per person in total.

For an accompanying main-course dish allow 3oz (75g) per person; for rice allow 2-3oz (50-75g) uncooked weight; for dried lentils, 1oz (25g).

These quantities are given for guidance only. Appetites vary enormously. One person may eat two or even three times as much as another. Also, the composition of an Indian meal could be one main dish with rice, or a number of main dishes with rice and bread. So, as with all aspects of cooking, common sense should prevail.

If you wish to cook for one person, either scale down the quantities or use the freezer. If you wish to cook for more than four, scale up. Taste and adjust as you go – if you feel a particular dish needs more spices – add some. Flexibility is, as always, the key.

SERVING AND DINING

Part of the fun of Indian food is the serving. This is best done by placing the curries, rice and dhals into metal or porcelain serving bowls and placing them in the centre of the table so that diners help themselves. Chutneys and pickles are attractive in little side bowls with teaspoons. Eat on dinner plates with dessertspoon and fork. Knives are only useful to cut bread. Provide a side plate for bread when you serve it. Don't be afraid to use your fingers – especially for Tandoori Chicken etc. After all, using fingers (of the right hand) is the polite and traditional way. In India even the most exclusive society is happy using fingers, and it was a recent Persian Royal Shah who said 'eating with a knife and fork is like making love through an interpreter'.

Normally with the main course one would expect to serve a side dish and/or a bread, a main dish and maybe one or two secondary dishes plus a number of chutneys and pickles. For a big party, you can increase the number of dishes. In the days of the Moghul emperors, the number of dishes you served indicated your wealth and prestige, so it was quite common for a banquet to contain hundreds of dishes and last for days. I doubt that you'll want to emulate that, but I'm sure you'll want to try a big feast at least once – it's ideal for parties. It is tasty, varied, colourful and different – with lots for your guests and yourself to talk about. Yet even the most complicated array of dishes can largely be prepared well in advance of your guests' arrival.

Bases for vegetable curries can be prepared in advance and the vegetables themselves can be blanched, then cooled in cold water, on the morning of the event. Papadoms and rice can be cooked in the afternoon and kept warm until required – even bread dough can be on standby. With careful planning, all you should need to do 'on the night' is to finish off any stir-fry dishes, reheat pre-cooked dishes in your oven and roll out and cook your breads.

When entertaining, avoid stretching yourself too far. Do not attempt a recipe which requires a technique you have never tried before, and do not cook a meal which requires more cooking rings or space than you have available.

One word of warning which may sound obvious here, but could be embarrassing 'on the night'. If you are inviting new guests and you do not know whether they eat spicy foods, the best advice I can give is 'don't'. Nothing is worse for hosts and guests than having a guest struggling with a disliked food. So don't serve curry at all. Play safe and invite only those whom you know will enjoy it. Then you'll all have a ball.

ALCOHOL AND BEVERAGES

Curry has a peculiar reputation when it comes to drink. One school of opinion states that no Indian drinks alcohol, for religious reasons. Another states that the only alcoholic beverage which goes with curry is lager and that wines are wasted. Neither is correct. Most Indians are Hindus and they have no laws regarding alcoholic consumption. It is the Moslems who are not permitted to drink alcohol. As for lager, if you like it then you'll enjoy it with curry. The same can be said, in my view, about wine, despite warnings from many critics that wine is wasted on spicy food.

The facts are simple: wine, red or white, is perfectly acceptable with curry. The more delicately spiced the dish, the more sophisticated can be the wine. More than one top-class Indian restaurant offers *premier cru* Bordeaux on its wine list. But such a wine would be wasted if your palate craved a searingly hot or pungently spiced dish.

I find Australian Shiraz, a rich and highly flavoured red wine, goes well with the hotter curries.

Reds from the Rhône and Roussillon regions, using Grenache or Syrah grapes, have a peppery quality which can cope with strong spices.

The Gamay grapes of Beaujolais and Touraine, though light reds, stand up well and make a marvellous change served chilled. Oaky Spanish Riojas are also appropriate.

Rosés are lighter and some go well with the richer creamier curries, such as Tikka Tandoori Masalas. The ultra fruity Château La Jaubertie Bergerac is recommended.

Whites are well represented by the oaky Chardonnays and the spicy Gewürztraminers. '*Gewürz*' means 'spice' in German, but go for the drier New World versions rather than the sweeter originals of Alsace. Torrés Viña Esmerelda from Spain effectively blends Muscat and Gewürztraminer and its overall spicy aromatic flavour makes it a popular choice.

Advice is readily available from high-street wine stores, where training is extremely good – but ask the manager rather than the Saturday help.

There is a flourishing alcohol industry in India. Lager-style beers are brewed and bottled all over the country, particularly in Bangalore where the climate and water suit the brewing process. One Bangalore brewery exports the especially fine Cobra lager to the UK. Cobra has been developed to accompany curry.

In certain areas wines are produced. The best of these is indisputably the 'champagne' produced in the Bombay area under French consultancy and marketed as 'Omar Khayam'. Although it cannot technically be called champagne, because it is not grown in the champagne area, the result is indistinguishable. The Indian white wine Veena is lightly spiced and makes a pleasant change, but their red wines and many other whites are rather heavy and resinous. Indian spirits – whisky, gin, brandy and vodka – are equally rough but they are relatively cheap.

All of these alcoholic processes were introduced to India by her European conquerors, notably the Portuguese and the British, so they have only been established in the country in relatively recent times (in the last few centuries). It is not surprising, therefore, that the habit of drinking alcohol has not overtaken a population whose civilisation began thousands of years ago. To this day, although the middle and wealthy classes enjoy the odd tipple (and the best present you can take an Indian host is a bottle of Johnny Walker 'Black Label' Scotch whisky – the price in India is six times what it is in Scotland), most people enjoy fruit juice and yoghurt drinks.

The traditional Indian beverages with the meal are fresh lime or yoghurt lhassi, and I include recipes for yoghurt and other drinks on pages 264-7.

It is always a good idea to have a jug of iced water on the table. It's not that the food is so hot that you need to gulp it down – in fact dieticians say it is wrong to drink too much during a meal – but it is very refreshing, and clears the palate from time to time.

My extravagant favourite beverage with curry is champagne if the occasion warrants it (and any excuse will do). Blow the expense . . . pink or white, not too dry. It just goes brilliantly with curry. Cheers!

The Curry Workshop

Much of the appreciation of Indian food comes from an understanding and correct use of the rather large amount of ingredients required in its cooking. I have given a lot of this information in my previous Indian cookery books but its importance must not be understated, and here, for the first time, it has been amalgamated and updated. I have entitled the chapter 'The Curry Workshop' because it contains a number of recipes which are important as bases or flavourings for subsequent recipes.

Although the information is presented in as logical an order as is possible, items as diverse as coconut and ghee, yoghurt and tamarind appear as neighbours. What they have in common is that they are much used in Indian curry cooking, and you will constantly need to use them in the recipes that follow.

My suggestion is that you initially skim-read this chapter so that you roughly know what's here. Then set aside a 'Curry Workshop' morning or afternoon when you can make up batches of everything you need in bulk, using the freezer as necessary. The great advantage of doing this is that you minimise the work, mess, washing-up and the smells to one outburst now and again.

OILS AND FATS

Edible oil and fat can be produced from many vegetables and nuts and from meat, fish, poultry, etc. It can also be produced from milk in the form of butter.

Curry cooking depends very greatly on the use of oil to establish both taste and texture, particularly in the early stages of cooking. And there is no argument that using *more* oil creates a better curry than using less. There is a limit to this, of course. We are all probably familiar with curries swimming in oil served in some restaurants. In such a case, too much oil was used in the first place, and no matter how good the end result, the excess oil spoils the dish. It could so easily have been spooned off at the end of its cooking while still in its saucepan. Once a properly cooked curry is taken off direct heat and allowed to rest, all the oil rises to the top and can then be ladled off for future use in curry cooking.

In this country we can get many suitable oils. For deep-frying I use a good quality odourless corn oil. This will do for all your Indian cookery actually, but for added interest I also use mustard oil which gives a distinctive flavour to the more delicate Southern Indian dishes. It is made from mustard seeds and smells a bit strong until it is cooked, when it becomes quite sweet in flavour. A light oil – sunflower oil, for example – is superb for lightly stir-fried vegetable dishes. It is odourless and is ideal in that it does not affect delicate and subtle dishes.

These days nutritionists are aware of health risks concerning certain fats and oils. Solid fats are described as saturated and can lead to a build-up of cholesterol in the body. Saturated fats include rendered animal fat such as dripping and lard. Butter, clarified butter and butter ghee are in this category and to a lesser extent solid margarine and vegetable ghee. Ghee (pronounced with a hard G as in geese) is widely used in the cooking of northern India and its neighbours, and is clarified butter or margarine. It has a wonderful flavour and really improves things like parathas or pullao rice and some curries. It is expensive to buy in tins but easy to make. Oils described as polyunsaturated are said to be better, and these include certain vegetable oils such as sunflower and soya oil. Best of all are said to be monounsaturated oils which include peanut and mustard oils, both excellent for curry cooking. One oil you should *never* use in any Indian cooking is olive oil. It imparts a strong flavour which does not go at all well with Indian cuisine.

In many dishes the oil used affects the final taste very minimally, so most oils can be used instead of ghee. But in rice and bread cooking, ghee imparts an important flavour. I have tried to strike a happy balance in these recipes by specifying neither too much nor too little ghee or oil. You can always use more if that is to your taste, and remember to spoon off excess before serving.

Ghee

Ghee is a clarified butter, which is very easy to make and gives a distinctive and delicious taste. When cooled and set, it will keep for several months without refrigeration, as does dripping.

If you want to make vegetable ghee, simply use pure vegetable block margarine instead of butter.

2lb (900g) any butter

1. Place the butter blocks whole into a medium non-stick pan. Melt at a very low heat.

2. When completely melted, raise heat very slightly. Ensure it does not smoke or burn, but don't stir. Leave to cook for about 1 hour. The impurities will sink to the bottom and float on the top. Carefully skim off the floating sediment with a slotted spoon, but don't touch the bottom.

3. Turn off the heat and allow the ghee to cool a little. Then strain it through kitchen paper or muslin into an airtight storage jar. When it cools it solidifies, although it is quite soft. It should be a bright pale lemon colour and it smells like toffee. If it has burned it will be darker and smell different. Providing it is not too burned it can still be used.

MILK

Indians are great milk consumers. They use the milk of cows, buffalo and goats. They make cream and yoghurt, but cheese isn't traditional. Indian cheese *(paneer)* is a simple form of cottage cheese, actually the curds separated from the whey (page 22). The whey can be used as vegetable stock or in soups.

Condensed milk *(koya)* is used in Indian sweets and is made by continually stirring milk until it reduces to a thick texture. Powdered milk can be used in certain recipes in place of cream or koya. In every curry house you'll see a huge saucepan in a warm place in which the day's yoghurt is made.

Some Indian restaurant chefs use ordinary milk as a cooking ingredient in curry. It reduces to a nice thick gravy, and when it is added to curries with slightly acidic ingredients (tomatoes or vinegar, for example) the milk can 'curdle', i.e. turn into curds and whey. This is not an unpleasant effect as the curds are minute and virtually tasteless.

Evaporated milk can be used to obtain a creamy taste in kormas, etc.

YOGHURT

Yoghurt predates history, and how it came to be invented can only be speculation. It is milk into which a culture or bacteria is introduced at a controlled heat to cause fermentation, souring and coagulation. New yoghurt can be started by using some existing yoghurt as the culture. It is a chicken and egg story. So how did the first yoghurt start? One theory is that the ancient tribes, probably the dairy-farming Aryans, carried their spare milk in leather pouches. Some bacteria may have got into the pouch and the heat of the sun did the rest.

Home-made Yoghurt

Making yoghurt is a skill well worth mastering. Not only does home-made yoghurt cost a fraction of factory versions, but it is fresher and creamier too. To start a yoghurt you need fresh milk (not UHT) or powdered milk. You also need a live bacteriological culture called *bulgaris,* to start the process. As this is present in yoghurt itself you can use factory yoghurt as a starter, although this is weaker than proper culture and can result in a thinner yoghurt. This can be thickened (milk powder works well).

If you decide to make yoghurt regularly, a good investment is a cooking thermometer or, better still, an electric yoghurt-maker.

Makes about 15oz (425g)

1 pint (600ml) milk (not UHT)
1 tablespoon milk powder (optional but gets thick results)
1 tablespoon bulgaris *culture or fresh yoghurt*

1. Bring the milk to the boil, add the milk powder, then keep it simmering for 2-3 minutes. (Use a 4 pint/2.25 litre pan, and it won't boil over.)

2. Remove from the heat and allow to cool to just above blood temperature, about 20-30 minutes. (It should be no cooler than 104°F/40°C, no hotter than 113°F/45°C.) The age-old test in the Middle East is rather masochistic and un-hygienic – immersing the fingertips in the milk. Once you can keep them in it for 10 seconds it is ready.

3. In a mixing bowl combine the yoghurt culture or yoghurt with a few drops of the warmed milk. Mix well. Add more and more milk until it is at pouring consistency.

4. Pour this and the remaining milk into a non-metal bowl. Cover the bowl with cling film then put it in a warm, draught-free place to ferment (the airing cupboard or a pre-warmed switched-off oven).

5. Leave it fermenting undisturbed for at least 6 hours and no more than 8. (The longer it is left the sourer it becomes.) Put it into the fridge (to stop fermentation) for at least 2 hours.

Note: Fermentation will stop if temperature exceeds 130°F/54°C or goes below 98.6°F/37°C.

PANEER

This is a fresh home-made 'cheese' which does not melt when cooked. It is full of protein and easy to make. It resembles compacted cottage cheese and is very common in the sub-continent as a vegetarian dish.

Paneer is remarkably versatile. The recipe below produces a bright white neutral flavoured product, which can be used crumbled or cut to any shape. 'Solid' paneer can be marinated to absorb flavour and colour, for 2-6 hours. Then it can be deep- or shallow-fried, grilled or barbecued.

Home-Made Paneer

It is very easy to make paneer at home. Follow the recipe below and use in any of the recipes requiring paneer.

Makes about 8oz (225g)

4 pints (2.25 litres) full-cream milk (not UHT)
4-6 tablespoons any vinegar or lemon juice

1. Choose a large pan. If you have one of 12 pint (6.75 litres) capacity, the milk will only occupy a third of the pan and won't boil over (unless the lid is on).

2. Bring the milk slowly to the boil. Add the vinegar or lemon juice, stirring until it curdles – when the curds separate from the whey.

3. Strain into a clean tea towel placed on a strainer over a saucepan. Fold the tea towel over and press through the excess liquid – the **whey**. Keep for later use as stock.

4. Now place the curds – from now on called paneer – on to the draining board, still in the tea towel. Press it out to a circle about 1/2 inch (1cm) thick. Place a flat weight (the original saucepan full of water, for instance) on the tea towel and allow it to compress the paneer.

5. If you want **crumbly paneer**, remove the weight after 30-45 minutes. Crumble the paneer and use as the recipe directs. If you want the paneer to be solid, keep the weight on for 1¹/₂-2 hours. Then cut the paneer into cubes.

COCONUT

Coconut is used extensively in the cooking of Goa, South India and Bengal and all the curry lands to

the east of India. None of the labour-saving coconut products can equal the excellence of the real
thing. The hairy brown tufted oval familiar from
the fairground is readily available at the greengrocer. Cooks only use three parts of the coconut:
the liquid inside the nut, coconut water, as a drink
or as cooking stock, the white flesh itself, and
coconut milk which is made from flesh and water.

When buying a fresh coconut, shake it to ensure
it is full of liquid. (The more liquid it has, the
fresher it is.) Coconut without liquid or with
mouldy or wet eyes should not be used.

To open a coconut

1. Make a hole in two of the three eyes with a
clean screwdriver or nail. Drain off and keep
the liquid (**coconut water**) for stock.

2. Bake the empty coconut in the oven at
400°F/200°C/Gas 6 for 15 minutes.

3. While still hot, crack it with a hammer or
something heavy.

4. Remove the outer husk and discard.

5. Break the inner parts into manageable pieces.
Pare off the dark inner husk, using a small knife
or a potato peeler.

6. Use the flesh in chunks, or puréed in curries.

Ready-to-use coconut products

Desiccated coconut is one substitute for fresh
coconut, and can be used by adding it dry to your
cooking, or by simmering it in water and straining
it to create coconut 'milk'. Canned coconut milk is
much richer and thicker, and a new product to this
country is coconut milk powder – very finely
ground, dried coconut flesh – which has a creamier taste than desiccated, and mixes well with
water.

The familiar 7oz (200g) rich block of '**creamed
coconut**' is a combination of freshly grated coconut flesh and coconut oil, which sets solid. It
must be kept under refrigeration. To use, boil a
little water. Cut off the amount required and melt
it in the hot water. If you try to fry it without
water, it will burn.

Coconut oil comes set solid in bottles with no
instructions as to how to extract it. It is, however,
simple. Ensure the cap is screwed on tightly then
immerse the bottle in hot water for a few minutes.
The oil becomes transparent and pourable as it
melts.

Coconut Milk

1. Take the flesh of one coconut from Step 6 above
and cut into small cubes no bigger than 1 inch
(2.5cm) each. Put into the blender with the
coconut water, reserved from Step 1 above, plus
10 fl oz (300ml) water.

2. Mulch it into a purée.

3. Cover and refrigerate from 4-24 hours.

4. Strain the flesh and keep the liquid. Press the
flesh hard against the strainer to remove all
liquid. Use at once.

FLOUR

In many parts of the Indian sub-continent wheat is
the staple food, not rice. The basic flours used for
Indian breads are wholemeal flour (the Indian
version is called ata flour or chupatti flour and is
available from Asian suppliers or The Curry
Club), self-raising flour and strong plain white
flour. Ata flour is made from hard wheat and is
more finely ground than our flour. This combination makes it more glutinous.

You'll also find the following useful to keep in
stock: gram flour *(besan)* which is made from
chana dhal (lentils), and is used to make bhajias,
pakoras etc (see page 62); rice flour which is less
important but useful if you need to thicken a gravy
and don't want the wheat taste you get from
ordinary flour. It is also used to make sweetmeats.
You can actually make your own gram and rice
flour. See the Chef's Tip on page 213.

TAMARIND

Tamarind – also known as the Indian date – is a
major souring agent, particularly in southern

Indian cooking. The tamarind tree bears pods of about 6-8 inches (15-20cm) long which become dark brown when ripe. These pods contain seeds and pulp, which are preserved indefinitely for use in cooking by compression into a rectangular block weighing about 11oz (300g).

Tamarind Purée

To use the tamarind block, soak it overnight in twice its volume of hot water – about 23 fl oz (650ml) per 11oz (300g) block. The next day pulp it well with your fingers, then strain through a sieve, discarding the husks. The brown liquid should be quite thick, and there will be plenty of it. Freeze any spare.

Alternatively for a small portion cut off about an eighth of the block – a piece about 1½ inches (4cm). Soak this in about 3½ fl oz (100ml) water for half an hour or more. Pulp and strain as above.

Lemon or vinegar, which can be used as substitutes, will give completely different flavours.

GARLIC

Garlic is indispensable to curry cooking. It is best to buy one or more bulbs on which are clustered a number of individual cloves. The skin is discarded and you should be left with a creamy, plump firm clove. To use, I prefer to chop the cloves finely (you can use a spring vegetable chopper), but you can use a garlic crusher (I think these are messy to clean and wasteful). You can also simply crush them under the flat side of a knife blade. To purée garlic, use an electric food processor or mortar and pestle.

Indian restaurants often use large quantities of garlic powder in place of real garlic which saves a lot of time. It also helps to capture that distinctive restaurant flavour, assisted no doubt by the sulphur dioxide and chemical stabilisers it contains. It also seems to cause dehydration. How often have you woken during the night with a raging thirst after eating an Indian restaurant curry? Real garlic does not seem to do that. If you do use garlic powder use 2 teaspoons for every clove specified in

the recipe. Sometimes I like to use powder and sometimes fresh, and yet again a combination can be interesting.

An expensive (but good) product is garlic purée in tubes and a product I have used a lot recently (as do many restaurants) is dehydrated garlic flakes: to use, soak in an equal volume of water for 30 minutes then mulch down in a food processor or blender. The taste is nearly as good as the real (fresh) thing, and the texture is indistinguishable.

If you and your friends like garlic add more (a lot more if you like) to the recipes. If you are worried about what it will do to your career, your social or love life, you can cut down on the quantities or omit it altogether.

Garlic Purée

If you want to make your own garlic purée, make a large batch and freeze it in ice-cube trays. Mine have ten sections and each holds 1 tablespoon of purée. When I specify a portion of garlic purée in other recipes I mean either an ice-cube tray section or 1 tablespoon. One plump clove of garlic is the equivalent of 1 level teaspoon garlic purée.

Makes 10 portions

30 plump garlic cloves, peeled

1. Mulch the garlic cloves around in a blender or food processor, adding no water or a minimum amount.

2. Scrape the garlic purée out of the container, place in ten ice-cube moulds, and freeze raw.

3. Pop out of the moulds, and store in firmly sealed freezer bags, or preferably, small rigid containers.

GINGER

Ginger is a rhizome or root which grows underground, and is native to Asia and other suitable climates. It comes in three forms – fresh, whole dried, and as powder. Fresh is the best way, and it stays fresh for many months after being cropped. It is readily available at UK greengrocers. Size is not always a guide to quality. It should look plump, not withered, and have a pinky beige skin and a slight sheen. When cut the ginger should be a primrose-cream colour with no sign at all of blue or staleness. It is not possible to tell if it is stale until you cut it, so if you know your greengrocer well, ask him to cut it before you buy it. It should not be stringy or very dry and tough.

A lot of work can be saved by using ginger powder. Some of the recipes in this book do use powder but there is really no substitute for fresh.

Ginger is quite hot and pungent so do not over-do the quantity unless you are a ginger freak.

It is worth mentioning that turmeric is another rhizome related to ginger. It is *always* used in powder form which saves us all a lot of hard work, but watch out for it in chunks in some Indian pickles.

Ginger Purée

In my first book I stated that ginger had to be peeled before using. This is the way it has always been done. The skin of the ginger root causes a bitter taste, so it is said. But shortly after that, I started to experiment and found that if ginger is mulched down it does not cause bitterness if the skin is left on. Remove the really rough ends or dirty bits, but leave any nice pink skin. This saves a great deal of time.

Freeze ginger purée as for garlic purée. Once again, each of my ice-cube moulds holds a table-spoon of purée and a 'portion' in a recipe means 1 tablespoon or 1 ice-cube tray section.

Makes 10 portions

1lb (450g) fresh ginger, trimmed of hard knobs but unpeeled

1. Coarsely chop the ginger, then mulch it down in a blender or food processor.
2. Scrape out of the container, place in ten ice-cube moulds and freeze raw.

3. Pop out of the moulds and store in firmly sealed freezer bags or, preferably, small rigid containers.

ONION

Onions in India are relatively small, quite hot and have pink skins. They are not available in the UK but small English or, better, French onions have a similar flavour. Of course the smaller they are the more work there is in peeling them, and the hotter they are the more you'll cry. The restaurants prefer to use the large mild Spanish ones and so do I. These give you a good consistency for puréeing, and heat can quickly be added with chilli powder. Some restaurants use dehydrated onion flakes which is the least labour-intensive, though dear-est, way of preparing onions. Keep fresh onions in the light or they will sprout green leaves and be useless. (Potatoes, on the other hand, must be kept in the dark to prevent sprouting.)

Onion Purée

Onions do not freeze whole at all well. As they are very watery they become soggy when they thaw, which is fine for boiling and subsequent puréeing but no use if you want to chop and fry them. Raw chopped and puréed onion freezes and thaws satisfactorily.

Unlike garlic and ginger, I find that onion needs to be boiled (blanched) in hot water first before puréeing, otherwise it has a very bitter taste.

From around 5lb (2.25kg) of raw onions (the quantity used here), the average yield of purée is about 2$\frac{1}{2}$ pints (1.5 litres). Where a recipe calls for '1 recipe of onion puree', this is the quantity to use. When a recipe requires '1 portion of onion puree', you need only a tenth of the total quantity made here – or about 10-12 tablespoons. Yoghurt pots are ideal for freezing the purée in.

Makes 10 portions

10 Spanish onions, each weighing about 8oz (225g), peeled

1. Coarsely chop the onions and place them in boiling water. Strain well after 3 minutes.

2. Mulch down in a blender or food processor until very fine in texture.

3. Scrape out of the container, place in ten yoghurt pots, cover with lids or foil and freeze.

Onion Tarka

The *tarka* is the traditional crispy brown onion garnish sprinkled over several of the dishes in this book. I like to make a reasonably sized batch. If cooked correctly these dry crispy pieces will keep, like biscuits, in an airtight tin. To get them crispy, the trick is to dry the onion in a low oven, then to fry at medium heat. Serve hot or cold.

8oz (225g) onions, peeled
6-8 tablespoons vegetable or sunflower oil

1. Finely slice the onions into julienne strips (matchsticks) about $1^1/_2$ inches (4cm) in length.

2. Pre-heat the oven to 210°F/100°C/Gas $^1/_4$.

3. Spread the onion slices on a baking tray and place in the oven for anything between 30 and 45 minutes.

4. They should now be quite dehydrated, so heat the oil in a karahi or wok.

5. Add the onion slices and stir-fry for 10-15 minutes, until they go dark brown. A little blackening is fine, but control things to prevent an all-black situation.

6. When you have the colour you like, strain off the oil (use it for subsequent cooking). Drain on absorbent paper.

Quick Onion Tarka

Almost indistinguishable from the previous recipe, and it will save you about $1^1/_2$ hours. These too will keep in an airtight tin for several weeks.

Makes an ample amount

8 tablespoons sunflower oil
6oz (175g) dried onion flakes

1. Heat the oil, then add the onion flakes.

2. Briskly stir-fry for around 1 minute. (They will burn easily so keep them moving.)

3. Remove from the heat and drain. Serve hot or cold.

HERBS

The use of herbs in cooking performs a similar function to spices – to add flavour to food. They are usually fresh or dried leaves of plants cultivated exclusively for the purpose. They also add greatly to the appearance of a dish when used as garnishes. The use of herbs is, of course, widespread in Mediterranean countries such as France, Italy and Greece. Middle Eastern cooking uses almost as many spices as Indian, but it also uses a wide selection of herbs. Considering the historical relationship between the Arabs and India in terms of trade and invasions over the last 2,000-3,000 years, it is surprising that the use of herbs in Indian cooking is minimal.

Coriander

The main herb used is fresh coriander leaf which has a very distinctive, acquired, musky taste, a little redolent of the not unpleasant fragrance of candle wax. But it is very important, and contributes greatly to achieving both 'that restaurant taste' and authentic flavours. The leaves only are used, the stalks are a little bitter and are discarded (although guinea pigs and rabbits adore them, so if you or your friends or their kids . . .).

Fresh parsley can be substituted if you can't get coriander, which does not taste the same, but *looks* nice. Gardeners will probably be able to grow coriander but things like that are above and beyond me.

When purchasing fresh coriander, the problems are twofold. Firstly, although it is flown in fresh from Cyprus, Egypt and Greece daily, and it is also grown in the UK, some greengrocers stubbornly refuse to stock it. If you have some of those in your town, go to your local curry house and ask which greengrocer supplies them. Whoever it is will supply coriander. Second, although it is not expensive, coriander comes in great big bunches. A lot can be wasted if it's not used within a day or so. (Stand it in water, and change this daily: this will prolong its life.) A bunch will yield an average of 2-2½oz (50-70g), or 4-5 tablespoons of chopped leaf and light stalks.

An alternative to the purée method below is simply to chop fresh coriander, dry it if necessary on kitchen paper, and freeze by itself. Or you can freeze it chopped, in ice cubes, for adding to curries prior to serving.

Coriander Purée

Freezing coriander in a purée is my solution to the problem, and it retains the original flavour almost as well as if it were fresh. As with all my purées I like to make up a large quantity then freeze it in ice-cube moulds, transferring the cubes to a rigid container later. Each cube gives enough coriander for an average recipe for four.

Makes about 12oz (350g)

4 bunches fresh coriander, washed and trimmed of coarse stalks
4oz (110g) onions, peeled

1. Chop the coriander coarsely, including the smaller stalks. Also chop the onion.

2. Put both into a food processor and mulch into a purée.

3. Scrape out and freeze in ice-cube trays. When frozen, pop out of the trays and freezer-store as above.

Mint

The other herb which is used from time to time is mint, particularly spearmint. Its use will crop up in a few of the recipes which follow. A tiny pinch of dried mint livens up many curry dishes, giving them a fresh taste. Add it 10 minutes before the end of cooking.

Fresh mint is readily available in season, and easy to grow in pots or in the garden. You can freeze it as for coriander, or bottle it in vinegar (no sugar) for use out of season.

Please do remember that dried herbs are stronger than fresh, so use half quantities.

SPICES

In the next chapter we will meet individual spices and discover their individual qualities. Here I talk in general terms about their use, including their cooking.

Storing spices

Whole spices retain their flavour longer than ground, for one year or more sometimes. Ground spices give off a stronger aroma than whole, and of course this means their storage life is that much shorter. Three months is about right for most ground items. So plan your larder accordingly, and buy little and often and grind freshly. Keep the spices out of sunlight (better in a dark cupboard) and in airtight labelled containers. Clean coffee or jam jars are excellent.

Grinding spices

It is better by far to grind your own whole spices whenever you can. Firstly you can be sure of the quality and contents, and secondly they will be fresher and tastier. The traditional method is by mortar and pestle, but you can use an electric coffee grinder or the new electric spice mill. After a damp wipe a coffee grinder can still be used for coffee – it might even enhance the flavour! Use small quantities to prevent overloading the motor.

Don't try to grind dry ginger or turmeric. They are too fibrous for most small grinders, and commercial powders are adequate. Peppers – chilli, paprika and black or white pepper – are tricky, and commercially ground powders will suffice. The oilier spices such as cloves, nutmeg, brown cardamoms and bay leaves are easier to grind if roasted first.

In the recipes, when a spice is referred to as 'ground', this means factory ground. Where it requires the spice to be home-ground (usually after roasting), the recipe clearly states this.

Roasting whole spices

Whole spices contain essential or volatile oils. It is these which we can smell when handling a spice, and it is these which we must release when we cook with spices.

Roasting whole spices is my favourite way of releasing their essential oils. A roasted whole spice tastes quite different from a raw one and the release of flavour is pleasantly overwhelming.

The roasting process is simple and can be done in a dry pan on the stove, in a dry electric frying pan, under the grill or in the oven. Each spice should be heated until it gives off its aroma. The heat should be medium rather than hot and the time required is a few minutes. (Preheat the over to 325°F/160°C/Gas 3 and allow about 10 minutes.) The spice should not blacken, a light brown at most is sufficient. The original oil of the spice must not be totally cooked out or it will lose its flavour. A little experimenting will soon show you how to do it. In some recipes pre-roasted spices are important. (Incidentally, coffee is roasted in exactly the same manner as spices.)

Blending spices

This sounds rather grandiose. In fact it's simple. Every mixture is called a blend. Generally we mean ground spices, and of course the best-known blends of all (with the worst reputation) are curry powders. Many of my recipes use blends of two or more ground spices. So in effect we make our own 'curry powder' every time we use one of these recipes. 'Curry powder' gives a totally wrong image and is generally despised by cooks in all the curry lands, who call any mixture of spices the 'masala'.

Each recipe has its own masala and it is this unique combination of spices which makes Indian-style cooking so distinctive. The following curry powder recipe is a masala, but throughout my recipes I refer to the masala as 'spices' (whole or ground).

Masala – Mild Curry Powder

Commercial curry powder has two drawbacks in my view. Firstly, although the manufacturers are supposed to list the ingredients, some avoid it by simply stating 'spices'; and even if they do list them, they do not state the quantities. They often put in too much chilli, salt and, in some cases, chemical colourings and preservatives. Undeclared additives can include husks and stalks and other adulterations.

The second drawback is that the use of the same curry powder blend in all the recipes would make each dish taste virtually the same.

However, it is sometimes useful to have curry powder in the larder. You can purchase a commercial version or you can make up your own with this interesting mixture. It comes from the first cookery book given to a young bride who, with her husband, was posted to the British army base in Agra in 1904. The lady was my grandmother and that book was her bible. It was first published in 1870, so this masala has been recipe tested for 120 years, in itself an amazing fact.

A heaped teaspoon is about 5g (a tablespoon 15g). It's not easy to transpose to Imperial.

Makes about 9oz (250g)

60g coriander seeds
30g white cummin seeds
20g fenugreek seeds
25g gram flour (besan)
25g garlic powder
20g paprika
20g turmeric
20g aromatic garam masala (page 29)
5g dry ground curry leaves
5g asafoetida
5g ginger powder
5g chilli powder
5g yellow mustard powder
5g ground black pepper

1. Roast and then grind the first three spices.

2. Mix all together well and store.

3. Omit the final four spices for a totally mild curry powder.

4. For those who wish, salt and sugar (white granulated) can be added for flavour during the blending: add 2 tablespoons sugar and/or 1 teaspoon salt.

To make a dish for four you would need about 1oz (25g) of masala, so this will give you enough for ten curries. I prefer to make a reasonable batch like 9oz (250g) because it 'matures' or becomes better blended the longer it is stored. It can be used at once, of course, but after about a month it is perfect. Do not keep it for longer than 18 months – it tends to lose its subtle flavours, becoming bitter. Store in an airtight container in a dark damp-free place.

Garam Masala

Garam means hot and *masala* means mixture of spices, and there are as many combinations and recipes for garam masala as there are cooks who make it. Some use only five or six spices, but I have one recipe which lists as many as fifteen spices! This one has only nine and has been my favourite for years. Try it. For the next batch, you might like to vary the mixture to your own preference. That's the fun of Indian cookery. (Again I list in metric only, as that's the way I weigh out the spices for this and it doesn't transfer easily into Imperial.)

For an *aromatic* garam masala, use this recipe *without* the peppercorns and ginger. I came across a remarkably 'mild' garam masala recipe in Kashmir which uses no hot spices at all. In their place were saffron stamens and rose petals. If you wish to use saffron, add it whole at the very end of cooking.

Makes about 14oz (400g)

110g coriander seeds
110g cummin seeds
50g black peppercorns

30g cassia bark
30g cloves
30g brown cardamoms
15g nutmeg
10g bay leaves
15g ground ginger

1. Lightly roast everything except the ground ginger under a low to medium grill or in a low oven. Do not let the spices burn. They should give off a light steam.

2. When they give off an aroma remove from the heat, cool and grind in batches.

3. After grinding add the ground ginger, mix thoroughly and store in an airtight jar. Garam masala will last almost indefinitely, but it is always better to make small fresh batches every few months to get the best flavours.

Char Masala

'*Char*' in Hindi, Urdu and Pashto means four, and '*masala*', our familiar mixture of spices. This can be used as a substitute for garam masala if you wish to have a very fragrant mixture of spices with no heat.

The four spices are usually the same, though the proportions can vary. This recipe makes 60g worth (enough for four curries).

20g cassia bark
20g white cummin seeds
10g green cardamom seeds (not pods)
10g cloves

1. Roast, grind and store in a jam jar.

Panch Phoran

This is a Bengali mixture of five (*panch*) spices. There are several possible combinations, but this is my favourite.

Simply mix together equal parts of (a teaspoon of each is plenty):

white cummin seeds
fennel seeds
fenugreek seeds
mustard seeds
wild onion seeds

Aromatic Salt

Throughout this book, recipes call for aromatic salt. This is salt, preferably sea salt, to which is added a light spice mixture. Ordinary salt can be used in its place, but the spicing adds a delicacy and subtlety to a recipe. It is a trick I picked up from professional chefs, and I highly recommend it.

Here are two recipes, the first being light and aromatic, the second containing spicier tastes as well as nuts. Finely grind a reasonable size batch and store in a screw-top jar.

Lightly Spiced Salt
100g (4oz) coarsely granulated sea salt
1 teaspoon powdered cinnamon
1 teaspoon ground allspice

Spicier Aromatic Salt
1 quantity lightly spiced salt
1/2 teaspoon ground fenugreek seeds
1 teaspoon dried mint
1 tablespoon ground almonds
1/2 teaspoon turmeric

Cooking ground spices

Whole spices need to be 'roasted' to bring out their aromas (page 28). It is less obvious that ground spices must be cooked too. In fact it is even more important. Factory-ground spices are never pre-roasted so they have 'raw' tastes. Anyone who has had the misfortune to experience the old-style British canteen curry will know what this means. Curry powder is spooned straight into a bubbling stew. The result is appalling, and has single-

handedly set back this nation's appreciation of curry by decades.

It is easy to cook ground spices. They simply have to be fried. Some cooks just add powdered spices to hot oil. But it is all too easy to burn the spices this way. The most reliable way to cook ground spices is to make the dry masala into a wet paste by adding water.

The Masala Paste

When a recipe states 'mix and blend dry spices' (a masala), as in the earlier curry powder mixtures, it is necessary to cook those spices to remove the raw tastes. This is most safely done by making up a paste with water which prevents the spices from burning up when they are introduced to the oil in the *bhoona* or frying process.

1. Select a mixing bowl large enough to enable you to stir the masala.

2. Stir the masala until it is fully mixed.

3. Add enough water to form a stiff paste *and no more*.

4. Leave to stand for a minimum of 10 minutes. It does not matter how long it stands. This ensures that the ground spices absorb all the water.

5. Add a little water if it is too dry prior to using in the bhoona or frying process.

The Bhoona

The *bhoona* is the Hindi term for the process of cooking the spice paste in hot oil. This is an important part of the curry-cooking process which removes the raw taste of the spices and influences the final taste of the dish. Use the bhoona method whenever the recipes in this book state that you should 'fry the spices'. In fact, traditionally you should fry the spice paste first, then add the puréed or chopped onion second. This method can easily cause burned spices so I reverse the process and have found that it works very satisfactorily.

1. Take a round-sided pan such as a karahi or wok. If you don't have one, use an ordinary frying pan (a non-stick one is best).

2. Heat the oil to quite a high heat (but not smoking).

3. Remove the pan from the heat and at once gently add the onion purée. Return to the heat and commence stirring.

4. *From this point do not let your attention wander.* Keep stirring the purée until the oil is hot again, then gently add the masala paste. Beware of splattering.

5. Keep stirring. The water in the paste lowers the temperature. Do not let the mixture stick at all. Do not stop stirring, not even for a few seconds.

6. After a few minutes the water will have evaporated out and the oil will float above the mixture. The spices will be cooked. Remove the pan from the heat. Proceed with the remainder of the recipe.

The Bargar

Some of the recipes in this book require you to fry *whole* spices. The process is for the same reason as the bhoona (and the roasting of whole spices on page 28) — to cook out the raw taste from the spices. Again the oil should be hot, and the spices are put into the oil with no water or purée. You must use your judgement as to when they are cooked. Do not let them blacken. As soon as they begin to change colour or to float they are ready. It will not take more than a couple of minutes.

If you do burn the spices during the bhoona or bargar process *you must throw the result away and start again.* Better to waste a small amount of spices than taint a whole meal.

Curry pastes, gravy and stock

Anyone interested in Indian food must have encountered bottled curry pastes on the grocery shelves. There are many makes and types, but little explanation as to what they are or what they do. They are designed to take the labour out of blending a spice mixture, making it into a water paste and frying it. The manufacturers do it all for you, adding vinegar (acetic acid) and hot oil to prevent it from going mouldy. Unfortunately they also add salt and chilli powder which makes the pastes a little overpowering. They are very concentrated, and you only need a small quantity for cooking.

Curry pastes are already cooked, but to 'disguise' them you will probably need to add some other whole or ground spices, and you will certainly need to fry garlic, ginger, onion, etc. Simply add the spice paste after these three are fried and carry on with the rest of the recipe.

It's much better to make your own, and there are a few recipes following.

Mild Curry Paste

This mild paste can form the base for many curry dishes. Using vinegar (rather than all water) to make the paste will enable you to preserve it in jars. As with all pickling, sterilise the jars (a good hot wash in the dishwasher followed by a dry-out in a low-heat over will do). Top off the paste in the jar with hot oil and inspect after a few days to see that there is no mould.

Makes about 1¹/₂lb (675g)

1 recipe masala mild curry powder (page 28)
6-8 fl oz (175-250ml) vinegar (any type)
6-8 fl oz (175-250ml) vegetable oil

1. Mix together the curry powder spices.

2. Add the vinegar and enough water to make a creamy paste.

3. Heat the oil in a karahi or wok.

4. Add the paste to the oil. It will splatter a bit so be careful.

5. Stir-fry the paste continually to prevent it sticking until the water content is cooked out (it

should take about 5 minutes). As the liquid is reduced, the paste will begin to make a regular bubbling noise (hard to describe, but it goes chup-chup-chup-chup) if you don't stir, and it will splatter. This is your audible cue that it is ready. You can tell if the spices are cooked by taking the karahi off the stove. Leave to stand for 3-4 minutes. If the oil 'floats' to the top, the spices are cooked. If not, add a little more oil and repeat step 5.

6. Bottle the paste in sterilised jars. Then heat up a little more oil and 'cap' off the paste by pouring in enough oil to cover. Seal the jars and store.

Green Masala Paste

This curry paste is green in colour because of its use of coriander and mint. You can buy it factory made, but it does not have the delicious fresh taste of this recipe from Ivan Watson, journalist and regular correspondent to *The Curry Magazine*. You will come across green masala paste in the Indian home where it is used to enhance curry dishes and impart a subtle flavour that can be obtained in no other way.

As with all curry pastes, this one will keep in jars indefinitely if made correctly.

Makes about 1lb (450g)

1 teaspoon fenugreek seeds
6 garlic cloves, chopped
2 tablespoons finely chopped fresh ginger
1¹/₂oz (40g) fresh mint leaves
1¹/₂oz (40g) fresh coriander leaves
4 fl oz (120ml) vinegar
3 teaspoons salt
3 teaspoons turmeric
2 teaspoons chilli powder
¹/₂ teaspoon ground cloves
1 teaspoon ground cardamom seeds
4 fl oz (120ml) vegetable oil
2 fl oz (50ml) sesame oil

1. Soak the fenugreek seeds in water overnight. They will swell and acquire a jelly-like coating.

2. Strain the fenugreek, discarding the water.

3. Mulch down all the ingredients, except the oils, in a blender or food processor, to make a purée.

4. To cook, follow the previous curry paste method.

Curry Masala Gravy

Every curry restaurant has a large saucepan on the stove. In it is a pale orangey-gold gravy, quite thick in texture like apple purée. Taste and it's quite nice – a bit like a soup – or mild curry. Ask how it's made and like as not you'll get a shake of the head and a murmur about secrets of the trade. For this stock pot is one of the keys to achieving the restaurant curry. Recipes vary only slightly from chef to chef and restaurant to restaurant.

You can substitute this curry gravy for the individual garlic, ginger or onion purées given in many of the recipes which follow. Remember, this is just a mild base to which you can add other spices as required.

The average yield of this recipe is 4¹/₂ pints (2.5 litres) total. When I refer to a portion of curry masala gravy, I mean one-tenth of this, or 9 fl oz (275ml). For convenience freeze in large yoghurt pots, as they hold one portion perfectly.

Makes the gravy base for 10 curry recipes (each serving 4 people)

¹/₂ pint (300ml) ghee or vegetable oil
5 tablespoons (5 portions) garlic purée (page 24)
4 tablespoons (4 portions) ginger purée (page 25)
1 full recipe (10 portions) onion purée (page 25)
1¹/₂lb (675g) canned tomatoes and their juice
6 tablespoons tomato purée
3 teaspoons salt
2 tablespoons sugar

Spices
4 tablespoons masala mild curry powder (page 28)
2 tablespoons paprika
1¹/₂ tablespoons turmeric

1. Mix the spices with water to make a paste the consistency of tomato ketchup. Let it stand.

2. Using a 6-8 pint (3.5-4.5 litre) saucepan, heat 5-6 tablespoons of the oil. Stir-fry the garlic purée for 30 seconds, then add the ginger purée and cook for 30 more seconds. Add 5-6 more tablespoons of oil and when hot add the spice paste and stir-fry for 30 seconds more. Add the remaining oil and the onion purée and stir-fry gently for around 10 minutes.

3. Mulch down the canned tomatoes in a blender then add with the tomato purée to the pan. Mix in well and add enough water to achieve a medium thick soup consistency. Add sugar and salt to taste.

4. Simmer gently for at least 30 minutes and at most an hour. Aim for a reduction to a thickish but easily pourable apple purée texture. But if it starts to get too dry add a little water from time to time.

5. Pour into ten moulds, cool, cover with lid or foil, and freeze.

Akhni Stock

Some restaurants make a strained stock as well as or in place of the previous curry masala gravy. This flavoured clear liquid, sometimes called yakhni, is used exactly like any vegetable stock at any time the recipe directs 'add water'. You can keep it in the fridge for a couple of days, but it is essential to re-boil it after this time; it will be safe for several re-boils, but use it finally in a soup or other cooking. Add the brine or water from tinned vegetables to your stock. You can top it up with fresh or leftover ingredients as required.

Makes 1¹/₂ pints (900ml)

3 pints (1.75 litres) water
2 Spanish onions, chopped
1 teaspoon garlic purée (page 24)
1 teaspoon ginger purée (page 25)
1 tablespoon ghee
2 teaspoons salt

Spices (whole)
10 cloves
10 green cardamoms
6 pieces cassia bark
6 bay leaves

1. Boil the water, then add everything else.

2. Simmer for 1 hour with the lid on, by which time the stock should have reduced by half.

3. Strain and discard the solids.

The World of Spices

✱

Spices are vegetable matter, harvested from plants, shrubs, flowers or trees. Many are berries, seeds or pods, whilst others are leaves, roots, bark, bulbs and rhizomes. In one case, saffron, it is the stigma or stamen of a flower whilst in another case, the clove, it is the bud.

Most spices on their own are bitter, unpalatable and in some cases inedible (cassia or cinnamon bark for example), but used correctly in small amounts, singly, or in combination, they add both fragrance and flavour to food. There are over 60 whole spices that can be used in Indian cooking. Some of these are rarely used, whilst others are virtually indispensable. Some are used whole, some ground.

There are spices to give savoury tastes, and others to give aromatic, even sweetish, tastes. Others still, such as turmeric and fenugreek, are intended to give bitter tastes and should be used in moderation. Some spices are used to create colour, others texture. A few give intense heat.

Come with me in this chapter on a journey into the world of spices to meet those stars of Indian cooking which appear in this book.

Facing page: A collection of spices in traditional spice trays, (*masala dabbas*). The large leaves are from the cassia tree.

ALKANET ROOT *Ratin Jot*

This is a specialised spice used only for colouring purposes, not flavouring. It is a root related to borage. It is beetroot red and when dried it forms a wafer-thin bark. In India it is used as a deep red dye for make-up, clothing and food. Northern Indians and Kashmiris use it (or an alternative plant called cox comb) to colour food.

ANISEED *Saunf*

A tiny round striped grey-brown seed with a little tail, it is frequently confused in parts of India with its near relative in flavour, the fennel seed. Aniseed is slightly more powerful in dishes requiring an aromatic conclusion. Definitely worth having in stock.

ASAFOETIDA *Hing*

A sap which is collected from a giant perennial plant of the fennel family by cutting the stalk off at the root. The sap solidifies into a brown resin-like substance. This is factory ground into a grey-brown or bright greeny-lemon powder (depending on species).

It is the smelliest spice, giving rise to its other names — devil's dung and stinking gum. Fortunately, its unpleasant odour disappears in cooking. Used none the less in small quantities in fish and lentil dishes, it is supposed to aid digestion by combating flatulence.

BAY LEAF *Tej Pattia*

An aromatic dark green leaf from a tree which grows world-wide. In fact it is one of the few spices to be used in England, though not in India. There the *tej pattia* is the slightly larger leaf of the cassia tree, unobtainable outside India. Bay makes a good substitute and can be used fresh or dry.

Whole, it gives an incomparable fragrance and flavour to subtle curries, such as kormas. Ground, it is an ingredient in masalas.

CARDAMOM *Elaichi*

This is one of India's most elegant and exported spices, earning India considerable revenue and the spice itself the title, 'The Queen of Spice'. Cardamom is one of the most aromatic and expensive spices. It is a pod containing slightly sticky black seeds. There are three main types, all of which can be used whole or ground.

Brown (also called black) have a rather hairy, husky, dark brown casing about 20mm long. Used in garam masala, kormas and pullaos. They are quite pungent though still aromatic.

Green have a smooth, pale green outer casing about 1/2 inch (1cm) long. Used whole or ground, with or without casing, in many savoury and sweet recipes.

White are about the same size as green, with a slightly rounder white casing. Green and white have a similar flavour — more delicate than the brown.

CASSIA BARK *Dalchini*

This is the corky brown outer bark of a tree with a sweet fragrance related to cinnamon. Indeed there is some confusion between the two. Cassia, also known as Chinese cinnamon, is less fragrant and cheaper than cinnamon.

Cassia bark is usually much coarser, thicker and tougher than cinnamon, and it stands up to more robust cooking. It is used as an aromatic flavouring in more subtle meat and poultry dishes and as a major flavouring in pullao rice and garam masala. (See also Cinnamon.)

Although widely used in cooking, the bark cannot be eaten.

CHILLI Green *Hari Mirch*, Red *Lal Mirch*

Chillies are the fleshy pods of shrub-like bushes of the capsicum family. There are four species and 1,500 sub-species in the family, including the capsicum, sweet or bell pepper.

They range in size from a minute 1/3 inch (less than 1cm) to a huge 12 inches (30cm); in shape from conical or cherry to cucumber; in colour from green to white, yellow, orange, red and purple; in texture from fleshy to scaly; and in taste from sweet and mild to incendiary. Hottest of all are the tiny 'bird' or Tabasco chillies.

Best for use in Indian cookery are fresh green or red chillies about 2-4 inches (5-10cm) in length, and about 1/2 inch (1cm) in width.

Red chillies are also available whole dried, crushed, or ground to a fine powder. Depending on which chilli was ground, packet chilli powder can vary immensely in heat strength. The recipes in this book use normal chilli powder. 'Hot-heads' may like to use chilli powder labelled 'extra hot'.

Cayenne pepper originally came from French Guiana, but is now blended from many types of chilli, and is indistinguishable from chilli powder, though it is often dearer.

Chillies are native to the tropical forests of Latin America, and were not discovered until the 15th century when Spanish and Portuguese explorers stumbled across them, along with tobacco, cocoa, the potato, tomato, turkey and sweetcorn. It did not take long for the chilli to be carried across oceans to India. The Portuguese took them to their southern Indian bases, and the natives took to chillies like ducks to water. Up until that time, and for thousands of years before, black peppercorns had been the 'heat' agent.

Pepper and chilli have one factor in common – they create a burning sensation in the mouth. This causes the brain to activate the salivary glands to 'wash away' the irritant. The nose runs and the body perspires. Researchers believe this is one reason why chillies actually cool you down. They also believe that the high level of the alkaloid capsaicin – the measure of 'heat' in food – present in peppers is the reason why chilli in particular and curry in general is mildly addictive. (Capsaicin is related to caffeine, nicotine and morphine.) I for one enjoy 'hot' food and I get withdrawal symptoms if I have to abstain from my curry for more than a couple of weeks . . . I just have to take a fix! But the scientists assure us that this addiction is very slight and quite harmless.

More serious research has proved that no permanent harm comes to the innards of chilli eaters. Chillies are rich in Vitamin C and, like onion and garlic, actively help to reduce blood pressure and

cholesterol. Regular chilli eaters build up an increasing tolerance to chilli heat.

CINNAMON *Dalchini*

Originating in China, cinnamon has been used to flavour food for thousands of years, its sweetish aromatic flavour adding a haunting quality to food.

In Roman times Arabs were the middlemen between the Chinese and Romans. To protect their trade routes and their monopolies, the Arabs used to invent tall stories. They claimed, for example, that cinnamon bark came from the nest of a great man-eating horned eagle, the size of a horse, on top of a single high mountain peak. The Romans believed this and paid outlandish prices for their spices.

Cinnamon is the inner bark of a tree, available in parchment-thin, tightly rolled, pale brown quills of around 1/2 inch (1cm) in diameter by 4-6 inches (10-12cm) long. These quills are highly aromatic but can break up in robust cooking. Little pieces of cinnamon are inedible and unpleasant, so quills are best confined to infusing drinks and in pullao rice. Ground cinnamon is used in some dishes. (See also Cassia.)

CLOVES *Lavang*

Cloves are the most familiar UK spice, having been used continuously since the Romans brought them here. We use them in apple pies and to ease toothache. (They contain a pain-killing essential oil.)

Cloves grow on tall trees, native originally to two Indonesian Moluccan 'spice islands', Ternate and Tidore. Wars were fought over them and today cloves are to be found in India, Zanzibar and the West Indies. Cloves are the unopened buds of the tree's flowers. They are bright green at first, and must be picked when they turn pink. The flowers, if allowed to bloom, are red or dark pink about 1/2 inch (1cm) in diameter.

Cloves themselves are dark red-brown, bulbous at one end with tapering stalks, and about 1/2 inch

(1cm) in length. The Romans thought they looked like nails – *clavus* is Latin for nail, the origin of clove.

The clove is the world's second most important spice, earning India alone some £20 million a year. It takes some 8-10,000 cloves just to make up 1kg (2¼lb)!

CORIANDER *Dhania*

In terms of volume (but not value), coriander is the most important spice in Indian cookery. The country exports 80,000 tons a year. It is widely used in two forms – seed and fresh leaf. Its root is also used in India but we find it rather bitter.

Coriander was native to India but now grows world-wide. There are many species, so the appearance of the seed varies from small spherical buff-coloured seeds (about ⅛-¼ inch/4mm in diameter) to oval-shaped larger ones. The seeds are used whole or ground, forming the largest single ingredient in most masalas. They impart a sweetish flavour, and the seeds are delicious roasted – try them as a garnish.

Coriander leaves are mid-green and flat with jagged edges and are also important in Indian cookery – some people say indispensable. However, the leaves bear no resemblance in flavour to the seed, and not everyone enjoys their distinctive musky candle-waxy odour. Indeed, the word coriander derives from the Greek word *koris*, a bug, supposedly because its foetid smell resembles that of bed bugs. That's as may be, but coriander is widely available from UK greengrocers in large bunches. Before purchasing a bunch, always crush one to ensure it has 'that' smell and that it is not the similar looking but flavourless flat parsley.

CUMMIN, WHITE *Jeera* or *Zeera Safed*

Small yellow-green seeds, about ⅛-¼ inch (4mm) long. Whole, they are used fried for roasted at the early or final stages of cooking, or as a garnish. Ground cummin is one of the most important spices in curry cooking, imparting a savoury taste.

CUMMIN, BLACK *Jeera* or *Kala Zeera* or *Shahi Jeera*

Dark brown seeds slightly smaller and narrower than their white relative. In appearance, but not in flavour, it resembles caraway seed, a spice which is never used in Indian cookery. Black cummin is only used whole to great effect in such dishes as pullao rice and certain vegetable dishes.

CURRY LEAVES *Neem* or *Kari Phulia*

Small dark green leaf, about 1 inch (2.5cm) in length, which grows on a small tree, Despite its name it has a lemony fragrance, indeed the tree is related to the lemon family. Leaves are widely used whole in southern Indian cooking and impart a delicious flavour to dishes such as lemon rice. They are also used ground in many commercial powder blends.

Fresh curry leaves are imported into the UK by airfreight from Kenya, but are hard to locate. Dry ones make passable substitutes.

FENNEL *Sunf* or *Soonf*

A small pale greenish-yellow stripy seed slightly plumper than cummin, which grows to around ¼ inch (5mm) in length. They are quite sweet and aromatic. Though confused with aniseed in India, fennel has a slightly milder though similar flavour. It is used in aromatic and subtle dishes.

FENUGREEK *Methi*

Pronounced *maytee* in Hindi, fenugreek means 'Greek hay' in Latin. Two forms are used in Indian cookery – the seeds and the leaves.

The seeds are miniature ochre-gold nuggets harvested from a clover-like plant. Though seeming to smell of curry, they are quite bitter. Used in moderation they are an important flavouring in masalas. Light roasting gives the seeds an interesting depth, and another way of using them is to soak them overnight (see page 32). (Incidentally, the seeds can also be sprouted, like mung beans for beansprouts: they have a light curry flavour.)

The leaves are used fresh, but are more likely to be purchased dry from an Asian supplier. They produce a particularly delicious, pungently savoury flavour.

LOVAGE *Ajwain* or *Ajowan*

A minor spice with tiny round grey striped seeds, which are a little bitter. They have a slightly musky but quite distinctive flavour. They probably are an acquired taste, but once acquired you'll enjoy them in Bombay mix, snacks, and fish dishes.

MACE *Javitri*

A minor spice, mace forms a tendril-like net surrounding an inner seed – the nutmeg – inside a pithy inedible green case (resembling a horse-chestnut case). When the green case is first opened, the mace is a delightful crimson colour.

At this stage it is pliable and the croppers separate it from its nutmeg and flatten it before drying it in the sun. It then goes salmon pink in colour. Its use in Indian cooking is minimal. Its subtle flavour goes well with lighter fish, vegetable and sweet dishes. (See also Nutmeg.)

It is most often bought ground.

Below: The world of spices introduces us to a wealth of colour, fragrance and shape. Note the peppercorn vines in the mortar, and the turmeric roots (top left).

MANGO POWDER *Am Chur*

This is always used factory-ground. It is made from raw sour mangoes (*am*) which are seeded and dried, then ground to a fine grey-coloured powder. It is used as a souring agent in cooking, or it can be sprinkled over dishes as a condiment.

MUSTARD SEED *Rai*

We think of mustard as being a bright yellow powder or paste. In fact it is made from black and yellow seeds, the husks of which are discarded. Flour and turmeric for colour are also added.

Indian mustard seed is neither black nor yellow, but a dark brown, and it is almost always used whole. The seeds are spherical and minute. They are immensely popular in southern India where they appear in many recipes roasted or fried or as a garnish. One interesting fact is that tasted raw they are unappealing and bitter. When cooked, however, they become sweet and appetising, and are not as hot as you might expect.

NUTMEG *Jaifal*

Nutmeg needs no introduction. In Britain, the little hard, egg-shaped nuts offer their magic when grated into pudding and cake mixes, and over hot chocolate drinks and mashed potato.

See Mace for how they grow. Originally they only came from the tiny Indonesian Moluccan island of Ambon, but are now available elsewhere. The ancient Chinese knew of them, and the Arabs brought the trade to Europe.

Indian cooking does not call for nutmeg often as an individual spice, but it is excellent grated over desserts and it is an ingredient of garam masala.

PAPRIKA

Paprika is the Hungarian word for pepper, and it was they who made it synonymous with their native dish, goulash, that bright red tasty stew. In Hungary, there are many different qualities of paprika, ranging from mild to medium hot.

Paprika originated in Latin America (see Chillies). It is only available ground (from a mild pointed red pepper). It is used in curry primarily to give a red colour to dishes. It should be mild of course, but beware, some manufacturers add chilli.

PEPPER *Mirch*

We all know pepper – it comes out of a pot with two or three holes (which matches the salt pot with one hole), or it is dried shrivelled seeds which are ground out of the pepper mill. But there is a lot more to pepper than that.

It is India's major spice and revenue earner, and has been for thousands of years. The Romans brought it to England, where it was used as a form of money. In the 13th century you could buy a sheep for 3oz (75g) of pepper! Foreign ships entering London paid a levy of pepper, and it was a recognised form of paying due debts, such as (peppercorn) rent. Until the chilli was discovered in the 16th century, pepper was the main heat-giving agent in cooking.

Peppercorns are the fruit or berries of the pepper vine which grows only in monsoon forests. The heart-shaped leaves (*paan*) are used as digestives (page 271). The vine flowers triennially and it produces berries, called spikes, in long clusters, first green then changing colour through yellow to orange-red and eventually to crimson when ripe.

Depending on the colour of the spikes when cropped, you will get green, black, white or pink peppercorns, for they are all one and the same thing. Green peppercorns are very immature, and are either bottled in vinegar or brine immediately in order to retain their colour, or are air-dried or, more recently, freeze-dried. To obtain black peppercorns, the spikes are picked when they start changing colour to yellow. They are dried in the sun and within a day or so become black and shrivelled. To harvest white pepper, the spikes are left on the vines until they turn red. The outer red skin is removed by soaking it off, revealing an inner white berry which is then dried. Pink pepper is obtained in the same way from a specific variety of vine, and it is immediately air-dried to prevent it turning white.

POPPY SEED *Cuscus*

A minor spice. Minuscule seeds, creamy white in India (not the slate grey used in British bakery), used more for texture than for flavour.

SAFFRON *Zafron* or *Kesar*

Saffron is the world's most expensive spice, reflecting not just scarcity but the extraordinary intensity of labour required to crop it. It is the golden stigma (a kind of stamen) of a variety of crocus, but not the one which emerges in the spring in the English country garden – although the saffron crocus *was* once grown commercially in Britain, in and around Saffron Walden in Essex, for instance.

The edible variety grows mainly in Kashmir, Iran and the La Mancha district of Spain. Only three stigma grow in each crocus flower and it requires 70,000 individual crocuses, or 200,000 stigma to make 1lb (450g) of saffron worth over £1,000. This places it not far behind gold (currently £2,600 a lb), which is why saffron is called liquid gold. Fortunately 20-30 stigma are sufficient to impart amazing colour, flavour and fragrance to savoury and sweet dishes.

SESAME *Til*

This tiny creamy white disc-shaped seed originated in India where, though a minor spice and somewhat neutral in taste, it is used to texture delicate cooking. It is also used as a garnish and as one of the spices in panch phoran (page 29).

STAR ANISE

This must be the prettiest spice on earth. It is $^3/_4$-1 inch (2-2.5cm) in diameter, red-brown in colour and has a regularly spaced number of arms (star points) radiating from the centre (often eight or twelve).

Although it is Chinese, and hence has no Indian name, it is astounding used in pullao rice, as much for its shape as its flavour.

TURMERIC *Haldi* or *Huldi*

One of the most important spices, turmeric is a rhizome – a kind of underground root – which when cut fresh is bright orange, when it is used as a vegetable or in pickles. More usually, the rhizome is boiled then dried until it becomes as hard as granite. It is then cleaned and ground into the familiar fine yellow powder.

Its primary use is in colouring curries. It is very bitter so it must be used sparingly.

WILD ONION SEEDS *Kalonji*

Also called *nigella*, these jet black tiny nuggets are used whole as a pungent aromatic in recipes, especially in the Bengal area. They are one of the ingredients in panch phoran (page 29).

Before the Meal

One of the joys of an Indian meal is the preamble – the build-up of nibbling and crunching which we've all enjoyed at the Indian restaurant.

Bombay mix and papadoms are the stars of the show, and these are greatly enhanced by a selection of chutneys such as fresh onion, tart tamarind and crunchy carrot. They are all in this short chapter, along with some less requested but equally excellent pre-meal nibbles – Chevda special mix, Bombay duck and potato raquets.

Caution. Wonderfully delicious though all this is, don't forget it is just the appetiser, so only take tiny portions.

Facing page, clockwise from top: Chevda Special Mix (page 44); *Potato Raquets* (page 46); *Bombay Mix* (page 44); *Papadoms,* folded in half and quarters (page 45); *Carrot Chutney* (page 48); *Tamarind Chutney* (page 48), *Onion Chutney* (page 47).

BOMBAY MIX

In my previous book, *The Indian Vegetarian Cookbook,* I gave the various recipes which form the constituents of Bombay Mix, but most of us buy this indispensable *delicioso* from our local deli. Bombay mix is a combination of crunchy spiced 'straws' made from gram flour batter which is deep-fried. This comes in a thick version *(ganthia)* and a thin one of vermicelli dimensions *(sev)*. It also usually includes cooked dry chickpeas, green peas, lentils and nuts, and is spiced with chilli and salt.

CHEF'S TIP

If your Bombay mix goes stale and the crunchy 'straws' go soft, spread the whole mixture on a flat oven tray to a depth of $^3/_4$ inch (2cm) and put into the oven preheated to 225°F/110°C/Gas $^1/_4$ for 10 minutes or so. When it cools it will be crisp again.

Chevda Special Mix

Makes 2lb (900g)

Chevda is based on cooked dry basmati rice, split chana dhal, nuts, sultanas, salt and sugar. Try combining it with other ingredients for a truly outstanding mixture. You can scale your quantities up or down as you like.

INGREDIENTS

2 x 100g packets Bombay Mix
5 x 100g packets Chevda
3 teaspoons garam masala
2 teaspoons cummin seeds, roasted
2 teaspoons coriander seeds, roasted

1 teasspoon fennel seeds, roasted
$^1/_2$-1 teaspoon aromatic salt (page 30)
$^1/_2$-1 teaspoon granulated white sugar
chilli powder to taste

METHOD

Mix well. Store in an airtight jar or biscuit tin. Serve as required. Use within one month.

PAPADOMS

If proof were needed that Indian cookery is world class, the papadom must be it. Invented way back in the mists of time (when the Europeans were running about painted in woad), they are as unappetising as shoe leather until cooked, whereupon they become divine.

There are three ways of cooking them (see below), and there are innumerable spellings. They come plain and unspiced, and spiced with black pepper, cummin seed, chilli, whole lentils, etc. Originating in South India, papadoms are normally made from ground lentils. They range in size from 3 inches (7.5cm) to more than 12 inches (30cm) in diameter.

They are made by hand, usually by women, who have spent a lifetime learning their skill. This discs are slapped out by hand from dough in a trice, and laid out on huge trays to dry in the sun. They are then packed in dozens or twenties in packets, and it is in this form that most people buy and cook them.

To Cook Papadoms

Deep-fry one at a time in hot oil at 340°F/170°C for about 10 seconds, turning once. Remove from the oil with tongs, shaking off excess oil. Allow to cool or keep in a warm place for a few hours and each will be crispy and oil-free.

Alternatively, cook under the grill. Set the grill tray at a midway position and the heat to about three-quarters. Grill one or two papadoms at a time for about 10 seconds. Ensure that the edges are cooked. Being oil-free they can be served at once or stored until ready.

Papadoms can also be microwaved. Most machines are power-rated at 650 watts. Place two papadoms in and cook on full power for about 30 seconds. Inspect and apply more heat if necessary. Serve at once or store until needed.

CHEF'S TIP

Papadoms
Immediately after they come off the heat papadoms are soft enough to fold (albeit very hot). Halved or quartered makes a superb presentation.

BOMBAY DUCK

Of course, it is not a duck! It is a fish which abounds in the rivers and estuaries around Bombay. There it is known as Bommaloe Macchli or Machi. Presumably this was too hard for the British to pronounce so it became Bumbay Duck. As soon as the fish is caught, it is topped, tailed and filleted and then hung on cane frames to dry.

We receive it in this dried form, and anything smellier or more unappetising is hard to imagine. However, don't let that put you off! The end product, for the uninitiated, tastes a little like and has the texture of crispy bacon or pork scratchings.

It can be used in a curry or pickles or, more commonly, as a crispy salty nibble with an aperitif, or crumbled over your curry and rice as a garnish.

To cook, deep-fry until golden and serve warm. Its strong fishy smell diminishes on cooking. To avoid stinking out your house, though, it is best cooked well in advance. In fact a large batch can be cooked and stored in an air-tight container for weeks. To serve (from cold) or to make them crisp again, just warm in the oven for 5 minutes at 225°F/110°C/Gas ¼.

Potato Raquets

Makes about 1lb (450g)

It was the Indians who invented the potato crisp and potato straw, calling them *sali* and *jali* respectively.

I first encountered raquets in Bombay. To make them you need one of those hand cutting devices you often find being demonstrated by super-slick salesmen at exhibitions. I bought a V cutter with a raquet attach-ment which cuts cucumbers or potatoes into a tennis raquet shape. If you cannot get such a tool (some cookshops do sell them) simply cut the potatoes either into the thinnest slices or into matchsticks, and follow the recipe.

INGREDIENTS

4 large potatoes, peeled
vegetable oil for deep-frying

Spices
1 tablespoon garam masala

½ teaspoon turmeric
0-2 teaspoons chilli powder
aromatic salt to taste (page 30)

METHOD

1 Cut the potatoes into thin raquet shapes. Spread them on kitchen paper and cover them with it as well, to keep them as dry as possible.

2 Heat the oil in the deep-fryer to 375°F/190°C.

3 Put the potato pieces into the pan, a few at a time but quickly, to prevent them sticking together. When the surface area of the pan is full but not crowded, fry until they stop sizzling and the moisture is cooked out. They will be an attractive golden colour.

4 Remove them from the pan, shaking off excess oil, and place on kitchen paper until cool.

5 Repeat stages 3 and 4 until all the potato raquets are cooked and cool.

6 Put into an airtight container with the spices. Shake well to mix. Store and use as required.

Onion Chutney

Makes 1 ample serving

I've included the next three recipes in this chapter because it has become the norm now to enjoy chutneys with crispy nibbles. Their sharp acidic tastes cut through the fullness of the nibbles, perfectly arousing the appetite for the meal to follow.

Onion chutney is simple to make. Use red onions if you can get them. They not only look better, but their slightly stronger flavour suits this chutney.

INGREDIENTS

1 red onion, tennis ball size
1 tablespoon finely chopped
parsley, fresh coriander or green
spring onion leaves

a pinch of chilli powder (or paprika)
a pinch of aromatic salt (page 30)
a pinch of white sugar

METHOD

1 Finely cut the onion into 1 inch (2.5cm) strips.

2 Add the other ingredients.

3 Place into a dish. Cover, chill and serve when required. If left for 24 hours, or longer, the onions go more translucent, which some people prefer.

CHEF'S TIP

Freeze any leftover onion chutney, and use it in a subsequent curry.

Tamarind Chutney (Imli)

Makes ample

It requires a bit of effort to prepare tamarind (page 24), but believe me it is really worth it just to make this sweet and sour, hot and tart runny brown chutney. Use it as a dip for crispy papadoms or raquets.

This recipe makes plenty, but it's hard to say how long it will last – that depends on how much you eat! I find it keeps for weeks in the fridge, but use the freezer if necessary.

INGREDIENTS

6 fl oz (175ml) tamarind purée (page 24)
1-2 tablespoons dark brown sugar (to taste)
1 teaspoon garam masala

½ teaspoon aromatic salt (page 30)
water

METHOD

1 Mix all the ingredients together, adding water until you obtain pouring cream consistency.

Carrot Chutney

Makes ample

Indian carrots are often an attractive dark red colour. I've not seen them in the West so here's a compromise. Add beetroot, marinate for a few days and – hey presto – dark red carrot chutney.

INGREDIENTS

8oz (225g) carrots, scraped clean
2oz (50g) beetroot, peeled
1 teaspoon tamarind purée (page 24)
1 teaspoon garam masala

1 teaspoon salt
½ teaspoon mustard seeds
water
vinegar (any type)

METHOD

1 Slice the carrots into strips about 2 inches (5cm) long by ¼ inch (5mm) wide).

2 Do the same with the beetroot.

3 Mix both in a jar, adding the tamarind purée, garam masala, salt and mustard seeds.

4 Add 50/50 water and vinegar until the ingredients are covered.

5 Cap the jar and shake well. Leave to marinate for 2-3 days (or as long as you like) before serving.

CHEF'S TIP

Make sure all the ingredients are covered with the vinegary liquid or you will find that uncovered carrot and beetroot will go mouldy.

Soups, Starters and Snacks

The concept of the starter is definitely Western and does not emanate from India at all. *Larousse Gastronomique*, the indispensable cookery encyclopedia, describes it as '*hors d'oeuvre*, the (additional) first dish to be served at the meal. It should be light, delicate and decorative, stimulating the appetite for the heavier dishes to follow.'

So, as with pre-meal nibbles, it is best to make smaller portions, leaving your diners actively looking forward to their main course. The problem, of course, is that Indian starters are so delicious, and can be a meal in themselves. It is therefore quite acceptable to use them as such, and to 'mix and match' dishes from this chapter with main-course dishes.

Cold dishes are not the norm either in the sub-continent – because of the difficulties of preserving food in the intense heat – but I've given a number of cold starters here which can combine to make the picnic with a difference.

Facing page, clockwise from top: Chaat (page 63), Sag Paneer Samosas (page 60), Taj Shahi Kebabs (page 64), Shorba Malabar (page 56), and Murgh Shorba (page 53).

Mulligatawny Soup

Serves 4

Though originating in the deep south of India and Sri Lanka, as a very hot vegetarian consommé (*molegoo* meaning pepper and *tunee*, water), the British Raj changed it to a thick meat-based winter soup.

INGREDIENTS

1½ pints (900ml) water or akhni stock (page 33)
3 tablespoons vegetable oil
2-3 garlic cloves, finely chopped
4oz (110g) onion, finely chopped
2oz (50g) minced beef
2 tablespoons mild curry paste (page 31)
1 tablespoon vinegar (any type)
1 tablespoon tomato purée
1 tablespoon rice, uncooked
1 tablespoon red masoor lentils, uncooked

2oz (50g) potato, peeled and chopped
1 teaspoon aromatic salt (page 30)
chilli powder to taste

Garnish
desiccated coconut
chopped parsley, basil or fresh coriander

METHOD

1 Bring the water or stock to the boil in a 5 pint (2.75 litre) pan.

2 Whilst the water is heating, heat the oil in a karahi or wok. Stir-fry the garlic for a minute. Add the onion and stir-fry for a further 2-3 minutes. Add the mince and curry paste and continue to fry for 10 more minutes.

3 When the water boils, reduce the heat and keep simmering.

4 Add the remaining ingredients to the water, including those in the karahi.

5 Simmer for at least 30 minutes – but longer will not harm it. If it gets too thick, add water.

6 Serve when required, as cooked, or if you want a smooth texture strain it, place the solids with some of the strained soup into a blender, and mulch down.

7 Ladle into mugs or soup bowls, and sprinkle in some desiccated coconut and green chopped leaves.

CHEF'S TIP

A good measure of soup is 7 fl oz (200ml) and it may help to have a ladle of that size. Surplus soup can be frozen.

Murgh Shorba

· CHICKEN SOUP ·

Serves 4

This soup comes from the Dum Pukht restaurant in Delhi, where they describe it as, 'an ineffably fragrant clear chicken soup made from slow-cooking drumsticks with cloves, cinnamon and black pepper.' *Shorba* is derived from the Persian word 'sherbet' (which itself is derived from the Arabic word '*shariba*', to drink).

INGREDIENTS

1¹/₂ pints (900ml) water or
*   chicken stock*
4 chicken drumsticks, skin
*   removed*
2-3 bay leaves
1 x 4 inch (10cm) piece cinnamon
1 teaspoon black peppercorns
2 tablespoons ghee or butter
2 garlic cloves, sliced

1 inch (2.5cm) cube ginger, sliced
4oz (110g) onions, sliced
1 teaspoon fennel seeds
4 fl oz (120ml) milk
1 teaspoon aromatic salt (page
*   30)*
15-20 saffron strands
20-30 fresh coriander leaves

METHOD

1 Put the stock, drumsticks, bay leaves, cinnamon and peppercorns into a 5 pint (2.75 litre) pan, and bring to the boil.

2 Whilst it is heating up, heat the ghee in a karahi or wok. Stir-fry the garlic and ginger for 2 minutes. Add the onion and stir-fry for a further 5 minutes.

3 Add the fennel seeds and milk to the karahi.

4 As soon as the stock becomes hot add the karahi contents, then simmer on for at least 40 minutes.

5 Ten minutes prior to serving add the salt and most of the saffron and fresh coriander leaves.

6 Serve into bowls and garnish with the remaining saffron strands and coriander leaves.

Note: You can bone the drumstick prior to serving if you like.

Kudhi Karahi Kaju

· CASHEW NUT SOUP ·

Serves 4

Cashew nuts grow profusely in the hotter areas of India, and nowhere more lusciously than in Goa. There cashews are put to many uses, for example as an ingredient of an intoxicating liqueur called Feni. This rich soup uses the nuts and an alcoholic booster.

INGREDIENTS

*9oz (250g) raw white shelled
    cashew nuts
2 tablespoons sesame oil
1 teaspoon black mustard seeds
2 teaspoons white sesame seeds
2 garlic cloves, finely chopped
2-6 dry red chillies, chopped*

*³/₄ pint (450ml) whey (page 22) or
    water
³/₄ pint (450ml) milk
aromatic salt to taste (page 30)
2 fl oz (50ml) brandy
1 full recipe onion tarka (page 26)*

METHOD

1 Place some of the cashews into a blender and mulch down with enough water to create a smooth easily pourable sauce. Repeat until all the nuts are ground.

2 Heat the oil in a 5 pint (2.75 litre) pan. Stir-fry the mustard and sesame seeds for 30 seconds, then add the garlic and the chopped dry red chillies.

2 Remove from the heat and add the whey or water and milk and bring to a rolling simmer.

4 Add the puréed cashews and simmer for 20-30 minutes.

5 Salt to taste, add the brandy, and serve garnished with the tarka.

CHEF'S TIP

Fry or oven-roast a largish batch of raw cashews. Packets of 500g (just over 1lb) are convenient. When they are golden remove from the heat, cool, then keep in an airtight container.

Facing page: Kudhi Karahi Kaju garnished with tarka and extra mustard seeds.

Charu

· SPICY TAMARIND WATER ·

Serves 4

This recipe comes from Orissa, on India's north-east coast, which is rarely visited by tourists. It is one of my favourite states for handicrafts. This thin spicy soup is served cold and can be taken as a beverage throughout a meal.

INGREDIENTS

1¹/₂ pints (900ml) water
2 tablespoons tamarind purée
  (page 24)

2oz (50g) onions, finely chopped
1 teaspoon mango powder
aromatic salt to taste (page 30)

METHOD

Simply mix everything together and serve with ice cubes.

Shorba Malabar

· TOMATO AND COCONUT SOUP ·

Serves 4

The Malabar coast of India lies in the deep south where the coconuts grow huge and the spices lush. This recipe is equally good served hot or cold.

INGREDIENTS

1 pint (600ml) water
1lb (450g) plum tomatoes (see Chef's Tip, below)
2 teaspoons garlic purée (page 24)
2 tablespoons onion purée (page 25)
1 tablespoon tamarind purée (page 24)
1/2 pint (300ml) fresh coconut milk
3-4 tablespoons fresh coconut purée (page 23)
1-4 whole fresh red chillies (optional)

salt to taste
fresh coriander or parsley, finely chopped
thick pourable cream to garnish

Spices
1 teaspoon mustard seeds, roasted
1/2 teaspoon fenugreek seeds, roasted and ground
1/2 teaspoon crushed black peppercorns

METHOD

1 Bring the water to the boil in a 5 pint (2.75 litre) pan.

2 Place the whole tomatoes into the boiling water for 30 seconds. Remove from the water and when cool enough, peel off and discard the skins.

3 Meanwhile, into the simmering water put the garlic and onion purées, the skinned tomatoes, tamarind, coconut milk and purée, and chillies if using.

4 Add the **spices** and salt. Serve soon after, garnishing with the green leaves and a curl of cream.

CHEF'S TIP

Plum tomatoes provide a superb flavour. These are becoming increasingly available fresh. If they are not, use 50/50 fresh tomatoes/canned plum tomatoes.

SOUPS, STARTERS AND SNACKS

Toovar Rasam

· SOUTH INDIAN LENTIL CONSOMMÉ ·

Serves 4

*R*asam is a South Indian vegetable soup, traditionally served with rice, curds, lentil and vegetable dishes. It is thin and spicy, and is excellent on its own.

INGREDIENTS

2 tablespoons mustard or coconut
  oil
2 teaspoons garlic purée (page 24)
2 tablespoons onion purée
  (page 25)
$^1/_2$ teaspoon turmeric
1 pint (600ml) whey (page 22),
  akhni stock (page 33) or water
2oz (50g) toovar dhal, picked over
  for grit etc
1oz (25g) carrot, finely shredded
$^1/_2$ pint (300ml) tomato juice

2 tablespoons vinegar (any type)
1 teaspoon white sugar
aromatic salt to taste (page 30)
fresh coriander leaves

Spices (whole and roasted)
2 teaspoons coriander seeds
2-4 dry red chillies
1 teaspoon cummin seeds
1 teaspoon polished moong dhal
$^1/_2$ teaspoon black peppercorns
$^1/_2$ teaspoon mustard seeds

METHOD

1 Heat the oil in a 5 pint (2.75 litre) saucepan. Stir-fry the garlic and onion purées for 2 minutes. Stir in the turmeric.

2 Remove the pan from the heat and allow it to cool for a minute or two then add the liquid, plus all the other ingredients (except the salt, coriander and **spices**).

3 Bring to the boil, then simmer for 30 minutes or so.

4 About 5 minutes before serving, add the **spices** and salt.

5 Garnish with the leaves and serve piping hot.

> **CHEF'S TIP**
>
> If you enjoy this South Indian soup, make a batch of the masala (spice mixture) – simply multiply the quantities of the **spices** above (a factor of 10 will yield about 9oz/250g). Roast and store in an airtight jar.

Dal Surwa

· NEPALESE LENTIL SOUP ·

Serves 4

It is often bitterly cold in Nepal, being high in the Himalayas, so thick nutritious soups are popular and warming. This *surwa* (the Nepalese derivation of *shorba*) would traditionally be served as part of the main meal.

INGREDIENTS

2 tablespoons sunflower oil
4oz (110g) onions, chopped
2 teaspoons mild curry paste or
  masala (pages 28 and 31)
1½ pints (900ml) water or
  vegetable stock

1 large potato, peeled and diced
2oz (50g) dry red masoor lentils
aromatic salt to taste (page 30)
2 tablespoons chopped fresh
  coriander or parsley

METHOD

1 Heat the oil in a 5 pint (2.75 litre) saucepan. Stir-fry the onion until lightly golden. Add the curry, mix in well, then add the water or stock, potato and lentils.

2 Simmer for 30 minutes.

3 Salt to taste, then add the coriander or parsley. Serve hot within a few minutes.

Goolar Kebab

· STUFFED KEBAB ·

Makes 16

These Kashmiri meatballs are stuffed with a sweet and sour chutney. A Goolar is an Indian wild fig, whose spherical shape this delightful recipe resembles.

INGREDIENTS

Kebabs
1lb (450g) fillet steak, weighed
   after discarding unwanted
   matter
1 pint (600ml) water or akhni
   stock (page 33)
2oz (50g) chana dhal, cleaned
2 eggs
salt
vegetable oil for deep-frying

Spices
1 tablespoon masala (page 28)
1 tablespoon garam masala (page 29)

Chutney
4 tablespoons raisins
2 tablespoons chopped fresh mint
2 tablespoons chopped fresh
   coriander
0-4 fresh green chillies, chopped
1 tablespoon brown sugar
1 teaspoon mango powder

The Kebab Case

1 Mince the steak several times until very smooth.

2 Bring the water or stock to the boil in a 5 pint (2.75 litre) pan. Add the mince and dhal. Bring it back to the simmer then cover and cook until the liquid has reduced completely and the mixture is dry. (Stir frequently and take care that it doesn't burn.)

3 Allow the mixture to go cold then mix in the eggs, **spices** and salt to taste. Divide into sixteen pieces.

The Chutney

4 Put all the ingredients into the food processor. Mulch into a stiff paste. Divide into sixteen equal portions.

To cook

5 Take one kebab case. Flatten it in your palm. Place a portion of chutney in the centre and form the kebab into a ping-pong-ball shape. Repeat until all sixteen are made.

6 Preheat the deep-fryer to 375°F/190°C. Place the first kebab into the oil. Follow with the next seven. Fry for 7-8 minutes. Remove and keep warm while you repeat with the second batch.

7 Serve hot on a bed of salad with lemon wedges.

Sag Paneer Samosa

· SPINACH AND CHEESE-FILLED PASTRY ·

Makes 16

The *samosa* is one of the best-known Indian delicacies. It has relatives in Afghanistan where it is called the *samboosa*. In the Middle East the *sambuska* is crescent-shaped though the concept is the same, whilst in Turkey the triangular stuffed pastry is called the *borek*.

There are a number of ways of achieving the triangle shape, each equally valid. This version uses a rectangular strip. Sizes, varying from large to tiny, will be determined by the size of the strip. That described here produces samosas with sides of about 3 inches (7.5 cm).

As to pastry, shortcrust is the norm, but puff pastry is good too. Filo pastry or spring roll wrappers produce cracklingly effective results. Whichever you choose to use, the thinner you roll the pastry, the better the effect.

INGREDIENTS

Vegetable oil for deep-frying

Filling
1lb (450g) spinach, fresh, frozen or canned
2 tablespoons ghee or vegetable oil
2-4 garlic cloves, finely chopped
4oz (110g) onions, finely chopped
2 tablespoons mild curry paste (page 31)
4oz (110g) crumbly paneer (page 22)
4 tablespoons chopped fresh coriander

4 tablespoons chopped fresh mint
1 tablespoon garam masala
1/2 teaspoon aromatic salt (page 30)
0-4 green chillies, finely chopped

Pastry
1 tablespoon sesame oil
8oz (225g) strong white plain flour or 16 rectangular sheets of filo pastry, approx. 3 x 8 inches (7.5 x 20cm)

METHOD

The filling

1 Make the filling first, to allow it sufficient time to cool. Clean and finely chop the spinach. Boil it until cooked (15 minutes), or follow packet or label instructions. Strain off as much liquid as you can (it makes good soup stock).

2 Meanwhile heat the ghee or oil and stir-fry the garlic, onion and curry paste for about 10 minutes. Add the spinach, paneer and all the remaining ingredients. Mix well, bring to the sizzle then place in a strainer and allow to become completely cold.

The Pastry

3 Mix the oil, flour and enough water to make a dough which, when mixed, does not stick to the bowl. Leave it to stand for about an hour.

4 At the same time mix 1 extra tablespoon of flour with enough water to make a glue-like paste (to stick each samosa together).

5 Divide the pastry into four pieces then shape each piece into a square. Roll it out and cut four rectangles 3 x 8 inches (7.5 x 20cm). Remember the thinner you can roll, the crisper your samosas will be.

The Samosa

6 Take one rectangle. Place a teaspoon of filling on it (see below). Make the first diagonal fold, then the second and third.

7 Open the pouch and top up with some more filling. Do not *over*fill, or it will burst when cooked.

8 Brush some flour and water paste on the remaining flap, gluing it over the opening to seal in the filling. Trim off the excess.

9 Deep-fry in hot oil at 375°F/190°C for 8-10 minutes.

10 Serve with tamarind chutney (page 48).

CHEF'S TIP

Some Asian stores sell packets of 'samosa pads' containing about 40 sheets of thinly rolled pastry strips.

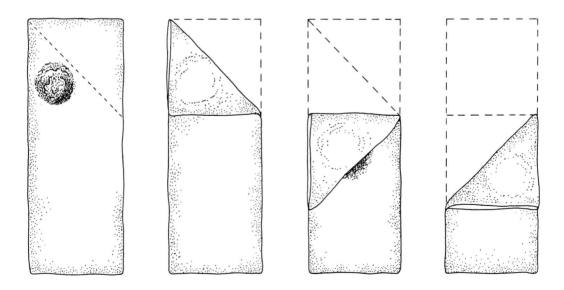

Singhara

· SPICY FRITTERS ·

Makes 8

One of the sub-continent's most famous finger snacks is the onion *bhajia* or *pakora*. Here is the Bangladeshi variant, the *singhara*. Their principal joy is the seemingly endless variations of both batter and filling.

I frequently do cooking demonstrations in such exalted food places as Harrods, Bentalls and the Army and Navy Stores in Victoria, and one of the things I demonstrate is these spicy fritters. The point is to show people how easy and inexpensive they are – and how fast and tasty too. Though deep-fried, they should be very light and not in the least bit greasy. To achieve this the following observations must be adhered to:

1. No less than 50 per cent of the flour used must be gram flour.
2. The batter must not be too wet.
3. The fritters must be deep-fried. Shallow-frying makes them stodgy.
4. The oil temperature must be 375°C/190°F (the same as for chip-frying).
5. The 'filling' ingredients must be raw for optimum crispness.

The batter is combined with any filling of your choice. The most common, and my favourite, is onion, but you can use any alternative. Some suggestions include potato, aubergine, carrot, turnip, parsnip or white radish (*mooli*), all best shredded. Small cauliflower florets, mushrooms, pepper and chillies work well. So do paneer cubes. Dry or fresh fruit is excellent.

This batter recipe comes from one Bangladeshi friend and the filling suggestion from another: the result is a singhara of great culinary excellence.

INGREDIENTS

Vegetable oil for deep-frying

Batter
3oz (75g) gram flour (besan) plus
  1oz (25g) coconut milk powder,
  or 4oz (110g) gram flour
2 garlic cloves, chopped
1 tablespoon mild curry paste
  (page 31)
1 tablespoon lemon juice
1 teaspoon garam masala
1 teaspoon cummin seeds, roasted
1 teaspoon coriander seeds,
  roasted

1 teaspoon fenugreek leaf, dry
1 tablespoon fresh chopped mint
1 teaspoon aromatic salt
  (page 30)
sufficient water to make a thick
  batter

Filling
4oz (110g) onions, chopped into
  fine 1 inch (2.5cm) strips
2oz (50g) mashed cooked potato
2 tablespoons chopped cashew
  nuts
2 tablespoons Bombay mix

METHOD

1 Mix the batter ingredients together to achieve a thickish paste which will drop sluggishly off the spoon. Let it stand for at least 10 minutes, during which time the mixture will fully absorb the moisture.

2 Next add the filling. Mix in well and leave again for about 10 minutes to absorb the batter mixture.

3 Meanwhile, heat the deep-frying oil to 375°F/190°C. This temperature is below smoking point and will cause a drop of batter to splutter a bit, then float more or less at once.

4 Inspect the mixture. There must be no 'powder' left. It must be well mixed. Then simply scoop out an eighth of the mixture and place it carefully in the oil. Place all eight portions in, but allow about 30 seconds between each one so the oil will maintain its temperature.

5 Fry for 10 minutes each, turning once. Remove from the oil in the order they went in, drain well and serve with salad garnishes, lemon wedges and chutneys.

Chaat or Chat

· CHICKEN AND/OR POTATO COLD SNACK ·

Serves 4

There aren't many cold curries in the Indian repertoire, but *chaat*, pronounced 'chart' is one. It can, of course, be served hot, but somehow it tastes better cold, and it is never better than on a spicy picnic.

INGREDIENTS

1lb (450g) cooked chicken meat or boiled potato, or a 50/50 combination, all cold
1 full recipe spicy tandoori marinade (page 80)

4oz (110g) onion, finely chopped
salt to taste
garam masala
fresh whole coriander leaves

METHOD

This recipe is for a 50/50 combination of chicken and potato.

1 Place the marinade in a pan and slowly bring it to the simmer, stirring frequently.

2 Simmer on the lowest heat for about 10 minutes, stirring frequently.

3 Turn off the heat and let it go quite cold.

4 Dice the cooked chicken into small pieces, and the potato the same, and add to the pan, with the onion. Salt to taste.

5 Serve at once or cover and refrigerate for no more than 24 hours.

6 Garnish with garam masala and leaves, and serve with salad.

Taj Shahi Kebab

· MINCED STEAK KEBAB ·

Makes 16

These remarkable round kebabs were demonstrated to one of our Gourmet Tour Groups in Agra. There were three points of interest – Chef Ajit Bangera used both Cheddar cheese and hard-boiled eggs in the recipe, and thirdly, the Taj Mahal was just a kilometre away.

Don't use butcher's mince to make kebabs. It has too much fat and gristle. Only the tenderest cuts of best quality meat, such as beef fillet, will give a tender kebab.

INGREDIENTS

1½lb (675g) fillet steak, weighed
   after stage 1
1 tablespoon dried onion
2 finely chopped garlic cloves
1 tablespoon grated Cheddar
   cheese
1 hard-boiled egg
2 tablespoons chopped spring
   onion leaves
1 tablespoon chopped fresh mint

   or 1 teaspoon dried mint
0-4 fresh green chillies, chopped
2 tablespoons ground almonds
1 tablespoon gram flour (besan)
1 teaspoon green cardamom,
   ground
1 teaspoon aromatic salt
   (page 30)
½ teaspoon nutmeg, grated

METHOD

1 Chop the meat into finger-sized strips, discarding any unwanted matter.

2 Run it through a hand or electric mincer two or three times until it is lump free and finely ground.

3 In a large bowl mix all the ingredients together by hand. The mixture should be fairly sticky.

4 Clean your hands (before and frequently during this stage). Divide the mixture into four. Take one batch and divide it again into four and make four ping-pong-sized balls.

5 Slip these on to a skewer. Repeat with three more skewers.

6 During stage 4, preheat the grill to medium. Place the skewers on to foil on a grill pan and place this in the midway position under the heat. Alternatively they can be barbecued.

7 Grill for 5 minutes. Turn and grill for another 5 minutes.

8 Serve on a bed of salad with a lemon wedge and tandoori chutney (page 49)

SHEEK KEBAB

Use the above ingredients and method to make four Sheek Kebabs (sausage shapes).

Kalejee, Gurda, Dill

· SPICY OFFAL STIR-FRY ·

Serves 4

Offal sounds so awful! The word actually derives from 'off-fall' or off cuts. This recipe combines the three most popular offal in a tasty and spicy stir-fry. Their attractive-sounding Hindi words are *kaleji* (liver), *gurda* (kidney) and *dill* (heart) You may omit one or two of the three offals, or you can add or substitute brain and/or sweetbreads (see Chef's Tip 1 below).

INGREDIENTS

1lb (450g) offal of choice, weighed after discarding unwanted matter, diced into bite-sized pieces
4 tablespoons ghee, coloured red (colouring optional, see Chef's Tip 2 below)
1 tablespoon garlic purée (page 24)

1 tablespoon ginger purée (page 25)
1 teaspoon cummin seeds
salt
garam masala
chopped fresh coriander

METHOD

1   Heat the ghee and colour it red if you like.

2   Add the garlic, ginger and cummin, and stir-fry for 30 seconds.

3   Add the offal, and briskly stir-fry until it is cooked through (about 8-10 minutes depending on type of offal and size of cut).

4   Serve on a bed of salad with a lemon wedge. Sprinkle with salt, garam masala and the chopped leaves.

CHEF'S TIP 1

Kidneys, brain and sweetbreads should be immersed in salted water for an hour or so to remove the blood, then dried on kitchen paper.

CHEF'S TIP 2

For a really attractive appearance you can colour the ghee beetroot red in the traditional Indian way. Obtain some alkanet root (*ratin jot*). Put about 6-8 flakes into the warm ghee and it will go red. Strain and discard the root when it stops oozing red. Cook this dish with the red oil.

Lazeez

· GREEN HERBAL CHICKEN KEBABS ·

Serves 4

Following the previous red recipe here is an attractive green one. The two go well together on the starter plate.

INGREDIENTS

1½lb (675g) chicken breast fillet (weighed after skinning and boning), cut into squares

Marinade
6 tablespoons green masala paste (page 32)
5oz (150g) yoghurt

1 tablespoon garlic purée (page 24)
2 teaspoons bottled mint in vinegar
1 teaspoon garam masala
1 teaspoon aromatic salt (page 30)

METHOD

1 Cut the chicken breasts evenly (see Chef's Tip below). Aim for a total of between six and eight pieces per person.

2 Mix the marinade ingredients together in a bowl and add the chicken pieces. Cover and leave in the refrigerator for at least 24 hours (maximum 48 hours).

3 Just prior to cooking, slip six to eight pieces on to a skewer. Repeat with three more skewers. Use any spare marinade in a curry or discard.

4 Pre-heat the grill to medium. Place the skewers on to a rack over foil on a grill pan and place this in the midway position under the heat. Alternatively they can be barbecued.

5 Cook for 5 minutes, turn and repeat. Cut one piece to ensure that it is fully cooked and white throughout. If not, cook on for a while longer.

6 Serve on a bed of salad with a selection of chutneys.

CHEF'S TIP

Chicken kebab pieces should be even bite-sized pieces of 1-1½ inches (2.5-4cm) square. To cut these squares will involve 'wastage' of breast. Save the off-cuts for another curry or for stock.

Facing page: Lazeez (above) served with Panat Bhat (savoury cold rice, page 75).

Uthapam

· SOUTH INDIAN SAVOURY PANCAKE ·

Serves 4

There is nothing, just nothing, to compare with this dish. I watched an expert chef make these pancakes on an inverted cast-iron karahi under which were white hot coals. He deftly spread out the batter, scraping it paper thin as it cooked, It was 18 inches (45cm) in diameter and as light as a feather.

This method uses his batter in a crepe pan, flat frying pan or tava. Variations on the batter are called *dosa*.

INGREDIENTS

Sunflower or light oil as required
1 full recipe koora uthapam
*   masala (page 172)*

Batter
3¹/₂oz (100g) polished urid dhal

9oz (250g) raw uncooked Basmati
*   rice*
9oz (250g) cold cooked rice
¹/₂ teaspoon fenugreek seeds,
*   roasted and ground*
salt to taste

METHOD

1 Mix all the batter ingredients except for the fenugreek and salt together in a bowl, then cover with ample cold water and leave to soak for a couple of hours.

2 Strain and rinse generously.

3 Grind the ingredients in a blender adding just enough water to create a smooth, easily pourable pancake batter. Return it to its bowl and leave it overnight in a warm place (so that it very slightly ferments).

4 You'll need a curry filling. The one on page 172 is perfect for the job.

5 Stir the batter, and add the ground fenugreek. Salt to taste.

6 Heat the flat pan with a few drops of oil. Pour in sufficient batter which, when 'swilled' around the pan makes a thin pancake. Pour off any excess – the thinner the better.

7 Cook until it goes solid. Turn it if necessary (a really thin one won't need it) and repeat. The whole process takes about a minute.

8 Remove from the pan (see Chef's Tip below). Place the stuffing across the centre. Fold loosely and serve with chutneys.

CHEF'S TIP

Pancakes of any type can be cooked in advance, stored between layers of foil and refrigerated for a day or frozen. Thaw, reheat in an oven or microwave, first removing the foil.

Dahi Vadai

· SPICY RISSOLE BALLS IN YOGHURT ·

Makes 16

Another of India's lesser-known wonder dishes is crispy spherical rissoles in tangy yoghurt. Served cold, they are great for a spicy picnic.

INGREDIENTS

18oz (500g) polished urid dhal
1½ teaspoons salt
vegetable oil for deep-frying

Spices
1½ teaspoons cummin seeds,
*   roasted*
1 teaspoon black peppercorns,
*   crushed*
0-4 green chillies, chopped

Garnish
10oz (275g) yoghurt
paprika
garam masala
fresh whole coriander leaves

METHOD

1 Soak the dhal in ample water for a couple of hours.

2 Strain and rinse generously.

3 Grind the dhal in a food processor, adding just enough water to create a pliable dough. Doubtless the grinder will leave some of the lentils whole or partly ground, but persevere until most are ground. Towards the end add the salt and **spices**.

4 Cover and leave for a couple of hours (up to 24 hours in the refrigerator) to allow the water to be absorbed.

5 Sprinkle some flour on to your work surface then roll out small ping-pong-sized balls, until all the dough is used.

6 Heat the deep-fryer or oil in a pan to 375°F/190°C.

7 Place the balls in one by one about 10 seconds apart (so that the oil temperature is maintained) until you have eight in the pan. Cook for 8-10 minutes. Remove and set aside.

8 Repeat with the next eight, and leave all to go cold.

9 Place the yoghurt into a serving bowl and the rissoles into the yoghurt.

10 Sprinkle with paprika, garam masala and green leaves on top. Serve cold with coconut chutney (page 253).

Batata Vada

· POTATO BALLS ·

Makes 12

Here is another kind of rissole. This one is made from mashed potato coated with batter and deep-fried. They are, believe me, scrumptious. You'll find them in the excellent Sabra's restaurant in London NW10.

INGREDIENTS

1lb (450g) mashed cooked potato
2oz (50g) chopped nuts (any type)
0-4 fresh green chillies or red
  chillies, chopped
2 teaspoons masala (page 28)
1 teaspoon salt

vegetable oil for deep-frying

Batter
3oz (75g) gram flour (besan)
2 tablespoons lemon juice

METHOD

1 Make the batter by adding the lemon juice to the gram flour, then enough water to make it thick but pourable. Let it stand during stages 2-4.

2 Mix together the potato, nuts, chilli, masala and salt.

3 Preheat the deep-fryer or oil in a pan to 375°F/190°C.

4 Sprinkle some extra dry gram flour on a work surface and roll the mixture into golf-ball-sized spheres.

5 Immerse a sphere in the batter then carefully lower it into the hot oil. Repeat with three more spheres. Fry for about 10 minutes, turning from time to time. Remove them and rest on kitchen paper. Repeat the process until all are cooked.

6 Serve hot or cold with salad and chutneys.

Kachori

· LENTIL BALLS IN BATTER ·

Makes 16

These are a combination in technique of the last two recipes. They hail from Central India, where you'll encounter them at every street corner.

INGREDIENTS

1 full recipe dahi vadai (page 69)
1 full recipe batata vada batter
  (above)

METHOD

1 Make sixteen dahi vadai up to stage 6 (i.e. omitting the yoghurt).

2 Make the batata vada batter.

3 Follow the previous recipe from stage 4 to the end.

Khamans

· SQUARE STEAMED LENTIL CAKES ·

Makes 16

These are unusual, firm but light textured savouries from the southern Indian repertoire.

INGREDIENTS

18oz (500g) gram flour (besan)
4 tablespoons yoghurt
2oz (50g) chopped nuts (any kind)
0-4 fresh green and/or red chillies, chopped
1 tablespoon chopped fresh coriander
1 teaspoon aromatic salt (page 30)

2 tablespoons mild curry paste (page 31)
lettuce leaves

Topping
2 teaspoons mustard seeds, roasted
4 tablespoons coconut chutney (page 253)

METHOD

1 Mix all the ingredients (except for the lettuce) with enough water to make a stiffish but pliable dough.

2 Roll or press the dough out to form a 6 inch (15cm) square about 1 inch (2.5cm) in thickness.

3 Line a steamer tray with lettuce leaves (to prevent the square from sticking). Then place the square on this.

4 Steam for 15-20 minutes (see Chef's Tip below).

5 Remove from the heat and allow the square to go cold.

6 Cut into 1½ inch (4cm) squares.

7 Mix the 'topping' ingredients and spread on to each square.

CHEF'S TIP

Steaming
A Chinese bamboo steamer basket with lid, of about 8 inches (20cm) in diameter, used in a wok complete with a wire rack, cannot be beaten. Put the rack in the wok. Pour in enough water to leave the rack standing clear. Bring the water to the boil. Put the lidded bamboo basket on the rack and steam away!

Green Salad with Sesame

Serves 4

This is an Indian rarity – a salad. The idea came from the chefs at one of India's supreme hotels – The Oberoi Grand in Calcutta. Serve it cold as a starter or at a picnic.

INGREDIENTS

1lb (450g) vegetables (all or some of these): green peppers, cucumber, custard marrow, watercress, fresh spinach leaves, green apple (weighed after discarding unwanted matter).
2 tablespoons sesame oil
2 tablespoons sesame seeds
1 teaspoon panch phoran (page 29)
1-3 garlic cloves, thinly sliced
3oz (75g) onion, thinly sliced
2oz (50g) desiccated coconut, preferably fresh

Dressing/Marinade
5fl oz (150ml) coconut water (page 23)
3 tablespoons sesame oil
2 tablespoons freshly squeezed lime juice
1 tablespoon white granulated sugar
1½ teaspoons aromatic salt (page 30)
½ teaspoon yellow English mustard powder

METHOD

1 First, prepare the aromatic base of the salad. Heat the oil in a karahi or wok and stir-fry the sesame seeds and panch phoran for 20 seconds. Add the garlic, onion and desiccated coconut and continue to stir-fry for 4-5 minutes. Remove from the heat and allow to go cold.

2 Make the dressing/marinade by combining all the ingredients.

3 Prepare the vegetables. Cut into bite-size shapes of your choice.

4 Mix everything together in a bowl. Cover it and refrigerate for up to 30 hours.

Crab Papad Rolls

Serves 4

This stunning invention is from Alice, a Goan chef whom I met at the Ramada Renaissance Hotel in Goa. She told me she always had the problem of using up papadoms which had lost their crunch.

Minced prawn or any other filling – meat, chicken, vegetables – are equally excellent in this recipe.

INGREDIENTS

4 large or 8 small cooked
  papadoms
6-8oz (175-225g) white and
  brown crab meat
2oz (50g) onion, finely chopped
2 tablespoons thick mayonnaise
1 tablespoon mild curry paste
  (page 31)

1 tablespoon chopped fresh
  coriander or parsley
0-4 fresh green chillies, chopped
aromatic salt to taste (page 30)
vegetable oil for deep frying

METHOD

1 Soak the papadoms in water in something large and flat, such as an oven tray, for a few minutes.

2 Mix the remaining ingredients into a spreading paste.

3 Remove the papadoms from the water and place on clean dry teatowels to dry them.

4 Preheat the deep fryer to 375°F/190°C.

5 Take one dryish, now pliable, papadom and keeping it flat, place a line of filling along the centre line. Then roll it up, like a stuffed pancake.

6 Carefully (to avoid spluttering from the damp papadom) lower it into the oil. Try to get the flap on to the bottom to avoid it unrolling. Fry for 5 minutes or so and remove it.

7 Repeat stages 5 and 6 until all are cooked. Serve with salad.

Teesryo

· COCKLES IN GINGER ·

Serves 4

A Goan speciality using a minute thumb-nail-sized cockle, native to Goa, which seems to be unobtainable elsewhere. Use small clams, cockles or mussels with or without shells. The dish is not unlike *moules marinière* in concept. Fresh is best, but bottled cockles will do.

INGREDIENTS

12oz (350g) cockles (weighed without shells)
2 tablespoons mustard oil
1 tablespoon mustard seeds
2-4 garlic cloves, finely chopped
2 inch (5cm) cube fresh ginger, chopped into strips
4oz (110g) onions, chopped
fresh coconut water from 1 nut (if available)
2oz (50g) fresh coconut flesh, chopped, or 4 tablespoons coconut milk powder

2 tablespoons fresh chopped coriander
aromatic salt to taste (page 30)
4 limes, quartered

Spices (ground)
2 teaspoons cummin
1 teaspoon coriander
1 teaspoon mango powder
1/2 teaspoon turmeric
chilli powder to taste

METHOD

1 Wash the cockles well and check them over to see that they are clean and perfect. Dry well.

2 Heat the oil in a karahi or wok and stir-fry the mustard seeds for 10 seconds. Add the garlic, ginger and onion and stir-fry for a further 5 minutes or so.

3 Mix the **spices** into a paste with a little water, and add to the karahi. Stir-fry for 2-5 minutes.

4 Add the fresh coconut water and flesh or the coconut powder and water. Stir well, then add the fresh coriander and finally the cockles. Make the sauce as runny as you like.

5 Salt to taste, and serve with lime wedges.

Facing page: Teesryo made with mussels (see above)

Panat Bhat

· SAVOURY COLD RICE ·

Serves 4

This is another amazing delicacy from South India. It must be served cold and believe me, despite its simplicity, it is just delicious. It's great for picnics, but take my advice and make plenty.

INGREDIENTS

12oz (350g) pre-cooked Basmati rice, chilled
1 tablespoon tasty oil such as pistachio, toasted sesame, walnut or hazelnut
2-3 tablespoons fresh lime or lemon juice

2 tablespoons onion tarka (page 26)
2 teaspoons mustard seeds, roasted
20 cashew nuts, fried and chopped
0-4 fresh green chillies, chopped
aromatic salt to taste (page 30)

METHOD

1 Mix all the ingredients together, but gently so as not to break the rice grains.

2 Serve with other cold dishes for a summer treat.

Dalo Temperadu

· DEVILLED SQUID ·

Serves 4

This recipe comes from the resplendent island of Sri Lanka where they enjoy things hot. This particular recipe, I was told, was developed from a Portuguese recipe bought to Sri Lanka some 400 years ago by traders. Buy large squid rather than small.

INGREDIENTS

12oz (350g) squid rings (after
  cleaning, see below)
4 tablespoons semolina
4 tablespoons plain white flour
vegetable oil for deep-frying

Spices (ground)
1 tablespoon cummin
1 tablespoon paprika
2 teaspoons coriander

1 teaspoon mango powder
$^1/_2$ teaspoon asafoetida

Garnish
lettuce leaves
chilli powder (optional)
garam masala
salt
desiccated coconut
4 limes, quartered

METHOD

1 Wash the squid well (after thawing, if frozen), and discard any unwanted matter. You may find there is an 'ink sac'. Wash until the dark liquid is removed. Cut off the heads and use for fish stock. Cut the bodies into rings (familiar to devotees of the Spanish *calamares*) and dry in a teatowel.

2 Preheat the deep-fryer to 375°F/190°C (chip-cooking temperature).

3 Mix the **spices** with the semolina and flour. Dip the rings in this mixture and put about twelve of them quickly, one at a time, into the fryer. Deep-fry for 5 minutes then remove.

4 Place on kitchen paper. Keep them warm, and repeat until all are fried.

5 Place on a serving dish lined with lettuce then sprinkle with chilli powder and/or garam masala, salt and desiccated coconut. Serve at once with lime wedges.

Momo or Yomari
· SPICY FILLED DUMPLINGS ·

Makes 8

Although divided by the peaks of the Himalayas, and with little contact between them, the food of Tibet and Nepal has some elements in common. These dumplings are one such dish. In Tibet they are called *momo*, and in Nepal they are *yomari*. The shape differs, but in essence, they are the same. They are eaten on their own as a snack with chutneys, or they can be incorporated into many vegetable dishes.

INGREDIENTS

1lb (450g) strong white or brown
  chupatti flour
3 tablespoons vegetable oil
1/2 teaspoon baking powder
1oz (25g) raisins or sultanas
  (optional)
1oz (25g) chopped almonds
2oz (50g) onions, thinly sliced
6oz (175g) cummin-spiced potato
  (page 183)
aromatic salt (page 30)

Spices
2 tablespoons sesame seeds,
  roasted
1 tablespoon cummin seeds,
  roasted
2 teaspoons dried fenugreek
  leaves
2 teaspoons masala (page 28)
2 teaspoons garam masala

METHOD

1 Mix together the flour, oil and baking powder with enough water to make a pliable dough. Knead then leave to rise in a warm place for 1/2 hour or so.

2 After it has risen, re-knead it, adding the sultanas (if you like a sweet taste), almonds, onion, curried potato, then **spices** and the salt. Knead and mix carefully and thoroughly.

3 Divide the dough into eight and roll into balls for *momo* and pear shapes for *yomari*.

4 The best way to cook the dumplings is in a double boiler or steamer (see Chef's Tip, page 71). Cook them for about 20 minutes. Inspect and turn over and carry on for a further 10-15 minutes.

Tandoori and Tikka Dishes

✳

Nothing else in the world resembles the taste of food cooked in the tandoor. This ancient clay-pot oven was invented thousands of years ago and has evolved to the perfect cooking appliance it is today. It is cylindrical in shape, with a narrow neck above which is the only hole, its top. The base is rounded (a flattened base would require more fuel). Sizes vary from 4 feet (1.2 metres) high to 1½ feet (45cm).

The principle is simple, but ingenious. Charcoal is placed in the oven's base, filling about one-quarter of the volume. It is fired and allowed to get as hot as possible. Food is placed on steel skewers, which themselves conduct heat so that the food cooks from both the inside and the outside at an extremely high temperature. The narrow neck of the oven causes a fast upward air flow which prevents instant incineration of the food, as well as imparting the flavour of the charcoal enhanced by the marinade dripping on to it. Serious home cooks should consider purchasing a domestic tandoor, although the following recipes give conventional oven methods.

Facing page, clockwise from top: Rubian (page 89), Lamb Tikka Gosht (page 83) and Paneer Tikka Makhmali (page 88).

Tandoori Dry Mix Masala

As with all pre-mixed masalas, this has the advantage of maturing during storage. Keep it in the dark in an airtight container, and it will be good for about 12 months.

Makes 310g

45g ground coriander
45g ground cummin
45g garlic powder
45g paprika
25g ground ginger
25g mango powder
25g dried mint
25g beetroot powder (deep red colouring)*
20g chilli powder
10g anatto seed powder (yellow colouring)*

1. Simply mix the ingredients together well, and store.

2. Use as described in the recipes.

*If you use food colouring powder instead use only 5g red and 3g sunset yellow. These small quantities will achieve a more vibrant colour than beetroot and anatto.

Tandoori Masala Paste

Most restaurants use bright red tandoori paste to colour and spice their marinade. It is not difficult to make your own. To cook, use one recipe of the previous tandoori dry mix masala and cook it following the method for mild curry paste on page 31.

Spicy Tandoori or Tikka Marinade

Yoghurt is used as a medium in which to 'suspend' the spices for tandoori or tikka marinade.

Enough for 1¹/₂lb (675g) meat

5oz (150g) yoghurt

3 tablespoons mustard oil
2 tablespoons bottled or fresh lemon juice
1 teaspoon garlic purée (page 24)
1 teaspoon ginger purée (page 25)
3 fresh green chillies, chopped
1 tablespoon fresh mint or 1 teaspoon bottled mint
3 tablespoons chopped fresh coriander leaves
1 teaspoon cummin seeds, roasted and ground
1 teaspoon garam masala
1 tablespoon mild curry paste (page 31)
2 tablespoons tandoori masala paste or dry mix masala (above)
1 teaspoon salt

1. Simply mix everything together.

2. Use as directed in the recipes.

Light Tandoori Marinade

Enough for 1¹/₂lb (675g) meat

5fl oz (150ml) milk
2 teaspoons garlic powder
1 teaspoon ginger powder
1 teaspoon chilli powder
1 teaspoon dried mint
1 teaspoon aromatic salt (page 30)
¹/₂ teaspoon deep red food colouring powder (optional)
¹/₂ teaspoon sunset yellow colouring powder (optional)

1. Mix all the ingredients together.

2. Use as directed in the recipes.

CHEF'S TIP

To marinate, do so in a bowl of sufficient size to be virtually filled with marinade and the ingredient. Do not use a metallic bowl, as the acids of the marinade can react with the metal (especially aluminium).

Murgh Aangar
· TRADITIONAL TANDOORI CHICKEN ·

Serves 2 as a starter

For best results try to obtain a farm-fresh double poussin (a 6-10 week old young chicken) whose 'oven-ready' weight is 1½-2lb (675-900g).

INGREDIENTS

1 double poussin (see above)
1 full recipe light or spicy
  tandoori marinade (page 80)

salad garnish
lemon wedges

METHOD

1 Halve the poussin, and remove and discard the skin. With the tip of a sharp knife make short gashes all over the flesh (this gives a greater surface area for the marinade). Rub all over with the lemon juice (this degreases it and makes the marinade penetrate better).

2 Mix the marinade ingredients in a large non-metallic bowl. Cover the chicken pieces with the marinade, massaging it into the gashes.

3 Cover the bowl and refrigerate for 24 hours. You can do so for longer providing you are certain that the chicken is absolutely fresh.

4 When you wish to cook, preheat your oven to its hottest temperature. This will vary enormously from oven to oven which in turn will mean the times below will vary.

5 Place each poussin half on a skewer lengthwise, and place on to a skewer rack or ordinary grill rack at the top of the oven. Put a tray with foil underneath to catch the drips.

6 Cook for 8-10 minutes, then turn over. Continue to cook for 5-10 more minutes, until cooked. Prick the leg. When clear liquid runs out (rather than red), it is cooked.

7 Serve with shredded lettuce, white cabbage, onion and lemon wedges, with naan bread and tandoori chutney (pages 241 and 253).

VARIATIONS

Any bird can be tandoori cooked, with equally satisfactory results. Remember they must be skinned (duck is hard to do), and timings must be adjusted, as stated below.

Duckling One of about 3½lb (1.5kg) will be required for two people as it has less meat than chicken. Cooking time: 25-30 minutes.

Hen Pheasant Tenderer than the cock. One bird for two people. Cooking time: 20-25 minutes.

Grouse, Woodcock, Partridge One bird per person. Cooking time: 20-25 minutes.

Snipe, Quail, Squab (young pigeon) Being very small, allow 1½-2 birds per person. Cooking time: 15-20 minutes.

Murgh Reshmi
· CHICKEN TIKKA ·

Serves 2
(starters)

Tikka means a piece of something. Chicken makes that divine and most popular tikka dish from the Indian sub-continent.

INGREDIENTS

12oz (350g) chicken breast
1 full recipe light or spicy
  tandoori marinade (page 80)

salad garnish
lemon wedges

METHOD

1 Cut the chicken breasts evenly (see Chef's Tip, page 67). Aim for a total of between six to eight pieces per person.

2 Place the pieces into a bowl and add the marinade. Cover and leave in the refrigerator for at least 24 hours (maximum 48 hours).

3 Just prior to cooking, slip six to eight pieces on to a skewer. Repeat with one more skewer. (Use spare marinade in a curry or discard.)

4 Preheat the grill to medium. Place the skewers on an oven rack above the foil-lined oven tray and place this in the midway position under the heat. Alternatively they can be barbecued.

5 Cook for 5 minutes, turn and repeat. Cut one piece to ensure that it is fully cooked white through. If not, cook on for a while longer.

6 Serve on a bed of salad with lemon wedges, naan bread and tandoori chutney (pages 241 and 253).

Tandoori Mixed Grill

Serves 8

This is ideal for a dinner party or any occasion where you have to cook for a large number. The selection is up to you but here is one suggestion.

INGREDIENTS

1 full recipe chicken tikka (above)
  (makes 8 pieces)
1 full recipe Taj Shahi kebab
  (page 64) (makes 16 pieces)
1 full recipe tandoori king prawn
  (page 89) (makes 4 pieces)

1 full recipe lamb tikka (page 83)
  (makes 8 pieces)
1 full recipe liver tikka (page 83)
  (makes 8 pieces)

Each portion will thus consist of one piece of chicken tikka, two round kebabs, half a king prawn, one piece of lamb tikka and one piece of liver tikka.

Though it sounds like a lot of work, it isn't really, if you make a large batch of marinade (multiply the recipe on page 80 by four) and then marinade everything together. (This is quite safe, as they are all cooked together.)

Make the kebabs on the day. Cook everything together in the oven. Times vary, so put the items that take the longest in first, and calculate to bring them all out at the same time. Serve hot in the normal way.

Tikka Gosht

· LAMB, MUTTON OR BEEF TIKKA ·

Serves 2

If you buy the very best-quality lean meat, you will have lovely tender meat pieces.

Other meat – veal, pork, goat (traditional in India) and venison – can be cooked using this method, but cook fully. Liver is good too, but cook at lower heat for 10-15 minutes.

INGREDIENTS

8-10oz (225-275g) lean fillet of beef, lamb or mutton weighed after cutting and trimming.

1 full recipe light or spicy tandoori marinade (page 80)

METHOD

1 Cut the meat into even chunks about 1¼ inches (3cm) square. (Use off-cuts for stock or curry.) Aim to cut four to six pieces per person.

2 Mix the marinade ingredients in a large non-metallic bowl.

3 Place the cubes of meat into the marinade, ensuring they are well coated. Cover the bowl and refrigerate for 24 hours (longer if you are certain the meat is fresh).

4 When ready to cook, preheat the oven to its hottest. Line an oven tray with foil and place an oven rack above the tray.

5 Divide the meat pieces and thread them on to two skewers, leaving a little space between each chunk (this helps heat transference).

6 Place the skewers on to a skewer rack or an oven rack, and cook for 15-20 minutes depending on your oven. A degree of pinkness or rareness in the middle of the meat may be preferred, and this is acceptable – adjust cooking times accordingly.

7 Serve on a bed of salad with lemon wedges and tandoori chutney (page 253).

Gosht Kata Masala

· MEAT TIKKA IN A TASTY SAUCE ·

Serves 4

The nutty spicy sauce enhances the tikka pieces and turns this into a saucy curry.

INGREDIENTS

1¹/₂lb (675g) lean fillet of beef
2 full recipes light or spicy
  tandoori marinade (page 24)

Sauce
2 tablespoons ghee
1 tablespoon garlic purée
  (page 24)
1 tablespoon ginger purée
  (page 25)
6 tablespoons onion purée
  (page 25)
1 tablespoon mild curry paste
  (page 31)

4fl oz (120ml) milk
1 tablespoon ground almonds
6fl oz (175ml) single cream
1 tablespoon chopped fresh
  coriander
aromatic salt to taste (page 30)

Spices (whole)
4 green cardamoms
2 x 1 inch (2.5cm) pieces cassia
  bark
1 teaspoon cummin seeds

METHOD

1 Prepare the meat tikkas as in the previous recipe and marinate them a day or two in advance.

2 Preheat the oven to its hottest and cook the tikkas as described in the previous recipe.

3 For the **sauce**, heat the ghee in a karahi or wok. Stir-fry the garlic for 1 minute, add the ginger and stir-fry for a further 2 minutes. Add the onion and continue to stir-fry for 5 more minutes. Add the **spices**, the curry paste and any spare marinade, and stir-fry for 2-3 minutes.

4 Spoonful by spoonful add the milk, keeping it simmering. Add the ground almonds.

5 As soon as the meat is cooked add it to the curry almond sauce, along with any spare juices on the oven tray.

6 Add the cream and fresh coriander, and stir briskly. Salt and serve when it is hot.

CHEF'S TIP

Marination
Freezing ingredients in a marinade works well, and enables you to prepare more than one batch at a time for the same amount of mess and washing up.

Tandoori Murgh Makhani or Makhanwalla

· TANDOORI CHICKEN IN A GHEE-BASED SAUCE ·

Serves 4

This is not a 'same-day' recipe because of the tandoori marination. But it is well worth the build-up, being one of the Indian restaurant's most popular dishes. *Makhan* means butter, and the dish is definitely not for weight watchers, being cooked in butter ghee and cream.

INGREDIENTS

2 double poussins (see page 81), each weighing about 1³/₄lb (800g)
2 full recipes light or spicy tandoori marinade (page 80)

Sauce
4 tablespoons butter ghee
2 garlic cloves, finely chopped
4oz (110g) onions, finely chopped
5fl oz (150ml) milk

2 tablespoons tomato purée
0-2 fresh green chillies, chopped
1 tablespoon chopped fresh coriander
2 teaspoons garam masala
7fl oz (200ml) single cream
salt to taste

Garnish
1fl oz (25ml) single cream
1 tablespoon hot butter ghee

METHOD

1 Follow the chicken tandoori instructions on page 81. Marinate the chicken in the double quantities of marinade, but keep aside 2 tablespoons for the sauce. Cook the chickens as page 81. Keep any spare raw marinade. Try to manage the timings so that the tandoori comes out of the oven and goes straight into the sauce at stage 4.

2 For the sauce, heat the ghee in a karahi or wok. Stir-fry the garlic for 1 minute. Add the onion and continue stir-frying for 5 minutes or more.

3 Add 4 tablespoons of the milk (to cool the contents a little), then the spare tandoori marinade from stage 1 plus the 2 reserve tablespoons of marinade, and the tomato purée. Stir-fry until sizzling.

4 Add the remaining milk, chilli and coriander and, once reduced a little, add the cooked chicken. It can be on or off the bone.

5 Simmer for 5 minutes, then add the garam masala and cream. Simmer for a final 5 minutes. Salt to taste.

6 Garnish with a curl of cream over which you run a curl of ghee. Serve with rice.

Rezala

· CHICKEN TIKKA WITH KEEMA ·

Serves 4 (starter)

This fine recipe can be likened to chicken Kiev. A fillet of chicken breast is slit to make a pocket and is then stuffed with spiced raw mince (kebab mixture) and baked or barbecued.

INGREDIENTS

4 x 6oz (175g) chicken breasts, weighed after skinning and boning
1 full recipe light or spicy tandoori marinade (page 80)

8oz (225g) taj shahi kebab mixture (page 64, prepared to end of stage 3)
salad garnish
lemon wedges

METHOD

1 Carefully cut a pocket into each chicken breast.

2 Make the marinade in a large non-metallic bowl, then cover the breasts completely with it. Cover the bowl and refrigerate for 24 hours.

3 When ready to cook, preheat the oven to its hottest. Line an oven tray with foil and place an oven rack above the tray.

4 Press the kebab mixture into the pockets of each breast.

5 Put the breasts on the rack and cook for 15-20 minutes.

6 When cooked completely serve on a bed of salad with lemon wedges and tandoori chutney (page 253).

Facing page: Rezala (above) served with *Jeera Mattar Pullao* (page 227) and a simple chutney made from chopped onion, peppers and parsley.

Paneer Tikka Makhmali
· TANDOORI INDIAN CHEESE SKEWERS ·

Serves 2

This recipe is a marvellous showcase for paneer – marinated tandoori-style, then grilled.

INGREDIENTS

1 full recipe paneer, cut into 16 pieces (page 22)
1 full recipe light tandoori marinade (page 80)
8 pieces green pepper (the same size as the paneer)

8 pieces onion (the same size as the paneer)
salad garnish
lemon wedges

METHOD

1 Combine the paneer cubes and marinade in a suitable non-metallic bowl. Cover and refrigerate for up to 6 hours.

2 When you wish to cook, preheat the grill to medium.

3 Intersperse eight pieces of paneer on a skewer with the green pepper and onion pieces. Repeat with the second skewer.

4 Place the skewers on a skewer rack or oven rack above an oven tray lined with foil. Place this in the midway position under the grill.

5 Cook for 3-4 minutes. Turn the skewers and cook for a further 3 minutes.

6 Serve with lemon wedges on a bed of salad. Try dry coleslaw and shredded spinach with this dish.

Machli Amritsari
· TANDOORI FLAT FISH ·

Serves 2

For a starter, the small North Atlantic dab fish or American sand dab is the perfect shape and weight for this recipe. Alternatively use the larger flounder.

INGREDIENTS

2 dab fish or flounders
1 full recipe light or spicy tandoori marinade (page 80)

salad garnish
lemon wedges

METHOD

1 Wash the fish. Trim off the fins and square off the tail. Dry the fish on kitchen paper.

2 Score the flesh with close diagonal cuts on both sides.

3 Make up the marinade in a flat, non-metallic, appropriately sized container which will enable the marinade to cover both fish. Cover and marinate in the refrigerator for 6-24 hours.

4 When you want to cook, preheat the grill to medium.

5 Line the grill pan with foil. Place the fish on the grill rack and put the pan into the midway position under the heat, and cook for 5-8 minutes. Turn the fish over and cook for a further 3-4 minutes.

6 Serve on a bed of salad with lemon wedges.

Rubian

· TANDOORI KING PRAWN ·

Serves 2

The miracle of freezing makes some remarkable seafood available to those of us in colder climes. The king prawn is one. To obtain large ones it is best to buy them from fishmongers.

INGREDIENTS

*4 x 2oz (50g) king prawns,
    uncooked with shells on
1 full recipe light tandoori
    marinade (page 80)*

*salad garnish
lemon wedges*

METHOD

1 Wash the prawns, discard the shells and slit the back to remove the vein. Wash again.

2 Mix the marinade ingredients together in a non-metallic bowl, then immerse the prawns. Cover the bowl and put it in the refrigerator for a maximum of 12 hours.

3 To cook, preheat the grill to medium.

4 Place the prawns on the grill rack and place it in the midway position under the heat. (Put some foil on the tray to catch the drips.) Grill for 5 minutes. Turn and grill for a further 5 minutes.

5 Serve on a bed of salad with lemon wedges and tandoori chutney (page 253).

Meat Dishes

Make no mistake about it, many of the peoples of the subcontinent are devout meat eaters. However, there are quite strict rules about who eats what. Hindus, for instance, cannot eat beef. Moslems and Jews, of whom there are a number in India, cannot eat pork, whereas Goan Christians breed and eat pigs as well as beef. The beef which is eaten in India will have come from the buffalo. Universally popular are mutton and goat. Lamb is rarely sold.

Very nearly every meat recipe in Indian cuisine keeps the meat on the bone. Indian cooks say it creates more flavour and that a great part of the enjoyment of eating it comes from sucking the meat from the bone. The recipes which follow are all off the bone, to suit Western tastes, but you can easily adapt them if you wish.

The meat we get in Britain is generally very much more tender than that in India, but mass production and the freezer have led to a decline in flavour. Use a reputable butcher, buy fresh, and in general choose the more expensive cuts (fillets, top of legs etc) for the tenderest and leanest meat. Poor cuts will produce less satisfactory results.

Use beef, veal, lamb, mutton, pork or even goat or venison in all of these recipes, unless specified.

Facing page, from the top: Hariyali Sag Gosht (page 99), Moglai Gosht Kesari (page 108) garnished with edible silver leaf, and Mirchwangan Korma (page 112).

Karahi or Kadai Gosht

· MEAT COOKED IN THE KARAHI ·

Serves 4

The karahi is India's celebrated two-handled cooking pot. Its pronunciation sounds like curry with an additional syllable – 'curr-ar-hee'. *Kadai* is an alternative but similar pronunciation. Both might have been the origins of the word curry.

INGREDIENTS

1¹/₂lb (675g) lean meat, weighed
    after discarding unwanted
    matter
3 tablespoons ghee
1 tablespoon garlic purée
    (page 24)
4oz (110g) onions, finely chopped
1 portion curry masala gravy
    (page 32)

1 green pepper, seeded and sliced
6oz (175g) tomatoes, chopped
1 tablespoon mild curry paste
    (page 31)
1 tablespoon tomato purée
2 teaspoons garam masala
1 teaspoon sesame seeds
salt to taste

METHOD

1 Cut the meat into cubes about 1¹/₂ inches (4cm) in size, remembering that they will shrink during cooking as the liquids come out.

2 Heat the ghee in a karahi or wok. Stir-fry the garlic for a minute then add the onion and continue for 5 minutes. Add the curry masala gravy and stir-fry for 3 minutes.

3 Using a 4-5 pint (2.25-2.75 litre) casserole with lid, combine the fried ingredients and the meat and place into an oven preheated to 375°F/190°C/Gas 5.

4 After 20 minutes, inspect and stir, adding water or akhni stock (page 33) if it is becoming too dry. Repeat 20 minutes later, adding the remaining ingredients. Cook for a further 20 minutes or until cooked to your liking.

CHEF'S TIP

The dishes on pages 92-6, 98-9, 108, 110, 112 and 113 are transferred to the oven after initial cooking on the hob. Alternatively they can be cooked solely on the hob. Reduce the heat to very low, and stir frequently. Add a little water if it looks like sticking. Cooking time will be longer.

Papata-ma-Gosht

· POTATO AND MEAT STEW ·

Serves 4

Visitors to Bombay should ask for the food of one of the local communities – the Parsees. It is highly distinctive and rarely found elsewhere. This dish is typical.

INGREDIENTS

1¹/₂lb (675g) lean meat, weighed
  after discarding unwanted
  matter
3 tablespoons ghee
2 teaspoons cummin seeds
1 tablespoon garlic purée
  (page 24)
1 tablespoon ginger purée
  (page 25)
1 portion onion purée (page 25)
1 tablespoon tomato purée
1-4 fresh red chillies, chopped

1 tablespoon brown sugar
8oz (225g) potatoes
3oz (75g) peas
aromatic salt to taste (page 30)
1 teaspoon cummin seeds, roasted

Spices (roasted and ground)
4 cloves
2 green cardamoms
1 brown cardamom
2 inch (5cm) piece cassia bark

METHOD

1 Cut the meat into cubes about 1¹/₂ inches (4cm) in size, remembering that they will shrink during cooking as the liquids come out.

2 Heat the ghee in a karahi or wok. Stir-fry the cummin seeds, garlic and ginger for a minute, then add the onion and continue for 5 minutes.

3 Using a 4-5 pint (2.25-2.75 litre) casserole with lid, combine the fried ingredients, the meat and **spices**. Place into the oven preheated to 375°F/190°C/Gas 5.

4 After 20 minutes, inspect and stir adding water or akhni stock (page 33) if it is becoming too dry. Repeat 20 minutes later, adding the tomato purée, chillies and sugar. Continue cooking for at least 20 minutes more until the meat is cooked to your liking.

5 During stage 4, peel and chop the potatoes into bite-sized pieces. Heat some further ghee in the karahi and fry them until golden. Add to the curry with the peas about 10 minutes prior to serving, salting to taste. Garnish with the roasted cummin seeds.

Gosht Ulathiyathu

· MEAT COCONUT FRY ·

Serves 4

Down in the deep south of India there is a wonderful beach resort called Kovalum. Its restaurant is called appropriately 'The Shells'. This memorable, very dry, very dark, subtly spiced curry enhanced with coconut is on their menu.

INGREDIENTS

1½lb (675g) lean meat, weighed after discarding unwanted matter
3 tablespoons ghee
1 portion garlic purée (page 24)
4oz (110g) onion, finely chopped
2oz (50g) plain white flour
3½oz (100g) creamed coconut (½ block)
1 tablespoon brown sugar
2 teaspoons tamarind purée (page 24) or vinegar

3oz (75g) fresh coconut, shredded
salt to taste

Spices (roasted and ground)
20 curry leaves, dry
3 teaspoons coriander seeds
1 teaspoon cummin seeds
1 teaspoon aniseed
1 teaspoon mustard seeds
4 cloves
4 green cardamoms
2 inch (5cm) piece cassia bark

METHOD

1 Cut the meat into cubes about 1½ inches (4cm) in size, remembering that they will shrink during cooking as the liquids come out.

2 Heat the ghee in a karahi or wok. Stir-fry the garlic for a minute, then add the onion and continue for 5 minutes.

3 Make the **spices** into a paste, using enough water to make it pourable, then add to the karahi and stir-fry for a couple more minutes.

4 Put the flour into a flat tray and dab the pieces of meat in it, ensuring that they are well coated.

5 Add the floured meat to the karahi. Lower the heat and simmer for 10-15 minutes, turning occasionally

6 Place the contents of the karahi into a 4-5 pint (2.25-2.75 litre) casserole with lid. Place into an oven preheated to 375°F/190°C/Gas 5.

7 After 20 minutes, inspect and stir, adding water or akhni stock (page 33) if it is becoming too dry. Repeat 20 minutes later, adding the remaining ingredients. Cook for a further 20 minutes or until cooked to your liking.

Redang Daging

· INDONESIAN MEAT CURRY ·

Serves 4

There is a thriving curry-eating population in the Indonesian isles. This is one of their most celebrated curries.

INGREDIENTS

1½lb (675g) lean meat, weighed
   after discarding unwanted
   matter
3 tablespoons ghee
4 garlic cloves, sliced
8oz (225g) onions, sliced
2 inch (5cm) cube ginger, sliced
½ teaspoon turmeric
1 portion curry masala gravy
   (page 32)

2-6 fresh red chillies, chopped
8oz (225g) tomatoes, chopped
2 tablespoons peanut butter
3oz (75g) grated fresh coconut
1 tablespoon dark soy sauce
2 tablespoons lemon juice
aromatic salt to taste

METHOD

1 Cut the meat into cubes about 1½ inches (4cm) in size, remembering that they will shrink during cooking as the liquids come out.

2 Heat the ghee in a karahi or wok. Stir-fry the garlic for a minute, then add the onion, ginger and turmeric and continue for 5 minutes. Add the curry masala gravy and stir-fry for 3 minutes.

3 Using a 4-5 pint (2.25-2.75 litre) casserole with lid, combine the fried ingredients and the meat. Add the chillies, tomatoes, peanut butter, coconut and soy sauce. Place into an oven preheated to 375°F/190°C/ Gas 5.

4 After 20 minutes, inspect and stir, adding water or akhni stock (page 33) if it is becoming too dry. Repeat 20 minutes later. Cook for a further 20 minutes or until cooked to your liking.

5 About 10 minutes before serving, add the lemon juice, and salt to taste.

Lamb Dhansak

Serves 4

This most famous Parsee dish is a Sunday lunch treat in Bombay, where it is served on a bed of rice. Here is a simple recipe for a usually complicated dish.

INGREDIENTS

1¹/₂lb (675g) lean meat, weighed after discarding unwanted matter
3 tablespoons ghee
1-2 teaspoons garlic purée (page 24)
4oz (110g) onions, finely chopped
1 portion curry masala gravy (page 32)
2 tablespoons mild curry paste (page 31)
8oz (225g) cooked plain dhal
7fl oz (200ml) tomato soup (about ¹/₂ can)

1 tablespoon brown sugar
2 teaspoons garam masala
1 tablespoon fresh coriander leaves
1 tablespoon fresh lemon juice
salt to taste
chilli powder to taste

Spices (roasted and ground)
3 brown cardamoms
1 teaspoon cloves
1 teaspoon fenugreek seeds
1 teaspoon fennel seeds

METHOD

1 Cut the meat into cubes about 1¹/₂ inches (4cm) in size, remembering that they will shrink during cooking as the liquids come out.

2 Heat the ghee in a karahi or wok. Stir-fry the garlic and the **spices** for a minute, then add the onion and continue for 5 minutes. Add the curry masala gravy and curry paste, and stir-fry for 3 more minutes.

3 Using a 4-5 pint (2.25-2.75 litre) casserole with lid, combine the fried ingredients and the meat, the dhal and the soup, and place into an oven preheated to 375°F/190°C/Gas 5.

4 After 20 minutes, inspect and stir adding water or akhni stock (page 33) if it is becoming too dry. Repeat 20 minutes later, adding the remaining ingredients. Add salt and chilli powder to taste. Cook for a further 20 minutes or until cooked to your liking.

Boris Tikkea Malai

· BAKED MARINATED MEAT PIECES ·

Serves 4

All over India there are small communities of religious sects. In the primarily Hindu, vegetarian state of Gujarat live some meat-eating Moslems, the Boris community. Their food is outstandingly different from anywhere else in India, as this dish proves.

INGREDIENTS

1¹/₂lb (675g) lean meat, weighed
   after discarding unwanted
   matter
2oz (50g) breadcrumbs
2 eggs
3 tablespoons ghee
1-3 garlic cloves, chopped
2oz (50g) onions, finely chopped
aromatic salt to taste (page 30)
1 full recipe onion tarka (page 26)

Marinade
8fl oz (250ml) double cream
1 tablespoon garlic purée
   (page 24)
1 tablespoon ginger purée
   (page 25)
1 tablespoon garam masala
1 tablespoon mild curry paste
   (page 31)
1 tablespoon paprika

METHOD

1 Cut the meat into cubes about 1¹/₂ inches (4cm) in size, remembering that they will shrink during cooking as the liquids come out.

2 In a large non-metal bowl, mix together the **marinade** ingredients. Add the cubed meat, cover and put into the refrigerator for 24-30 hours.

3 When you want to cook, preheat the oven to 350°F/180°C/Gas 4. Line an oven tray with foil.

4 Remove the meat cubes and piece by piece roll in breadcrumbs mixed with the eggs. Place on to the foil-lined tray.

5 When complete place the tray into the oven and bake for 20-30 minutes.

6 During stage 5 heat the ghee in a karahi or wok. Stir-fry the garlic for a minute, then add the onion and continue for 5 minutes. Add the leftover marinade and, stirring frequently, simmer for about 5 minutes. Salt to taste.

7 To serve, place the meat on to each diner's plate, then pour the sauce over the meat as decoratively as you can. Garnish with the onion tarka.

Roghan Gosht

· AROMATIC MEAT CURRY ·

Serves 4

One of the most popular curries and one of my favourites. In my previous books, I have given authentic recipes for this dish. Here I give an interpretation from the Oberoi Tower Hotel in Bombay.

INGREDIENTS

1¹/₂lb (675g) lean meat, weighed after discarding unwanted matter
3 tablespoons ghee
1 portion garlic purée (page 24)
4oz (110g) onions, finely chopped
1 portion curry masala gravy (page 32)
1 tablespoon mild curry paste (page 31)

2 tablespoons ground cashew nuts
2fl oz (50ml) yoghurt
1 tablespoon tomato purée
1 tablespoon paprika
2 teaspoons garam masala
1 tablespoon fresh chopped coriander
salt to taste

METHOD

1 Cut the meat into cubes about 1¹/₂ inches (4cm) in size, remembering that they will shrink during cooking as the liquids come out.

2 Heat the ghee in a karahi or wok. Stir-fry the garlic for a minute, then add the onion and continue for 5 minutes. Add the curry masala gravy and paste, and stir-fry for 3 more minutes.

3 Using a 4-5 pint (2.25-2.75 litre) casserole with lid, combine the fried ingredients and the meat. Add the nuts, yoghurt and tomato purée and place into an oven preheated to 375°F/190°C/Gas 5.

4 After 20 minutes, inspect and stir, adding water or akhni stock (page 33) if it is becoming too dry. Repeat 20 minutes later, adding the remaining ingredients. Cook for a further 20 minutes or until cooked to your liking.

Bhoona Gosht

· DRY MEAT CURRY ·

Serves 4

The 'bhoona' method on page 30 is the vital process of stir-frying the rawness and water out of the curry paste. *Bhoona* or *bhuna* also describes a traditional curry which is mild to medium, and is pan-fried to create a very dry dish without the normal accompanying rich gravy.

INGREDIENTS

1¹/₂lb (675g) lean meat, weighed
after discarding unwanted
matter
3 tablespoons ghee
1 tablespoon garlic purée
(page 24)
4oz (110g) onions, finely chopped
2 tablespoons mild curry paste
(page 31)

1 red pepper, seeded and finely
chopped
2oz (50g) tomatoes, chopped
0-2 fresh red chillies, chopped
1 tablespoon paprika
1 tablespoon chopped fresh
coriander
aromatic salt to taste (page 30)

METHOD

1 Follow stages 1 and 2 opposite, omitting the gravy.

2 Using a 4-5 pint (2.25-2.75 litre) casserole with lid, combine the fried ingredients and the meat. Add the red pepper, tomato and chilli and place into an oven preheated to 375°F/190°C/Gas 5.

3 After 20 minutes, inspect and stir adding water or akhni stock (page 33) if it is becoming too dry, but remember the bhoona *should* be quite dry. Repeat 20 minutes later, adding the remaining ingredients. Salt to taste. Cook for 20 more minutes or until cooked to your liking.

Hariyali Sag Gosht
· MEAT COOKED WITH SPINACH ·

Serves 4

The combination of meat braised with spinach originated in the Punjab.

INGREDIENTS

1¹/₂lb (675g) lean meat, weighed
after discarding unwanted
matter
3 tablespoons ghee
1 tablespoon garlic purée (page
24)
4oz (110g) onions, finely chopped
1 portion curry masala gravy
(page 32)

1lb (450g) fresh spinach, cleaned
and chopped (frozen or canned
will substitute)
0-4 fresh green chillies, chopped
2 tablespoons green masala paste
(page 32)
1 teaspoon garam masala (page
29)
salt to taste

METHOD

1 Follow stages 1 and 2 opposite, omitting the paste.

2 Using a 4-5 pint (2.25-2.75 litre) casserole with lid, combine the fried ingredients and the meat. Add the spinach and the chillies and place into the oven preheated to 375°F/190°C/Gas 5.

3 Cook on as in stage 4 opposite.

Shak-Shu-Ka

· NEPALESE CURRIED MINCE ·

Serves 4

An unusual Nepalese dish of smooth, finely minced or ground lamb or beef, cooked in a delicate, mild sauce of cream, eggs and tomatoes. It accompanies dry meat dishes well, being of a creamy consistency, but is very rich, so I have given only a smallish quantity for four this time.

I have also given a recipe variation called Sasranga. Using precisely the same ingredients but less water, it is baked to a firm kebab-like consistency which is cut into slices, pie style, for an interesting main course or starter.

INGREDIENTS

1lb (450g) finely ground lamb or beef
4 tablespoons ghee
1 tablespoon ginger purée (page 25)
4oz (110g) onions, finely chopped
0-4 fresh green chillies, chopped
2 tablespoons chopped fresh coriander
4 tablespoons coarsely chopped roasted almonds

6fl oz (170ml) single cream whipped with 2 eggs
salt to taste

Spices
2 teaspoons garam masala
1/2 teaspoon mango powder
1 teaspoon garlic powder

METHOD

SHAK-SHU-KA

1 Grind the lamb down as finely as possible either by mincing three times or by mincing once then using a food processor.

2 Heat the ghee and stir-fry the ginger for 2 minutes, then the onion for 4 minutes. Add the chilli and coriander, and continue frying.

3 When soft add the mince with about 6fl oz (175ml) water. Stir-fry for 10 minutes.

4 Add the **spices**, stir-fry for 5 more minutes then add all the remaining ingredients. Simmer for 10 more minutes, keeping the consistency creamy (add a little water if needed).

SASRANGA

1 As stage 1 above.

2 As stage 2 above but add the **spices** and stir-fry for 2 more minutes.

3 Preheat the oven to 325°F/160°C/Gas 3. Place half the mince in a 6 inch (15cm) round baking tin, then make a layer of the fried items. Sprinkle all the nuts on then half the cream and egg mixture. Add the remaining mince and top with the remaining cream and egg.

4 Bake for 20-25 minutes. Serve hot.

Kofteh Char Masala

· AFGHAN AROMATIC MEAT BALLS ·

Serves 4

When the first invaders passed through wild mountainous Afghanistan on the way to India, thousands of years ago, it was uninhabited. Today's fierce Pathan warriors are descendants of these conquerors, as are these tasty meat balls, which became the Kofta of India. This Afghan sauce is quite thin.

INGREDIENTS

Kofteh
1¹/₂lb (675g) fillet steak, weighed
   after discarding unwanted
   matter
4 tablespoons dehydrated onion
1 tablespoon dried mint
0-4 dry red chillies, chopped
1 teaspoon aromatic salt
   (page 30)

Sauce
2 tablespoons ghee or vegetable
   oil
2-6 garlic cloves, thinly sliced
2 inch (5cm) cube of fresh ginger,
   sliced

2oz (50g) onions, thinly sliced
1 pint (600ml) akhni stock (page
   33) or water
2-3 tomatoes, chopped

Kofteh spices (ground)
2 tablespoons char masala
   (page 29)
1 teaspoon garlic powder

Sauce spices
1 teaspoon ground coriander
¹/₂ teaspoon turmeric
¹/₂ teaspoon whole black
   peppercorns

METHOD

1 Make the **kofteh** kebabs following stages 1-4 of the recipe on page 64, using the ingredients listed plus the **kofteh spices**. Make 24 instead of 16.

2 Preheat the oven to 375°F/190°C/Gas 5. Line an oven tray with foil and place the kebabs on to the foil, ensuring they don't touch each other. Place the tray into the oven and bake for 15 minutes.

3 During stage 2, make the **sauce**. Heat the ghee in a 3 pint (1.75 litre) saucepan. Stir-fry the garlic for a minute. Add the ginger and stir-fry for a further minute. Add the onion and the **sauce spices** and continue to fry for about 5 minutes.

4 Add the stock or water and the tomatoes, and simmer for 10 minutes or so, or until the kofteh are ready.

5 Serve the kofteh and the thin sauce in bowls.

Masuko Pakoda

· NEPALESE BATTERED STEAKS ·

Makes 4

The Nepalese eat this dish on one of their two festival days. Goat, buffalo and pork would be the Nepalese choice, but beef minute steaks are ideal for this unusual dish. Serve with a lentil dish and plain rice.

INGREDIENTS

4 beef minute steaks, each
  weighing about 5-6oz
  (150-175g) after trimming
1 teaspoon vegetable oil per steak

Batter
3oz (75g) plain white flour

2oz (50g) gram flour (besan)
1 egg
6fl oz (175ml) milk
1 tablespoon garam masala
1 teaspoon salt

METHOD

1 For the **batter**, sieve the flours into a bowl, then whisk in the egg, milk, garam masala and salt.

2 Heat the oil in a frying pan.

3 Coat one slice of meat with the batter and place it into the pan.

4 Repeat with the other three steaks.

5 After 5 minutes, turn the steaks over and fry for a further 5 minutes. (If all your steaks don't fit into the frying pan in one go, fry separately, keeping cooked steaks warm, or use more than one pan at once.)

Cochin Jewish Curry

Serves 4

Another once vast, now tiny, community are the Jews of Cochin. They have been there for 2,000 years, and an area of Cochin, containing a synagogue, is called Jew Town. Strict Kosher rules apply to their cooking. This curry is traditionally slowly cooked over coals to be eaten on the Sabbath. If you have an electric slow cooker use that, otherwise follow this method, which I encountered whilst staying at the delightful Malabar Hotel in Cochin.

INGREDIENTS

2lb (900g) leg of mutton on the bone, cut into smallish pieces (your butcher will oblige)
8 garlic cloves, sliced
8 oz (225g) onions, coarsely chopped
2-6 red or green fresh chillies, chopped
3fl oz (85ml) vinegar (any type)
salt to taste

Spices
1 teaspoon whole black peppercorns
1 teaspoon turmeric
1 tablespoon ground coriander
2 bay leaves

METHOD

1 Easy! Preheat the oven to 375°F/190°C/Gas 5. Combine all the ingredients in a lidded casserole, and cook in the oven for 25 minutes.

2 Turn off the heat but leave in the oven to finish slow cooking for a further 6 hours. If you can't wait that long, keep heat going for at least a further 25 minutes, or until the meat is tender, and serve at once.

Facing page: Masuko Pakoda (see opposite, above). The lethal-looking knives are called kukri and are used by the Gurkhas.

Medium Curry

Serves 4

This curry is a restaurateur's invention, and I have included it and the others opposite by popular request. First is one of my earlier recipes for Medium Curry from *The Curry Club Indian Restaurant Cookbook*. This forms the base, and the variants that follow show how the restaurants easily adapt the theme. Apologies to the purists!

The additional ingredients of the varying 'national' curries should be added to the medium curry base with **spices 2** at stage 6.

INGREDIENTS

1¹/₂lb (675g) lean meat (or chicken)
3 tablespoons vegetable oil
1 portion onion purée (page 25)
1 tablespoon tomato purée

1 teaspoon paprika
1 teaspoon chilli powder (more if you like heat)
1 teaspoon ground ginger
1 teaspoon garlic powder

Spices 1
1 teaspoon ground cummin
1 teaspoon ground coriander
1 teaspoon turmeric

Spices 2
1 teaspoon garam masala
1 dessertspoon dry fenugreek leaves

METHOD

1 Cut any fat off the meat. (Skin the chicken, on or off the bone.)

2 Heat the oil and fry the onion purée until it is good and hot (don't let it stick).

3 While this is happening, add a little water to **spices 1** to make a paste, and preheat the oven to 375°F/190°C/Gas 5.

4 Add the spice paste to the hot onion purée, and stir continuously. Reduce the heat if it starts to stick. Take about 5-8 minutes over this (the bhoona operation), as it is important that the spices are cooked and the water content removed. When the oil floats to the top it is done.

5 Put the meat and onion and tomato purées into a casserole dish, stir, and put in the oven. Cook for 45 minutes.

6 Stir and add **spices 2**. Cook on for a further 10 minutes, then serve.

CEYLON CURRY

¹/₃ block creamed coconut (2¹/₂oz/65g)
5fl oz (150ml) milk
1 tablespoon freshly squeezed lemon juice
0-4 fresh green chillies, chopped

KASHMIRI CURRY

8-12 fresh peeled lychees, or canned lychees
1 tablespoon granulated white sugar
4-8 Maraschino cherries, to garnish

MADRAS CURRY

14oz (400g) can tomatoes
2 tablespoons tomato purée
1 tablespoon ground almonds
2 tablespoons freshly squeezed lemon juice
2-4 fresh or dried red chillies, chopped
1 teaspoon white sugar
1 teaspoon chilli powder

MALAY CURRY

¹/₄ block creamed coconut (2oz/50g)
3fl oz (85ml) milk
2fl oz (50ml) double cream
12-16 small cubes fresh or canned pineapple

VINDALOO RESTAURANT STYLE CURRY

5-6oz (150-175g) boiled potato in bite-sized pieces
4-8 fresh or dried red chillies, chopped
2 plus teaspoons chilli powder

Takatan

· PAN-FRIED CURRY ·

Serves 4

This dish is quite fascinating and derives its name from the metallic clacking that the special metal tool makes on the huge frying pan (*tava*) as the dish is prepared – *taka-taka-taka-taka*.

A sauce base is prepared as is the principal ingredient which can be meat, chicken, seafood, vegetables, even leftovers. Spices are fried into the sauce (up to 30 spices can be used to taste). Then the showmanship begins. The chef takes the two steel, flat-edged spatulas and bangs them one after the other on to the pan to mash and mix the ingredients. Then the pre-cooked chicken or meat, vegetable or seafood is added and heated.

The first time I encountered this dish was under a star-studded black velvet sky at a barbecue in India. The chef demonstrating it, himself a Pakistani, had grown up with this dish in his home town of Karachi. He later apprenticed at the extremely elegant Al Bustan Restaurant at the Karachi Sheraton Hotel. Try it for a fun change at your next barbecue. Use a tava and knives.

INGREDIENTS

1½lb (675g) skinless breast of
chicken or meat, cubed, or
seafood or mixed vegetables
4 tablespoons ghee or oil
2 large onions, peeled and finely
chopped
2 garlic cloves, finely chopped
2 inch (5cm) cube fresh ginger,
finely chopped
1 tablespoon tamarind purée
(page 24) or vinegar
4 fresh tomatoes, or canned
strained tomatoes, chopped
2 tablespoons chopped fresh
coriander

2-4 fresh green chillies, chopped

Spices (whole)
½ teaspoon black cummin seeds
1 teaspoon white cummin seeds
1 teaspoon mustard seeds

Spices (ground)
1 teaspoon coriander
1 teaspoon paprika
½ teaspoon chilli powder
(minimum)
½ teaspoon fenugreek seed
½ teaspoon turmeric

METHOD

1 Simply pre-cook your chosen principal ingredient in a little ghee or oil
until ready, then keep warm while preparing the takatan sauce.

2 Fry the **whole spices** in the remaining ghee or oil until they pop (about
20 seconds).

3 Add the onion, garlic and ginger and fry until translucent (about 10
minutes on medium to high heat).

4 Meanwhile make a paste of the **ground spices** using the tamarind
purée or vinegar, plus water if needed.

5 Add the paste to the onion mix and fry on, stirring (and clattering
taka-taka-taka if you wish) for 5 minutes.

6 Add the tomato, coriander, chilli, and the main ingredient. Fry until
really hot. Serve with naan bread (page 241).

Moglai Gosht Kesari

· MEAT IN SAFFRON GRAVY ·

Serves 4

The great Moghul emperors obtained India by violence, then settled down to a life of sophistication and beauty such as the world had never known before or since. The Taj Mahal was one result. So was this dish – which is outstandingly subtle, enhanced with the world's most expensive spice, and garnished with the optional but decidedly opulent edible silver or gold leaf.

INGREDIENTS

1¹/₂lb (675g) lean meat, weighed after discarding unwanted matter
3¹/₂oz (100g) pistachio nuts
2fl oz (50ml) milk
30 saffron strands
3 tablespoons butter ghee or vegetable oil
2 teaspoons garlic purée (page 24)
6oz (175g) onions, finely chopped
4fl oz (120ml) double cream
salt to taste

edible silver or gold leaf (optional)

Spices
1 teaspoon white poppy seeds
1 teaspoon sesame seeds
1 teaspoon fennel seeds
¹/₂ teaspoon coriander seeds
¹/₂ teaspoon green coriander seeds
¹/₂ teaspoon cummin seeds

METHOD

1 Cut the meat into cubes about 1¹/₂ inches (4cm) in size, remembering that they will shrink during cooking as the liquids come out.

2 Keep a tablespoonful of the nuts aside. Blend the remainder with enough water to make a very smooth, pourable paste.

3 Bring the milk to warm, not hot, and put the saffron strands in. Leave them to exude their powerful orange-yellow colour.

4 Heat the ghee in a karahi or wok. Put the **spices** in and 30 seconds later add the garlic, followed 30 seconds later by the onion. Stir-fry all the time, continuing for a further 5 minutes.

5 Using a 4-5 pint (2.25-2.75 litre) casserole with lid, combine the fried ingredients and the meat and place into an oven preheated to 375°F/190°C/Gas 5.

6 After 20 minutes, inspect and stir, adding water or akhni stock (page 33) if it is becoming too dry. Add the nut paste, mixing it in well. The contents should not be too runny. Return to the oven for 20 more minutes.

7 Mulch the saffron in the milk to ensure all the colour is extracted. Mix it with the cream. Add it to the casserole and give it another 10-15 minutes in the oven. Salt to taste.

8 Garnish with the edible silver leaf (see Chef's Tip below) and the remaining whole nuts.

CHEF'S TIP

Edible silver or gold leaf: Vark
Vark, pronounced *varak*, was invented by the 17th-century Moghul emperors (who else?). It is made from a nugget of either pure gold or silver which is hammered between leather pads by craftsmen, until thinner than paper. Each piece measures about 3 x 5 inches (7.5 x 13cm), and it is available in packs of six sheets. Each sheet is sandwiched between newspaper or tissue.

To use, do not touch it; it will stick to your fingers and disintegrate. Carefully remove the top covering sheet of paper, leaving the vark resting on an under-sheet. Invert it then dab the undersheet on to the food. It is best to break it up a little on the food or else it looks rather unappetising, like cooking foil!

What does it do? It looks interesting. It is vegan, and of course it is a major talking point. The emperors enjoyed displaying their wealth – they used to include gold life-sized pieces (cloves, cardamoms etc) in certain dishes (the diners were supposed to return them to the emperor!). More than that, the Moghuls claimed it to be aphrodisiac. Whether it is or not is for you to say, not me.

Goan Pork Vindaloo

Serves 4

This is the real thing! Pronounced *vin-dar-loo* with the emphasis on the second syllable it makes the restaurateurs' standard hot curry pale into insignificance. The derivation of the word comes from the Portuguese words for wine and garlic. Goa was their Indian base, and Goa's inheritance to this day is Christianity, pigs and this sensational red-hot dish.

INGREDIENTS

1½lb (675g) lean leg of pork, weighed after discarding unwanted matter
3 tablespoons ghee or vegetable oil
8oz (225g) onions, finely chopped
2 tablespoons green masala paste (page 32)
4 long green chillies, chopped
1 tablespoon brown sugar
1 teaspoon salt

Marinade
6-8 fresh red chillies
1 red pepper, seeded
4 garlic cloves
2 inch (5cm) cube fresh ginger
1 tablespoon tamarind purée (page 24)
7fl oz (200ml) red wine

METHOD

1 Cut the meat into cubes about 1½ inches (4cm) in size, remembering that they will shrink during cooking as the liquids come out.

2 For the **marinade**, grind together the chillies, red pepper, garlic, ginger, tamarind and the red wine in the food processor or blender.

3 In a large non-metallic bowl, mix the meat and the marinade. Cover and put into the refrigerator for 24 hours.

4 To cook, heat the ghee or oil in a karahi or wok. Stir-fry the onion for about 10 minutes. Add the green masala paste, chillies and sugar.

5 Using a 4-5 pint (2.25-2.75 litre) casserole with lid, combine the fried ingredients and the meat, and place into an oven preheated to 375°F/190°C/Gas 5.

6 After 20 minutes, inspect and stir adding water or akhni stock (page 33) if it is becoming too dry. Repeat 20 minutes later. Salt to taste. Cook for a further 20 minutes or until tender.

Haleem

· WHEAT AND MINCE CURRY ·

Serves 4

Hyderabad is a rich Moghul, largely Moslem, city in central southern India. This unique dish combines meat and whole wheat which are cooked with pungent and hot spices until they become a gruel. Do this by including stage 6, or try my version which keeps the meat very soft, but in chunks.

INGREDIENTS

1lb (450g) lean minced meat
8oz (225g) whole wheat grains
3 tablespoons ghee
6-8 garlic cloves, chopped
2 inch (5cm) cube of fresh ginger, chopped
8oz (225g) onions, chopped
1 portion curry masala gravy (page 32)
4-8 fresh red chillies
5oz (150g) yoghurt

1 tablespoon garam masala
salt to taste
1 tablespoon chopped fresh coriander
1 tablespoon chopped fresh mint

Garnish
1 full recipe onion tarka (page 26)
2oz (50g) fresh coconut, shredded
2 eggs, hard-boiled and chopped

METHOD

1 Soak the wheat in water for 24 hours, changing the water a couple of times. Just prior to stage 2, strain it.

2 Heat the ghee in a karahi or wok. Stir-fry the garlic for a minute, then add the ginger and stir-fry for a further minute. Add the onion and continue for 5 minutes. Add the curry masala gravy and stir-fry for 3 minutes.

3 Add the mince and stir-fry it for about 8-10 minutes to brown it. Add the strained wheat, chillies and yoghurt, and stir-fry for a further 10 minutes.

4 Place the contents of the karahi in a 4-5 pint (2.25-2.75 litre) casserole with lid, and into the oven preheated to 375°F/190°C/Gas 5.

5 After 20 minutes, inspect and stir. Maintain sufficient water to cook until the wheat grains are very soft, by which time the water should have reduced out. Inspect again after 20-30 minutes.

6 Either proceed straight to stage 7, or purists may like to run the cooked dish through a food processor to achieve the traditional gruel-like consistency. Then reheat in the casserole prior to stage 7.

7 Add the garam masala, salt to taste, the coriander and mint. Give it a final 10 minutes, then serve with a garnish of tarka, coconut and chopped egg.

Mirchwangan Korma

· RED-HOT CHILLI KORMA ·

Serves 4

This recipe is as far removed from the formula curry as Kent is from Kashmir, whence it comes. Having been lulled into thinking korma meant 'mild', this searingly hot korma puts the record right. In fact korma actually describes a method of cooking, where the water content is reduced out completely leaving the ghee or oil (see page 14).

At a Kashmiri wedding feast, it is traditional to serve a number of kormas – a white one (using cream and ground nuts), a green one (using herbs), and this one, using the blood-red coloured Kashmiri chilli.

INGREDIENTS

1¹/₂lb (675g) lean leg of lamb, off
   the bone
3 tablespoons ghee
4-6 flakes alkenet root, optional
2-4 cloves garlic, finely chopped
8oz (225g) red onion, chopped
garam masala
salt to taste

Marinade
1 tablespoon tomato purée

1 tablespoon paprika
4fl oz (100ml) red wine
2fl oz (50ml) bottled beetroot
   vinegar
1 bottled beetroot, ping-pong-ball
   size, sliced
20 fresh deep-red chillies, or dried
   Kashmiri chillies, seeded and
   coarsely cut
1 red pepper, seeded and coarsely
   cut

METHOD

1 Cut the meat into cubes about 1¹/₂ inches (4cm) in size, remembering that they will shrink during cooking as the liquids come out.

2 Put into a blender the tomato puree, paprika, red wine and beetroot vinegar. Mulch into a loose paste.

3 In a large non-metallic bowl combine the paste with the rest of the **marinade** ingredients. Add the meat and coat well. Cover and refrigerate for 24-48 hours.

4 Heat the ghee, colour it red with alkenet root (see Chef's Tip 2 on page 65) or omit if unavailable. Stir-fry the garlic for one minute, then the onion for about 10 minutes.

5 Using a 4-5 pint (2.25-2.75 litre) casserole with lid, combine the fried ingredients with the meat and marinade and place into an oven preheated to 375°F/190°C/Gas 5.

6 After 20 minutes, inspect and stir adding water or akhni stock (page 33) if it is becoming too dry. Repeat 20 minutes later, adding the garam masala and salt to your taste. Cook for a further 20 minutes or until cooked to your liking.

Shahi Safeid Korma
· ROYAL WHITE KORMA ·

Serves 4

If the last recipe made you see red, here is an authentic Moglai Korma. It is white, aromatic, creamy and mild, and from the court of Shah Jahan, the builder of the Taj Mahal. He gave legendary moonlight banquets at which everything had to be white – clothes, decor and food. You'll find this dish at the UK's top Indian Restaurant, Chutney Mary in London, SW5.

INGREDIENTS

1¹/₂lb (675g) lean meat, weighed
    after discarding unwanted
    matter

Marinade
5oz (150g) yoghurt
2 teaspoons garlic purée (page 24)
2 teaspoons ginger purée
    (page 25)
6 tablespoons onion purée
    (page 25)
2 tablespoons ground almonds
4fl oz (120ml) double cream
2 teaspoons garam masala
salt to taste

Spices
2 teaspoons poppy seeds
1 teaspoon melon seeds
6-8 green cardamoms
3-4 bay leaves
2 × 2 inch (5cm) pieces cassia
    bark

Garnish
sprinklings of onion tarka
    (page 26)
almond flakes, roasted
green chillies, seeded then sliced
    longways and grilled
edible silver leaf (page 109)

METHOD

1 Cut the meat into cubes about 1¹/₂ inches (4cm) in size, remembering that they will shrink during cooking as the liquids come out.

2 Mix the **marinade** ingredients and the **spices** together in a large non-metallic bowl. Immerse the meat, cover and refrigerate for 24-48 hours.

3 Transfer the meat and marinade to a 4-5 pint (2.25-2.75 litre) casserole with lid, and place into an oven preheated to 375°F/190°C/Gas 5.

4 After 20 minutes, inspect and stir, adding water or akhni stock (page 33) if it is becoming too dry. Repeat 20 minutes later, and salt to taste. Cook for a further 10 minutes or until cooked to your liking.

5 Garnish with the tarka, nuts, chillies and silver leaf.

Chicken Dishes

The Latin word for a hen is *gallina,* and if you consult your dictionary, you will learn that gallinaceous birds are domestic poultry, bred especially for the table, including chicken, duck, goose, pigeon, turkey and guinea fowl. Game includes birds which are bred for the table, but also those which are 'hunted'. These include grouse, partridge, pheasant, quail, snipe, wild duck and woodcock.

Chicken is the most popular main ingredient for curry dishes in the UK. Over 55 per cent choose chicken in preference to meat, fish, seafood or vegetables. This is not surprising. It is inexpensive, has the reputation of being healthier than red meat, and it cooks quickly. More rummaging through reference books tells us that the chicken is one of the most successful domestic animals, reared in every country on earth. Left to its own devices, it is a self-sufficient, wily scavenger. Domestically, a good hen can lay up to 300 eggs a year. The ancestor of the chicken is Indian, a jungle fowl of the pheasant family, which was certainly bred in the Indus Valley over 4,500 years ago.

Most of my recipes are for chicken – two recipes use duck – but you can substitute other poultry in almost all of the recipes in this chapter. Try turkey, goose or guinea fowl, with minimal adjustment to cooking times.

Facing, from the top: Murghi Badam Korma (page 124), *Murghi Rohani* (page 126) and *Handi Murgh* (page 117).

Balti Murgh

· POT-COOKED CHICKEN ·

Serves 4

Balti is cooked and served in a two-handled dish called a *Karahi* in India, and a *Balti* in Pakistan. This particular recipe uses chicken drumsticks.

INGREDIENTS

4 large chicken drumsticks, skinned
3 tablespoons ghee or vegetable oil
2-4 teaspoons garlic purée (page 24)
2oz (50g) onions, finely chopped
1 tablespoon mild curry paste (page 31)
1 portion curry masala gravy (page 32)

5oz (150g) tomatoes, chopped
1 green pepper, seeded and chopped
1 tablespoon chopped fresh coriander
salt to taste

Spices
2 teaspoons garam masala (page 29)
2 teaspoons dry fenugreek leaves

METHOD

1 Heat the ghee in a karahi or wok. Stir-fry the garlic for a minute, then add the onion and continue for 5 minutes. Add the curry paste and curry masala gravy and stir-fry for 3 more minutes.

2 Using a 4-5 pint (2.25-2.75 litre) casserole with lid, combine the fried ingredients and the chicken and place into an oven preheated to 375°F/190°C/Gas 5. Cook for about 20 minutes.

3 After 20 minutes, inspect and stir, adding water or akhni stock (page 33) if it is becoming too dry. Add the tomato, green pepper, the **spices** and fresh coriander, and cook for a further 20 minutes.

4 Salt to taste and serve.

Handi Murgh

· SPICY PAN-FRIED CHICKEN ·

Serves 4

The *handi* is a round-bottomed Indian cooking pot. Here I use the karahi. This recipe, again using drumsticks, makes an interesting comparison with the previous recipe.

INGREDIENTS

4 large chicken drumsticks,
  skinned
3 tablespoons ghee
2-4 garlic cloves, finely chopped
2 inch (5cm) piece fresh ginger,
  shredded
2 tablespoons mild curry paste
  (page 31)
1 tablespoon tomato purée
8oz (225g) onions, finely chopped
5oz (150g) tomatoes, chopped

1 teaspoon dried mint
1 tablespoon chopped fresh
  coriander
0-4 fresh green chillies, chopped
  (optional)
salt to taste

Spices
2 teaspoons garam masala (page
  29)
2 teaspoons dry fenugreek leaves

METHOD

1 Heat the ghee in a karahi or wok. Stir-fry the garlic for a minute, then add the ginger and continue to stir-fry for a further minute. Add the curry paste and tomato purée and stir-fry until it sizzles, then add the onions. Continue to stir-fry for 5-6 minutes.

2 Add enough water to free the mix, but not swamp it. When bubbling, add the drumsticks. Reduce the heat and simmer for 20 minutes, stirring and turning occasionally.

3 Add the tomatoes, mint, coriander and chillies (if used). Continue to simmer and stir occasionally for a further 10 minutes or so.

4 Add the **spices** and salt to taste. Simmer for a few more minutes then serve.

Butter Chicken

Serves 4

This delicious dish must use butter not ghee for the best flavour, and chicken breast for the best texture. You can get away with a very short marination – but the longer you give it, the deeper the flavour, so for best results prepare in advance.

INGREDIENTS

*1¹/₂lb (675g) chicken breasts,
weighed after skinning and
boning*
*1 full recipe light tandoori
marinade (page 80)*

2oz (50g) salted butter
1 tablespoon cummin seeds

METHOD

1 Cut the chicken breasts into bite-sized chunks.

2 Make the light tandoori marinade in a non-metallic bowl, and immerse the chicken cubes in it. Cover and refrigerate for 1-24 hours.

3 To cook, heat the butter in a karahi or wok. Add the cummin seeds, then stir-fry the chicken until cooked (about 12-15 minutes).

4 Serve with rice, breads and chutney.

Facing page: Butter Chicken (above) served with *Tengai Sadam* (page 236) and mini white-flour *Puris* (page 242).

Jeera Chicken

Serves 4

This is a variation of the previous recipe. The colour of the chicken pieces is, in this case, yellow, due to the addition of turmeric.

INGREDIENTS

1¹/₅lb (675g) chicken breasts, weighed after skinning and boning
2oz (50g) salted butter
1 tablespoon cummin seeds

Marinade
1 teaspoon turmeric

1 tablespoon mild curry paste (page 31)
5 fl oz (150ml) water
1 teaspoon salt

Garnish
1 tablespoon cummin seeds, roasted

METHOD

1 Follow the previous recipe exactly, simply substituting the above **marinade**.

2 Garnish with the roasted cummin seeds.

Murgh Shole

· MARINATED GRILLED CHICKEN ·

Serves 4

This is another lightly marinated dish, which is quick and easy to make, and light on calories.

INGREDIENTS

1¹/₂lb (675g) chicken breasts, weighed after skinning and boning

Marinade
5oz (150g) yoghurt

1 tablespoon mild curry paste (page 31)
2 tablespoons tomato purée
1 tablespoon paprika
1 teaspoon salt

METHOD

1 Cut the chicken breasts into good bite-sized chunks.

2 Mix the **marinade** ingredients together in a non-metallic bowl, and immerse the chicken cubes in it. Cover and refrigerate for 1-24 hours.

3 To cook, pre-heat the grill to medium. Line the grill pan with foil. Shake excess marinade off the chunks of chicken and place them on the grill rack. Grill for 8 minutes.

4   Withdraw the grill pan from the heat. Turn the heat up to full. Pour the excess marinade over the chunks. Put the grill pan at a higher level and grill for just a couple of minutes so as to blacken the tips of the chunks. Serve with salad and rice.

Murgh Malai Kebab

· CHICKEN IN CREAM AND ALMONDS ·

Serves 4

This is the final variation in our quartet of quickly prepared chicken chunks. This one will turn out white in colour and mild in taste, but its cream and almond marinade make it higher in calories.

INGREDIENTS

1¹/₂lb (675g) chicken breasts, weighed after skinning and boning

1 tablespoon ground almonds
1 teaspoon aromatic salt (page 30)

Marinade
5 fl oz (150ml) single cream
1 teaspoon garlic purée (page 24)

Garnish
1 tablespoon sesame seeds, roasted

METHOD

1   Follow the previous recipe exactly, simply substituting the above marinade.

2   Garnish with the sesame seeds.

Murgh Zaibunissa Moglai

· CREAMY CHICKEN CURRY ·

Serves 4

This white curry is a variation of the previous recipe. The chicken pieces are finished off in a rich sauce containing double cream and yoghurt. Sinful, but oh so good!

INGREDIENTS

1¹/₂lb (675g) chicken breasts, weighed after skinning and boning

Marinade
5 fl oz (150ml) single cream
1 teaspoon garlic purée (page 24)
1 tablespoon ground almonds
1 teaspoon aromatic salt (page 30)

Sauce
3 tablespoons ghee or oil

1 teaspoon garlic purée (page 24)
3 tablespoons onion purée (page 25)
6 fl oz (175ml) double cream
6 oz (175g) yoghurt
2 teaspoons garam masala
salt to taste

Garnish
hot ghee or butter
edible silver leaf (page 109)
chopped pistachio nuts

METHOD

1 Follow stages 1-3 of the recipe for marinated grilled chicken (page 120).

2 Make the **sauce** before and during the grilling stage. Heat the ghee in a karahi or wok. Stir-fry the garlic for 20 seconds, then add the onion and continue for a further 5 minutes. Lower the heat.

3 Add the cream, yoghurt, garam masala and any excess marinade, and stir-fry until it comes to the simmer.

4 Add the grilled chicken pieces, and salt to taste.

5 Serve garnished with a drizzle of ghee or butter, edible silver leaf and pistachio nuts.

Kadai Murch

· PAN-COOKED CHICKEN ·

Serves 4

The chicken meat is given a short half-hour marination, then it is stir-fried in the kadai or karahi. If you have them, serve in small serving karahis.

INGREDIENTS

1¹/₂lb (675g) chicken breasts, weighed after skinning and boning
2 tablespoons lemon juice
2 tablespoons vinegar (any type)
3 tablespoons ghee or vegetable oil
4-6 garlic cloves, finely chopped
2 inch (5cm) piece fresh ginger, finely chopped
4oz (110g) onions, finely chopped
¹/₂ red pepper, seeded and finely chopped
0-4 green chillies, cut into thin strips
2 tablespoons mild curry paste (page 31)

1 tablespoon tandoori paste (page 80)
3 tablespoons chopped fresh coriander
3 tablespoons single cream
2 teaspoons garam masala
1 tablespoon dry fenugreek leaf

Spices
1 teaspoon turmeric
1 teaspoon black mustard seeds
1 teaspoon white cummin seeds

Garnish
1 tablespoon cummin seeds, roasted

METHOD

1 Dice the chicken breasts into bite-sized pieces, and place in a bowl with the lemon juice and vinegar. Mix and leave for at least 30 minutes.

2 Heat the ghee in a karahi or wok and fry the **spices** for 1 minute. Add the garlic and fry for 1 minute, then the ginger for a further 2 minutes. Add the onion, pepper and chilli and fry until soft (about 3 minutes).

3 Add the chicken pieces and marinade, and stir-fry in the karahi for about 15 minutes.

4 Now add the curry and tandoori pastes, and stir well. Add 2 table-spoons of the coriander, the cream, garam masala, and fenugreek leaf.

5 Cook for about 10 more minutes, stirring occasionally. When ready to serve, transfer to four karahi serving bowls. Garnish with the roasted cummin seeds and the remaining chopped coriander.

Murghi Badam Korma

· AROMATIC SPICED ALMOND CHICKEN ·

Serves 4

The emperor's favourite and one of mine too. Its cooking and spicing is absolutely traditional – so it won't resemble the formula restaurant version.

INGREDIENTS

1¹/₂lb (675g) chicken meat, weighed after skinning and boning (2¹/₂lb/1.1kg if kept on the bone)
3 tablespoons ghee or vegetable oil
2 teaspoons cummin seeds
4 garlic cloves, finely chopped
1 inch (2.5cm) cube fresh ginger, finely chopped
8oz (225g) onions, finely chopped
2oz (50g) almonds, chopped
2 teaspoons garam masala
1 tablespoon chopped fresh coriander
salt to taste

Marinade
5oz (150g) yoghurt

2 fl oz (50ml) double cream
1 tablespoon white sugar
1 teaspoon salt
¹/₂ teaspoon turmeric

Spices
4 bay leaves
4-6 cloves
2 inch (5cm) piece cassia bark
6-8 green cardamoms
1 teaspoon fennel seeds
1 teaspoon coriander seeds

Garnish
a curl of cream
sprinklings of fresh coriander, edible silver leaf (page 109) and chopped or flaked almonds

METHOD

1 Cut the chicken into bite-sized pieces.

2 Mix the **marinade** ingredients and the **spices** together in a non-metallic bowl. Add the chicken, coating it completely. Cover and refrigerate for 24-48 hours.

3 To cook, heat the ghee in a karahi or wok. Stir-fry the cummin seeds for a few seconds, then add the garlic and continue for 30 seconds. Next add the ginger, and continue to stir-fry for a further 30 seconds. Finally add the onion and almonds, and carry on for 5 minutes.

4 Preheat the oven to 375°F/190°C/Gas 5. Using a 4-5 pint (2.25-2.75 litre) casserole with lid, combine the fried ingredients and the chicken with all its marinade. Put the casserole into the oven.

5 After 15 minutes, inspect and stir, adding water if becoming too dry.

6 After 15 more minutes, repeat, and add the garam masala and fresh coriander. Salt to taste.

7 Cook for a final 15 minutes or so then serve, sprinkled with the garnish ingredients.

Murgh Khushk Purdah

· SPICY CHICKEN PIE ·

Serves 1

Purdah is the custom of dressing eligible females behind the veil – thus keeping from aspiring males the secret of the face until the appropriate time. This dish, from the master hand of Lucknow's Chef Qureshi, maintains the same secrecy. He describes it as a 'resplendent chicken, cured in a scented marinade, grilled, then finished on *dum*, with an assortment of vegetables and a sprinkling of mace, behind a purdah of flaky pastry.' Somehow 'Spicy Chicken Pie' sounds totally devoid of mystery, but wait until you taste it.

METHOD

1 Follow stages 1-6 of the method for Murghi Badam Korma (opposite) using boneless chicken meat. Add **8oz (225g) sliced button mushrooms** and **20-30 strands of saffron** to the cooked chicken and set aside.

2 Increase the oven temperature to 425°F/220°C/Gas 7.

3 Flour your work surface and rolling pin and roll out **8oz (225g) ready-made puff pastry**. Divide the pastry into two portions, one slightly larger than the other.

4 Gently roll the larger part out to line the pie dish to a thickness of no less than 1/4 inch (5mm). Gently press this into the dish, allowing a slight overhang.

5 Carefully put the warm filling in. Roll out the remaining pastry to make the 'lid' or crust. Place the lid in place and press the overhang and lid together, wetting the rim with a pastry brush to ensure it is well sealed.

7 Cut away surplus pastry and decorate the edge. Make a small vent hole in the centre (which allows steam to escape). Use surplus pastry to decorate the lid with leaves, curls or strips.

8 Bake for 25-30 minutes, and serve hot with pullao rice.

Murghi Rohani

· STIR-FRY KASHMIRI CHICKEN ·

Serves 4

This is a highly prized Kashmiri dish, served at special occasions with the Kashmir staple – sticky rice. Indeed the Kashmiri word for food also means rice. If you like 'sticky' rice, use round-grained risotto rice, Japanese sticky rice or Thai fragrant rice.

INGREDIENTS

1½lb (675g) chicken breasts, weighed after skinning and boning
4 tablespoons butter ghee
6-8 flakes alkanet root (optional, see Chef's Tip 2 on page 65)
6oz (175g) red onions, chopped
3oz (75g) mushrooms (any type) chopped
3oz (75g) cherry tomatoes, halved
2oz (50g) red cabbage, shredded

1oz (25g) bottled beetroot, chopped
1 teaspoon brown sugar
salt to taste
2 teaspoons garam masala

Spices (whole)
1 teaspoon fennel seeds
2 inch (5cm) piece cassia bark
4-6 cloves
4 brown cardamoms, halved

METHOD

1 Cut the chicken into bite-sized pieces.

2 Heat the ghee in a karahi or wok. Add the alkanet root if you wish to colour it deep red. Stir-fry the **spices** for 30 seconds, then add the onion and continue stir-frying for 3-4 minutes.

3 Add the chicken pieces and stir-fry for about 10 minutes.

4 Add the mushroom, tomato, red cabbage, beetroot and sugar. Stir-fry for a further 10 minutes, adding a little water as needed. (It should be fairly dry.) Salt to taste.

5 Sprinkle in the garam masala and serve with sticky rice or pullao rice.

Moorgi Mollee or Mouli

· CHICKEN IN COCONUT ·

Serves 4

The *mollee* or *mouli* is a favourite style of cooking from South India where coconut is the base. *Moorgi* is a variation of the word *murgh* (chicken). The turmeric gives the white of the coconut a glowing bright yellow colour.

INGREDIENTS

1¹/₂lb (675g) chicken meat, weighed after skinning and boning (2¹/₂lb/1.1kg if kept on the bone)
1 fresh coconut, or 2oz (50g) coconut milk powder
3 tablespoons sesame or light oil
2 teaspoons mustard seeds
¹/₂ teaspoon whole peppercorns
0-4 fresh green chillies, sliced lengthwise

¹/₂ teaspoon turmeric
15-20 curry leaves, dry or fresh
milk
salt to taste

Garnish
coconut shreds
fresh coriander leaves

METHOD

1 Decide whether to cook this dish in the traditional manner – on the bone – or off the bone. Cut accordingly into manageable pieces.

2 Make a batch of coconut milk using one fresh coconut (page 23) or the powder, to achieve a runny paste.

3 Heat the oil in a karahi or wok. Add the chicken pieces and 'seal' them with a brisk 5-minute stir-fry. Remove the pieces from the oil and set aside.

4 Heat the oil again, and add the mustard seeds, peppercorns, chilli, turmeric and curry leaves. Stir-fry for just 10 seconds, then cool the mixture down by stirring in the coconut milk.

5 Add the part-cooked chicken, and simmer for 20 minutes. Stir frequently, and keep adding enough milk to achieve a thin rather than thick sauce. Salt to taste.

6 Serve garnished with coconut and coriander, and with plain or lemon rice.

Chicken Jalfrezi
· STIR-FRY CHICKEN ·

Serves 1

As this dish is one of my favourites, I make no apology for the fact that it appears in my previous books. This recipe takes 2-3 minutes to prepare, and no more than 20 minutes to cook, dispelling the myth that Indian food takes hours to make. For a change here is a recipe for a single serving (double up for two, quadruple for four).

INGREDIENTS

6-8oz (175-225g) chicken breast, weighed after skinning and boning
1 tablespoon ghee, butter or vegetable oil
1/2 teaspoon cummin seeds
1 garlic clove, chopped
3/4 inch (2cm) cube ginger, chopped
1/3 teaspoon turmeric
1 1/2 teaspoons mild curry paste (page 31)

0-2 fresh green chillies, sliced
3-4 pieces green and/or red pepper, sliced and cut into diamonds
3-4 cherry tomatoes, halved
3 tablespoons coconut milk (page 23)
3/4 teaspoon garam masala (page 29)
a few leaves of fresh coriander
salt to taste

METHOD

1 Cut the chicken breasts into bite-sized chunks.

2 Heat the oil in a karahi or wok. Stir-fry the cummin seeds for a few seconds. Add the garlic and continue stir-frying for 30 seconds. Add the ginger and continue for a minute. Add the turmeric and a splash of water, and when sizzling again, add the curry paste.

3 Now add the chicken pieces and stir until they are evenly coloured yellow and are lightly sizzling. Add the chillies, pepper and tomato and stir-fry for 10 minutes. During this stage, add the coconut milk spoonful by spoonful to maintain a good liquid level.

4 Add the garam masala, fresh coriander and salt to taste, then stir-fry for a final 5-10 minutes. Check that the chicken is cooked through, then serve at once, with Indian bread or fluffy plain rice.

Kukhurako Tarkari

· NEPALESE CHICKEN CURRY ·

Serves 4

Some older Nepalese Brahmins will not eat chicken, considering it to be 'exotic'. They will, however eat jungle fowl and peacock. We doubtless view it the other way around, and like most ordinary Nepalese we prefer straightforward chicken.

INGREDIENTS

1 x 2¹/₄lb (1kg) chicken
3 tablespoons ghee or vegetable oil
1 tablespoon garlic purée (page 24)
1 tablespoon ginger purée (page 25)
4oz (110g) onions, chopped
1¹/₂ pints (900ml) akhni (page 33) or chicken stock
1-6 fresh red chillies, chopped

2 tablespoons chopped fresh coriander
3 fl oz (85ml) single cream
aromatic salt to taste (page 30)

Spices
6 cloves
2 teaspoons cummin seeds
2 inch (5cm) piece cassia bark
4 bay leaves
1 teaspoon paprika

METHOD

1 Quarter the chicken and skin it.

2 Heat the ghee (called *ghui* in Nepal!) in a karahi or wok and fry the **spices** for 30 seconds. Add the garlic and stir-fry for a further minute. Add the ginger and continue stir-frying for a further minute. Add the onion and stir-fry for at least 5 more minutes.

3 Add the stock and when simmering add the chicken pieces. Simmer for around 15-20 minutes.

4 Add the final ingredients and cook for a further 10 minutes or so.

Kabuli Murgh

· AFGHAN CHICKPEA CHICKEN ·

Serves 4

I've had this recipe in my collection for a long time – in fact it is modified from my Granny's cookbook. Her notes, penned in 1904, say that this is an Afghan recipe called Kabul-e-Murgh (chicken from the Afghan capital city). It contains chickpeas (kabli chana) so either interpretation is valid.

INGREDIENTS

4oz (110g) dry chickpeas
2 poussins or 1 double poussin,
*   total weight around 2lb (900g)*
*   (see Chef's Tip below)*
4oz (110g) fresh tomatoes,
*   quartered*
4oz (110g parsnips, peeled and
*   chopped into small pieces*

Marinade
5oz (150g) yoghurt
1 tablespoon tomato purée
1 tablespoon mild curry paste
*   (page 31)*
2 teaspoons char masala (page 29)
1 teaspoon aromatic salt (page
*   30)*

METHOD

1 Pick through the chickpeas to remove small stones which are often there. Then rise them several times. Finally put them into a large bowl with ample water and leave them for 12-24 hours, to soften and swell.

2 At the same time joint and skin the chicken. In a non-metallic bowl, mix the chicken with the marinade ingredients. Cover and refrigerate for the same time as the chickpeas.

3 To cook, preheat the oven to 375°F/190°C/Gas 5.

4 Strain and rinse the chickpeas. Place them and the chicken with all its marinade into a 4-5 pint (2.25-2.75 litre) lidded casserole. Mix well and add enough boiling water just to cover the chicken. Place in the oven and cook for 30 minutes.

5 Inspect, stir and add a little water if it is a little dry – the chickpeas will absorb a lot of water. Continue to cook for a further 20 minutes.

6 Repeat stage 5, adding the remaining ingredients, and salt to taste. Serve with an Indian bread.

CHEF'S TIP

A poussin weighs 1-1½lb (450-560g), and is aged between 4 and 6 weeks. It serves one. A double poussin weighs 1½-2lb (675-900g), and is aged between 6 and 10 weeks. It serves two to three.

Chicken Cafreal

· GRILLED GOAN CHICKEN ·

Serves 4

I don't mind telling you that Goan food is a favourite of mine. This hot, sour marinade gives the chicken a wonderful flavour when grilled. Drumsticks are best.

INGREDIENTS

4 large chicken drumsticks, skinned
2 tablespoons fresh lemon juice

Marinade
10 garlic cloves, chopped
2 inch (5cm) cube fresh ginger, chopped
6-8 fresh green chillies, chopped

4 tablespoons chopped fresh coriander
1 tablespoon garam masala
1 tablespoon cummin seeds, ground
1½ teaspoons salt
2 fl oz (50ml) distilled malt vinegar

METHOD

1 In the blender make a paste of the marinade. It must be super smooth, and it is worth finishing it off with a mortar and pestle. Add water if it is too thick.

2 Cut small gashes into the drumsticks with a sharp knife. Rub the drumsticks with the lemon juice to degrease the meat.

3 Work the paste on to the drumsticks and into the gashes. Put into a suitably sized bowl, covering with all the excess marinade. Cover and refrigerate for 24-48 hours.

4 To cook, preheat the grill to medium. Place the drumsticks on an oven rack placed over a foil-covered oven tray.

5 Grill for 15-20 minutes, turning and basting with the excess marinade at least twice.

6 Serve with savoury fried potatoes (see page 189).

Murgh Khas Avadh

· STUFFED CHICKEN BREASTS ·

Serves 4

This is a rich delicacy from the city of Lucknow, formerly the base of the outstandingly rich Nawabs. The chicken breasts are stuffed with spicy cottage cheese, and are then simmered in yoghurt and cream. This recipe was demonstrated to a Curry Club Gourmet Tour group by Chef Kachru at Agra's beautiful Mughal Sheraton Hotel.

INGREDIENTS

4 x 6oz (175g) chicken breasts, weighed after skinning and boning
2 fl oz (50ml) milk
20-30 saffron strands
3 tablespoons ghee or vegetable oil
4 fl oz (120ml) single cream

Paste
8oz (225g) onions, chopped
3¹/₂oz (100g) cashew nuts
4oz (110g) yoghurt
1 teaspoon aromatic salt (page 30)

Stuffing
4oz (110g) cottage cheese or crumbly paneer (page 22)
¹/₂ teaspoon black cummin seeds
¹/₂ teaspoon aromatic salt (page 30)
¹/₂ teaspoon white peppercorns, ground
0-4 fresh green chillies, finely chopped
1 tablespoon cold soft ghee or butter

Garnish
a sprinkling of garam masala, mint leaves and flaked almonds

METHOD

1 Warm the milk in a small saucepan, and infuse the saffron in it.

2 Blend the paste ingredients in the blender or food processor.

3 For the stuffing, mix the cottage cheese or crumbly paneer with the cummin, salt, pepper, chilli and ghee.

4 Carefully cut a pocket into each chicken breast, and fill each pocket with stuffing. Don't *over*-stuff.

5 Heat the ghee or oil in a karahi or wok, add the cashew paste and stir-fry for about 5 minutes.

6 Carefully (to avoid spilling the stuffing) place the breasts into the karahi, reduce the heat and allow them to cook for about 12-15 minutes. Lower the heat.

7 Mulch the saffron in the milk to exude as much golden colour as possible. Add it and the cream to the karahi, turn the breasts, and simmer for 5 or so more minutes.

8 Place one breast on each diner's plate and garnish with the garam masala, mint and almonds.

Tikka Masala Curry

Serves 4

This is an Indian restaurant favourite, and can also be made with fillet steak or lean lamb instead of chicken. The sauce is savoury and rich with a whisper of sweet and hot, and with the addition of the tikka pieces, it is pure magic, matching anything the French have to offer.

INGREDIENTS

1¹/₂lb (675g) lean fillet steak,
   lamb or chicken
2 full recipes light or spicy
   tandoori marinade (page 80)

Sauce
4 tablespoons butter ghee
1 teaspoon white cummin seeds
1 tablespoon garlic purée (page
   24)
6 tablespoons onion purée (page
   25)
1 full recipe tandoori masala paste
   (page 80)
2 tablespoons mild curry paste
   (page 31)

1 tablespoon tomato ketchup
1 tablespoon brown sugar
1 tablespoon sweet tomato
   chutney (page 251)
1 tablespoon ground almonds
2 teaspoons garam masala
1 tablespoon chopped fresh
   coriander leaves
7 fl oz (200ml) single cream
3 fl oz (85ml) coconut milk
salt to taste

Garnish (optional)
edible silver leaf
fresh coconut, shredded

METHOD

1 Marinate and cook the tikkas following the recipes for Murgh Aangar or Murgh Reshmi (pages 81 and 82). Keep any spare marinade. Try to manage the timings so that the tikkas come out of the oven and go straight into the sauce at stage 5.

2 For the sauce, heat the ghee in a karahi or wok. Stir-fry the cummin seeds for 30 seconds then the garlic for 1 minute. Add the onion and stir-fry for 2-3 further minutes.

3 Next add the tandoori masala and stir-fry for 5-6 minutes.

4 Add the curry paste, ketchup, sugar, chutney and ground almonds.

5 When simmering, add the cooked tikkas and the remaining ingredients. Simmer until it reduces a little.

6 Garnish with optional edible silver leaf and fresh coconut.

Above: Harash Barra

Harash Barra

· SPICY DUCK STEAK IN SAUCE ·

Serves 4

Traditionally, Indian food is either pre-cut or it is cooked until tender enough to fall literally off the bone. This enables the food to be eaten with the fingers without knives and forks. This 'steak' is therefore a modern Indian recipe, being in one piece and served with a sauce, but it is tasty and tender.

INGREDIENTS

4 duck breasts, about 8oz (225g) each
1 full recipe light tandoori marinade (page 80)

Sauce
2 tablespoons vegetable oil
2 teaspoons cummin seeds
1/2 teaspoon turmeric

2-4 garlic cloves, finely chopped
1 inch (2.5cm) cube fresh ginger, finely chopped
4oz (110g) onion, finely chopped
6 cloves
6 green cardamoms
5 fl oz (150ml) tomato juice
4 fl oz (120ml) single cream
salt to taste

METHOD

1 Remove the fatty skin from the breasts. Score shallow long cuts diagonally on both sides of the breasts.

2 Put the marinade and breasts into a non-metallic bowl. Cover and refrigerate for 24-48 hours.

3 To cook, preheat the oven to 325°F/170°C/Gas 3. Cover an oven tray with foil. Put the breasts on to a rack above the tray, reserving any excess marinade. Cook for 15-20 minutes.

4 Inspect and baste the breasts with marinade. Increase the heat to 375°F/190°C/Gas 5. Return the duck to the oven and cook for a further 15-20 minutes.

5 Start the sauce during stage 3. Heat the oil in a karahi or wok. Place the cummin seeds into the pan followed by the turmeric, garlic, ginger, onion, cloves and cardamoms. Stir-fry for about 10 minutes, then lower the heat.

6 Add the tomato juice and cream, and simmer gently until you need the sauce.

7 Remove the steaks from the oven. Place them into the sauce in the karahi, along with any excess marinade, and simmer for about 10 more minutes. Just prior to serving, salt to taste.

Itak Rempah

· MALAY DUCK ·

Serves 4

Compare this authentically flavoured Malay dish with the Indian restaurant's version which appears on page 105. If you can't get lemongrass or shrimp paste, omit them, but there will be a slight absence of flavour.

INGREDIENTS

4 duck breasts, about 8oz (225g)
   each
4 garlic cloves, whole
4oz (110g) onion purée (page 25)
2oz (50g) fresh coconut, shredded
2-6 fresh red chillies
1 bulb fresh lemongrass, or
   several stalks dried
1 tablespoon brown sugar
1 tablespoon light soy sauce
1 tablespoon tomato purée
1 teaspoon Worcestershire sauce
1 tablespoon blachan (shrimp
   paste)
salt to taste

Spices
1 teaspoon coriander seeds,
   ground
$1/2$ teaspoon cummin seeds,
   ground
$1/2$ teaspoon turmeric
2 inch (5cm) piece cassia bark
6 cloves
1 teaspoon fennel seeds
2 star anise

METHOD

1 Skin the duck breasts, and chop the breast meat into bite-sized pieces.

2 Preheat the oven to 375°F/190°C/Gas 5.

3 Combine all the ingredients, including the **spices** in a 4-5 pint (2.25-2.75 litre) lidded casserole. Mix them well then press them down flat. Add enough boiling water to just cover them. Place in the oven and cook for 20 minutes.

4 Inspect, stir, add a little water if it is a little dry. Continue to cook for a further 20 minutes.

5 Repeat stage 4. At the end of this (an hour in all), salt to taste and serve with plain rice.

CHEF'S TIP

Duck Breasts
A very good French product is vacuum-packed *magret de canard*. There are two breasts per pack and they are perfect for the recipe above and on page 134.

Murgh Bargara

· CHICKEN BURGER IN SPICY SAUCE ·

Serves 4

This remarkable invention is from my good friend and great guru, Satish Arora, Chef Director of cuisine of the Taj Group of Hotels, based in Bombay. He is responsible for the output of over 1,500 chefs all over India. Recently he cooked dinner for the entire British Royal family.

INGREDIENTS

1¹/₂lb (675g) chicken breasts, weighed after skinning and boning
4oz (110g) onions, chopped
2 garlic cloves, chopped
0-4 fresh green chillies, chopped
2 tablespoons chopped fresh coriander
2 tablespoons ground almonds
1 cold fried egg (the soft yolk to aid binding)
1 teaspoon salt

Spices
1 teaspoon cumin seeds
1 teaspoon pomegranate seeds
¹/₂ teaspoon green cardamom seeds, ground
¹/₂ teaspoon chilli powder

METHOD

1 Place all the ingredients, including the **spices**, into the food processor, or run several times through a mincer to obtain a pliable cohesive mixture.

2 Divide it into eight equal parts, then shape into round burger discs.

3 Cook under the grill with the heat at medium, on a rack above the foil-lined grill pan, for 5-6 minutes.

4 Turn and carry on for 3-4 minutes, and serve burger style (in a sesame bun with onion rings), or in a gravy or sauce (choose from those on pages 32, 84, 85, 101, 122, 133, 142, 147, 149, 171, 193 and 194).

Fish and Seafood

✳

Did you know that there are over 20,000 species of fish? And I'll bet that every single one has been eaten at some stage in mankind's culinary evolution.

In this chapter, I have attempted to be adventurous by offering a wide choice of ingredients from the deep. The first half of the chapter deals with fish, with recipes for salmon, cod, whitebait, mackerel, smoked haddock, pomfret, plaice, flounder, dab or sole, and even eel. The second half deals with crustaceans and molluscs, with delicious recipes involving shrimps and prawns, scampi, crab and lobster. (We also met crab, cockles and squid among the Starters.)

India's coastline stretches for many thousands of miles. The types of fish found in her rivers, lakes and seas differs from those available in our fishmongers, so I have adapted the recipes to suit our fish. Remember all fresh fish (unless farmed) are seasonal, so do not hesitate to substitute one fish for another if you wish.

Fish and shellfish are high in protein, low in fat and are generally said to be excellent for health.

Facing page, from the top: Sukhe Jhinga Bhoona (page 150), Bangoe Puli Munch (page 144) and Mahi Kaliya (page 143)

> **CHEF'S TIP**
>
> *Buying Fish*
> When buying fresh fish, look for the following:
> 1. Firm red gills, hard to open. Fins not flabby.
> 2. Scales all in place. Body moist, eyes bright not sunken, flesh firm.
> 3. White fish should not have a blue tint.
> 4. No adverse smell.
>
> Cook fresh fish on the day of purchase.

Machli Recheade
· GOAN GRILLED SPICY FISH ·

Serves 4

This is a quick and easy recipe for spicing up sole fillets – lemon or Dover. *Recheade* is one of several ground pastes from Goa. Teams of women go from door to door daily, and stone-grind any masalas required by the household cook that day. They use large portable stone grinders. I wish we had such a daily service in Haslemere!

INGREDIENTS

4 x 8oz (225g) Dover or lemon sole, skinned and filleted
2 tablespoons freshly squeezed lemon juice
1 teaspoon salt
1/2 teaspoon white peppercorns, ground
2 lemons, quartered

Paste
1 tablespoon tamarind purée (page 24)

1 teaspoon prawn powder
1 teaspoon white sugar
1 teaspoon garlic purée (page 24)
1 teaspoon ginger purée (page 25)
1 teaspoon cummin seeds, ground
1 teaspoon turmeric
1/2 teaspoon garam masala
1/2 teaspoon chilli powder
vinegar (any type)

METHOD

1 Mix the lemon juice, salt and pepper in a dish. Season the fish with it and leave to stand for about 15 minutes.

2 Meanwhile, put the paste ingredients into the food processor or blender, using enough vinegar to achieve a smooth pourable paste.

3 Rub the **paste** on to both sides of the fish.

4 Preheat the grill to medium. Line a grill pan with foil to catch drips. Put the fish in the pan rack and under the heat at the midway position. Grill for 8-10 minutes.

5 Turn and grill for a further 5-8 minutes. Serve, garnished with lemon wedges, with a rice dish.

Machli Mysori Wadiyar

· COCONUT COD ·

Serves 4

Mysore is one of my favourite Indian cities. It is in the mid-south and still has an ex-Maharajah who is descended from a family, the Wadiyars, who ruled Mysore for centuries. He lives in a palace whose dome is covered in gold plate said to weigh over 2 tons. This recipe is from one of his royal chefs.

INGREDIENTS

1¹/₂lb (675g) cod steaks, weighed after skinning and filleting
4 tablespoons vegetable oil
1 tablespoon ginger purée (page 25)
6 tablespoons onion purée (page 25)
2 fresh tomatoes
3 tablespoons tamarind purée (page 24)

2 tablespoons coconut powder
salt to taste

Spices (whole)
1 teaspoon fenugreek seeds
1 teaspoon mustard seeds

Spices (ground)
2 teaspoons coriander
1 teaspoon chilli powder
1 teaspoon turmeric

METHOD

1 Cut the cod into 1¹/₂ inch (4cm) cubes.

2 Heat the oil in a tawa or flat frying pan. Stir-fry the **whole spices** for 1 minute, then the ginger for a further minute, followed by the onion for 3 minutes.

3 Make a paste of the **ground spices** using a little water. Add to the frying pan and fry together for 2 minutes.

4 Add the tomatoes, tamarind purée and coconut powder. Stir-fry until simmering.

5 Put the fish cubes in the pan and simmer for 15 minutes, adding water as required to keep the dish liquid.

Above: Min Tulika with its spicy sauce

Min Tulika

· CRISPY SPICED WHITEBAIT ·

Serves 4

Tiny fish abound in the coastal waters of south-west India. There appear to be several species all about 1¹/₂-2 inches (4-5cm) long. As far as I can ascertain, these are not whitebait, but being totally 'taken' by this dish, I used whitebait and found it as good as the real thing. Serve with lemon wedges, dhal and rice.

INGREDIENTS

1lb (450g) whitebait or sprats
oil for deep-frying
plain flour for dusting

Sauce
3 tablespoons sesame oil
2-4 garlic cloves, chopped
4oz (110g) onions, chopped
1 teaspoon turmeric
10-12 curry leaves, dry or fresh
2-6 fresh green chillies, chopped
2 teaspoons white sugar
1 fresh coconut, flesh and water

made into a purée (page 23), or
4 tablespoons coconut milk
powder mixed with milk
1 tablespoon chopped fresh
coriander
salt to taste

Garnish
2 teaspoons mustard seeds,
roasted
chopped fresh chives
chilli powder

METHOD

1 First make the sauce. Heat the oil in a karahi or wok. Stir-fry the garlic for 30 seconds, then the onion for 2 minutes. Add the turmeric, curry leaves, chillies and sugar. Stir-fry for a further 5 minutes.

2 Add the coconut and coriander, and salt to taste.

3 If the whitebait are fresh, wash them. If frozen thaw them, then wash them. Dry by patting on kitchen paper.

4 Preheat the deep-fryer to 375°F/190°C. Sprinkle some flour on your work surface, and use to dust the whitebait. Place them into the deep-fryer one at a time quickly (to prevent them sticking together). So as not to overload the pan, do them in three batches, frying each batch for 5-6 minutes. Keep the earlier batches warm until all are cooked.

5 To serve place the crispy whitebait on the dining plates and pour the sauce on top, garnishing with the mustard seeds, chives and chilli powder.

Mahi Kaliya

· SALMON CURRY ·

Serves 4

Salmon is a cold-water fish and so is not found in India. In Europe, we regard it as the king of fish, and treat it rather reverentially. However, its delicate flavour and pink colour can be enhanced with equally delicate spicing.

INGREDIENTS

*4 salmon steaks, skinned and
  filleted, each weighing about
  6oz (175g)*

Paste
2 garlic cloves, chopped

4oz (110g) onions, chopped
2 teaspoons paprika
2 teaspoons char masala (page 29)
1 teaspoon salt
milk

METHOD

1 Mix the paste ingredients in the food processor, using just enough milk to make quite stiff.

2 Wash the steaks, then pat them dry and coat generously with the paste. Wrap them loosely but completely in kitchen foil.

3 Preheat the grill to medium. Place the steaks on the grill pan at the midway position. Cook for about 25 minutes, then serve with plain rice.

Bangoe Puli Munch
· GRILLED MACKEREL ·

I remember once eating mackerel freshly caught in Cornwall. Their blue back markings were electric, not at all faded, and the taste was stunning. So please use fresh mackerel for this dish from South India.

INGREDIENTS

4 fresh mackerel, about 12oz
   (350g) each, cleaned

Marinade
3oz (75g) onions, chopped
3oz (75g) tamarind purée (page
   24)

2-6 fresh red chillies
1 teaspoon turmeric
1 teaspoon salt
lemon wedges

METHOD

1 Wash the fish and dry them as thoroughly as possible. Make several slashes in each side of the fish with a sharp knife.

2 Grind the marinade ingredients together with just enough water to obtain a thickish paste.

3 Work the marinade into the fish, cover and set aside for 2-3 hours.

4 To cook, preheat the grill to medium. Line the grill pan with foil. Place the fish on the grill rack and place it in the midway position.

5 Grill for about 8 minutes. Turn them over and finish off with a further 5-6 minutes. Serve with lemon wedges and Indian bread or rice.

Machli Bardez
· HADDOCK IN A MILKY SAUCE ·

Serves 4

This is another fine recipe from Goa.

INGREDIENTS

1¹/₂lb (675g) smoked haddock,
   weighed after skinning and
   filleting
3 tablespoons coconut oil (page
   23), or light vegetable oil
8oz (225g) onions, chopped
7 fl oz (200ml) milk
salt to taste
2 teaspoons garam masala (page
   29)

Paste
flesh and water from one fresh
   coconut (page 23)
2-6 fresh red chillies
2-4 garlic cloves, peeled
1 inch (2.5cm) cube fresh ginger
1 teaspoon tamarind purée (page
   24)

METHOD	1 Cut the haddock into 1¹/₂ inch (4cm) cubes.
	2 Put the paste ingredients into the blender, and purée, adding enough water to make a thinnish paste.
	3 Heat the oil in a karahi or wok, and stir-fry the onion for 10 minutes.
	4 Add the paste and stir-fry for 5 minutes.
	5 Add the milk little by little until simmering, then add the fish and simmer for 15-20 minutes. Salt to taste.
	6 Serve sprinkled with the garam masala.

Machhi Kothmiri

· MARINATED POMFRET ·

Serves 4

Pomfret is a most popular flat fish in India. In Britain it is available frozen and even fresh from some fishmongers, and is worth looking for. Substitute plaice, flounder, dab, small sole or brill for a similar effect. Get the fishmonger to skin it for you.

INGREDIENTS

4 small flat fish, each weighing
* 7-8oz (200-225g) after skinning*
freshly squeezed lemon juice
salt to taste

Marinade
3 tablespoons butter

3 tablespoons green masala paste
* (page 32)*
3 tablespoons chopped fresh
* coriander*
1 tablespoon chopped fresh mint,
* or ¹/₂ tablespoon dried mint*

METHOD

1 Cut diagonal score marks on each side of the fish, rub them with some lemon juice and salt, and set aside during stage 2.

2 Mix the marinade ingredients in the blender or food processor using just enough of the lemon juice to achieve a very smooth paste.

3 Liberally rub the paste into the fish, especially the scores. Use it all. Wrap each fish into a loose parcel in kitchen foil.

4 Preheat the oven to 375°F/190°C/Gas 5. Put the fish on an oven tray and bake for 20 minutes. Serve with rice.

Maachi Kadhi

· FISH AND YOGHURT SAUCE ·

Serves 4

The sweet and sour flavours of Gujarat predominate in this recipe. Adjust the number of chillies to suit your taste.

INGREDIENTS

2¼lb (1kg) flat fish, weighed after stage 1
2 teaspoons turmeric
2 teaspoons salt
3 tablespoons mustard oil
1 inch (2.5cm) cube ginger, finely chopped
8oz (225g) onions, finely chopped
0-4 fresh green chillies, chopped
7oz (200g) yoghurt
1 tablespoon sultanas

1 tablespoon brown sugar
a sprinkling of chopped fresh coriander
salt to taste

Spices
2 bay leaves
2 inch (5cm) piece cassia bark
4-6 green cardamoms
4-6 cloves
1 teaspoon lovage seeds

METHOD

1 Cut the fish into fairly large pieces, discarding heads, tail and fins. Wash the pieces and dry them on kitchen paper.

2 Mix the turmeric and salt together and rub into all parts of the fish.

3 Heat the oil in a karahi or wok. Fry the fish for about 5 minutes, turning once. Do this in two batches. Remove from the karahi, leaving the juices behind.

4 Into the karahi put the **spices** and stir-fry for 30 seconds. Add the ginger, onion and chillies, and stir-fry for 5 minutes.

5 Add the yoghurt, sultanas and sugar and briskly stir-fry up to the simmer.

6 Add the fish and fresh coriander. Simmer for 10 minutes or so. Salt to taste.

Machhli Ka Salan

· COD STEAK CURRY ·

Serves 4

A delicious dish in a rich red curry sauce.

INGREDIENTS

4 cod steaks, cut from the middle section of the fish, and each weighing 8oz (225g)

Sauce
4 tablespoons butter ghee
1 teaspoon white cummin seeds
1/2 teaspoon lovage seeds
1 tablespoon garlic purée (page 24)
6 tablespoons onion purée (page 25)
1 full recipe light or spicy tandoori marinade (page 80)

2 tablespoons mild curry paste (page 31)
1 tablespoon brown sugar
1 tablespoon tomato ketchup
1 tablespoon sweet red tomato chutney (page 251)
1 tablespoon ground almonds
2 teaspoons garam masala
1 tablespoon chopped fresh coriander leaves
7 fl oz (200ml) single cream
3 fl oz (85ml) coconut milk
salt to taste

METHOD

1 Prepare the sauce first. Heat the ghee in a karahi or wok. Stir-fry the cummin and lovage seeds for 30 seconds, then the garlic for 1 minute. Add the onion and stir-fry for 2-3 further minutes.

2 Next add the tandoori marinade and stir-fry for 5-6 minutes.

3 Add the curry paste, sugar, tomato ketchup, chutney and the ground almonds.

4 Allow to simmer gently while you cook the fish.

5 Put the fish in a steamer basket and steam over boiling water for about 10-15 minutes.

6 Add garam masala, coriander, cream, coconut milk and salt to the sauce. Then add the fish, simmer for about 5 minutes more, then serve.

Taja Bommaloe Macchli

· GRIDDLE-COOKED EEL ·

Serves 4

We met Bombay duck on page 46 in its dried form. On one occasion when I was in Bombay I saw local fisherwomen carrying baskets of freshly caught silvery eel-like fish. They hung the fish by their tails on racks to dry out in the sun and become the familiar Indian condiment. This recipe uses the fresh fish and I have converted it to use eels, traditionally rubbed in a spicy mixture and griddle-cooked (page 14).

INGREDIENTS

4 fresh eels, each weighing 6-8oz
(175-225g) after stage 1
plain flour for dusting
lemon

Paste
4-6 fresh red chillies
1 tablespoon paprika
1 teaspoon turmeric

METHOD

1 Remove the head and tail and (optionally) fillet the eel. Clean it, cut into pieces about 6 inches (15cm) long, and dry on kitchen paper.

2 Grind the paste ingredients together in the blender with enough water to make a thick paste. Then rub it into the fish, inside (if filleted) and out. Dust with flour.

3 Heat the griddle pan. Use no oil and place the fish on to the pan.

4 Griddle for about 10 minutes, turning as required. Serve with a squeeze of lemon and Indian bread.

CHEF'S TIP

Prawns

Prawns and shrimps are one and the same thing, say the professionals, who measure them by how many you get to the pound (450g). The tiniest are $1/3$ inch (6mm) in length (eaten whole) and the biggest are as much as 9 inches (23cm) long, weighing as much as 8oz (225g).

There are some fifteen species of cold-water prawns and twenty warm-water species. They are available alive sometimes, or cooked with shell on or off, and head on or off. Shelled and head off, you should get 200-300 to the pound for small ones. King prawns range from 21-25, 16-20 and 8-12 to the lb (450g), whilst tiger prawns can be under 5 to the pound.

Jinga Masaladar

· PRAWNS IN TANDOORI GRAVY ·

Serves 4

A tasty and popular prawn dish that can be served with rice.

INGREDIENTS

1¹/₂lb (675g) prawns, weighed
   after shells and heads are
   removed and, if appropriate,
   thawed

Sauce
4 tablespoons butter ghee
2 garlic cloves, finely chopped
4oz (110g) onions, finely chopped
5 fl oz (150ml) milk
1 full recipe light or spicy
   tandoori marinade (page 80)

2 tablespoons tomato purée
1-2 fresh green chillies, chopped
   (optional)
1 tablespoon chopped fresh
   coriander
2 teaspoons garam masala
7 fl oz (200ml) single cream
salt to taste

Garnish
1 fl oz (25ml) single cream
1 tablespoon hot butter ghee

METHOD

1 De-vein and wash the prawns (see Chef's Tip below).

2 To make the sauce, heat the ghee in a karahi or wok. Stir-fry the garlic for 1 minute, then add the onion and continue stir-frying for 5 minutes or more.

3 Add 4 tablespoons of the milk (to cool the contents a little), then the tandoori marinade and the tomato purée. Stir-fry until bubbling.

4 Add the remaining milk, the chillies and coriander, and simmer until reduced a little, then add the prawns.

5 Simmer for 5 minutes, then add the garam masala and cream, and simmer for a further 5 minutes. Salt to taste.

6 Garnish with a curl of cream over which you can run a curl of ghee.

CHEF'S TIP

Prawns or Shrimps
There is no such thing as cheap prawns or shrimps. Yet prices can vary enormously, particularly of frozen sachets. Cheap products can include a large percentage of water and chlorine (up to *half* the weight of the packet!).

Best are live prawns. Cook in boiling water for 5-8 minutes depending on size, or until they go pink. Rinse in cold water to enable you to shell them. Always remove the **vein** running down the back using a sharp knife tip. Use or freeze on the same day.

Sukhe Jhinga Bhoona

· FRIED PRAWN CURRY ·

Serves 4

This pan-fried medium curry is cooked by the *balti* method to produce a dry dish without the usual accompanying rich gravy.

INGREDIENTS

1¹/₂lb (675g) medium to large prawns, weighed after removing shells and heads and, if appropriate, thawed
3 tablespoons ghee
1 tablespoon garlic purée (page 24)

4oz (110g) onions, finely chopped
3 tablespoons mild curry paste (page 31)
1 tablespoon fresh coriander leaves
aromatic salt to taste (page 30)

METHOD

1 De-vein and wash the prawns (see Chef's Tip on page 149).

2 Heat the ghee in a karahi or wok. Stir-fry the garlic for 30 seconds, then add the onion and continue for 5 minutes. Add the paste and bring to the simmer.

3 Add the prawns and briskly stir-fry for 2-3 minutes. Then allow to simmer for about 5 more minutes (or until cooked, the larger the prawns the longer). Add sprinklings of water and keep it moving.

4 About 2 minutes before serving add the coriander and the salt.

Khinga Nishat

· SKEWERED SPICY BATTER PRAWNS ·

Serves 4

I was given this dish and its recipe in the Nishat garden at the Mughal Sheraton Hotel in Agra. The garden is named after its counterpart, the Nishat Bagh in Kashmir, which was established in 1600 for the emperor Jahangir who, it is said, delighted in fishing. In the pool of the garden he kept large trout. In their noses he put gold rings which enabled him to fish them, and return them unharmed to the pool. Their descendants still swim today in the Kashmiri gardens, sadly without rings. The emperors no doubt relished giant shrimps, and this recipe would do justice to their tables. Use the largest shrimps or prawns that you can buy.

INGREDIENTS

4 giant shrimps or prawns, total flesh weight 2lb (900g), thawed if necessary
4 tablespoons freshly squeezed lemon juice
1 tablespoon garlic purée (page 24)
1 tablespoon ginger purée (page 25)

2 eggs
4 tablespoons single cream
2 tablespoons gram flour (besan)
1 teaspoon lovage seeds
1/2 teaspoon turmeric
1/2 teaspoon salt

METHOD

1 Remove the heads, tails and shells of the prawns, and de-vein them (see Chef's Tip on page 149). Wash and dry them thoroughly.

2 Mix them with the lemon juice, garlic and ginger for 20 minutes.

3 Mix together all the other ingredients then mix in with the prawns, coating thoroughly. Keep in the refrigerator for a further 15 minutes or so.

4 Cook on skewers over charcoal or shallow-fry for 10-15 minutes then place on skewers with tongs and serve.

Below: fishermen casting their nets

Scampi Patia

· SWEET AND SAVOURY SCAMPI ·

Serves 4

Scampi, or Dublin Bay Prawn, Langoustine or Norway Lobster as they are also known, are wonderful if you can obtain them fresh or cooked, but not frozen and breadcrumbed. A great substitute for any seafood recipe is monkfish.

INGREDIENTS

1¹/₂lb (675g) scampi, weighed after removing shells, heads and, if appropriate thawing, or monkfish, skinned and filleted
3 tablespoons ghee or vegetable oil
1 tablespoon garlic purée (page 24)
1 tablespoon ginger purée (page 25)
1 tablespoon brown sugar
4oz (110g) onions, peeled and finely chopped
2 tablespoons mild curry paste (page 31)
2oz (50g) beetroot in vinegar, drained and finely chopped

2oz (50g) creamed coconut
1 tablespoon chopped fresh coriander
salt to taste

Spices
2 teaspoons tandoori dry mix masala (page 80)
1 teaspoon white sesame seeds
1 teaspoon aniseed
1 teaspoon paprika
¹/₂ teaspoon lovage seeds
¹/₂ teaspoon cummin seeds, roasted
¹/₂ teaspoon chilli powder

METHOD

1 Make a thick paste of the **spices** using a little water, and set aside.

2 De-vein the scampi (see Chef's Tip on page 149), and wash and dry thoroughly. If using monkfish, cut it into 1¹/₂ inch (4cm) cubes.

3 Heat the ghee in a karahi or wok. Stir-fry the garlic and ginger for 3 minutes. Add the spice paste and stir-fry to a sizzle. Add the sugar and onion and stir-fry for around 5 more minutes.

4 Add the curry paste and the beetroot, then, when sizzling, add the scampi or monkfish.

5 Simmer for 8 minutes or so.

6 Heat the creamed coconut in sufficient water to make a pourable paste (page 23) and add it at any point during stage 5.

7 Add the coriander and salt to taste. Simmer for a further 5-10 minutes or until cooked. The dish should be dryish, but control this with a little water at any stage.

Bhare Crabs

· STUFFED CRABS ·

Serves 4

This recipe is again from Goa, a paradise for seafood. I had these stuffed crabs at a barbecue. Most of us will purchase fresh cooked whole crabs (rather than live ones), but see Chef's Tip below.

INGREDIENTS

4 edible brown crabs, each
   weighing around 1lb (450g)
2 tablespoons vegetable oil
2 garlic cloves, finely chopped
4oz (110g) onions, finely chopped
4 teaspoons mild curry paste
   (page 31)
0-4 fresh red chillies, chopped

1 teaspoon lovage seeds
1 slice white bread, crust
   discarded, crumbled
1 tablespoon coconut milk
   powder
salt to taste
lemon wedges

METHOD

1 Heat the oil in a karahi or wok. Stir-fry the garlic for 30 seconds, then add the onion and stir-fry for 5 more minutes.

2 Add the curry paste, chillies and lovage seeds, and stir-fry for a further 5 minutes.

3 Add the bread, coconut and the crab meat. Stir-fry to the simmer then lower the heat and cook until dry – around 10 minutes, stirring frequently. Salt to taste.

4 Stuff the shells using all the filling. Flash it under the grill just to brown it. Serve with a twist of lemon.

CHEF'S TIP

To Prepare a Crab

1. If alive, immerse the crab in warm water for 30 minutes, to prevent it shedding its claws, then bring to the boil and boil for 10 minutes per pound (450g). Drain and allow to cool.

2. Place it on its back and pull off the claws and legs. Extract the flesh using pliers and a pick.

3. Remove and discard the tail then twist the body out of the shell with a knife.

4. Discard the finger-like grey gills and the stomach behind the eyes. Keep both the white and brown meat.

5. Wash the body shell. Using pliers crack off the top shell and discard. Wash again.

The yield from a 1lb (450g) crab is about 6-8oz (175-200g).

Lobster Hawa Mahal

· GRATIN OF LOBSTER ·

Serves 4

This dish was created by Satish Arora, Chef Director of the Taj Hotel Group, at the Taj Mahal Intercontinental Hotel in Bombay when the ex-Maharajah of Jaipur was staying there for a diplomatic convention. The dish is remarkable because it uses 'gratin' techniques which are more French than Indian, and this is one of Chef Arora's masterpieces. He named it after the Hawa Mahal (Palace of the Winds), one of India's architectural masterpieces (see page 219).

INGREDIENTS

2 whole lobsters, each weighing
$2^1/_4$lb (1kg), or 4 large crawfish
4 tablespoons ghee
1 tablespoon white cummin seeds
1 teaspoon garlic purée (page 24)
1 teaspoon ginger purée (page 25)
8 tablespoons onion purée (page 25)
1-6 fresh green chillies, finely chopped
4 fresh tomatoes, chopped
2 tablespoons chopped fresh mint, or 1 tablespoon dried mint
4 teaspoons chopped fresh coriander

5 fl oz (150ml) single cream
crushed or milled black pepper
salt to taste
4oz (100g) Cheddar cheese, grated

Sauce
$1^1/_2$lb (675g) fresh tomatoes
4oz (110g) ghee
8 fl oz (250ml) single cream
1 teaspoon white peppercorns, ground
1 tablespoon tandoori masala paste (page 80)
salt to taste

METHOD

1 If the lobsters are fresh, see the Chef's Tip opposite. If frozen, thaw them, then proceed to the next step.

2 When cold, halve the shells (see Chef's Tip again), and remove meat from the shell, claws, etc. Keep the shells. Chop the meat into small pieces.

3 Heat the ghee, and fry the cummin seeds for 1 minute, then the garlic for 1 minute, the ginger for 2 minutes, and the onion for 3 minutes.

4 Add the chillies, tomatoes, mint and coriander. Cook until this mixture is quite dry.

5 Add the lobster pieces, cream, pepper and salt to taste, then load this mixture back into the lobster shells.

6 For the sauce, purée the tomatoes in a blender or food processor. Heat the ghee and simmer the tomato purée until it changes colour to red from pink. Add the remaining ingredients and simmer for a further 5 minutes. Pour some of this over the lobster halves.

7 Sprinkle cheese over the halves and grill for 2 minutes until brown. Serve, pouring spare sauce on each plate.

Above: Lobster Hawa Mahal.

CHEF'S TIP

To Prepare a Lobster
1. Though unappealing, it is easy to cook a live lobster. Place it into boiling water for a minimum of 3 minutes (for uncooked flesh) and for 20 minutes (for cooked flesh).

2. Twist off the legs and pincers. Extract the flesh using pliers and a pick. Discard cartilage.

3. If using the shell, halve it by simply cutting down the centre line. Keep the tail on. Wash the shell halves when the flesh has been removed.

4. Discard the hard and soft material in the head area. Cut the flesh away from the shell, and separate it. Spoon out the creamy white liver and the red eggs (coral) if present.

5. Cut up and mix all the meat, liver and coral.

The yield of meat from a 1³/₄lb (800g) lobster is about 8oz (225g).

Lobster Balchao

Serves 4

Goan lobsters are huge and plentiful, and are fished for daily. The Indian lobster is in fact the spiny lobster, langouste, or crawfish, which does not have the huge claws of the European or American lobster. Crawfish can be as large as 20 inches (50cm). This recipe is traditionally served with an abundance of chilli. Temper it to your taste.

INGREDIENTS

1¹/₂lb (675g) cooked lobster meat
  (see Chef's Tip on page 155)
vinegar (any type)
2 tablespoons sesame or light
  vegetable oil
1 inch (2.5cm) cube ginger,
  chopped
4oz (110g) onions, chopped
20 curry leaves, fresh or dry

0-6 fresh red chillies, chopped
2-4 garlic cloves, chopped
salt to taste

Spices
3 teaspoons ground cummin
2 teaspoons ground black pepper
1-3 teaspoons chilli
1 teaspoon turmeric

METHOD

1 Mix the **spices** with enough vinegar to make a pourable paste.

2 Heat the oil in a karahi or wok. Add the ginger and onion together and stir-fry for 10 minutes.

3 Add the spice paste and stir-fry for a couple more minutes.

4 Add the lobster, the curry leaves, chillies and garlic and stir-fry for about 8 minutes, adding a little water to keep things from sticking. Salt to taste. Serve with rice.

Scampi Taleli

Serves 4

This is a quick-cook recipe of my own, using ingredients not available so far as I know in the sub-continent – breaded scampi. The idea is to spice and re-crumb the scampi then simply fry. (Scampi, by the way, is an Italian word for langoustines caught in the bay of Naples.) Serve dry with lemon wedges, puri and chutneys for a simple TV dinner.

INGREDIENTS

2lb (900g) breadcrumbed
  scampi, frozen
2 eggs
semolina
rice flour
oil for frying

Spices (ground)
¹/₂ teaspoon turmeric
¹/₂ teaspoon cummin
2 teaspoons coriander
1 teaspoon garlic powder
¹/₂-2 teaspoons chilli powder
¹/₂ teaspoon salt

METHOD

1 Thaw the scampi.

2 Mix the **spices** with the eggs. Coat the scampi thoroughly.

3 Mix equal quantities of semolina and rice flour and 'dry' the scampi in this.

4 Either deep-fry at 375°F/190°C (potato-chip temperature), or shallow-fry for 5 minutes or so. Serve with savoury fried potatoes (page 189).

Jhinge Koliwada Bhajia
· KING PRAWN FRITTERS ·

Serves 4

Use larger prawns, around 16-20 to the 1b (450g) for this colourful batter-coated deep-fried prawn dish. Serve with dhal and Indian bread.

INGREDIENTS

2lb (900g) prawns (see above), weighed after removing shells and heads and, if appropriate, thawing
vegetable oil for deep-frying

Batter
3oz (75g) gram flour (besan) plus 1oz (25g) coconut milk powder, or 4oz (110g) gram flour
2 garlic cloves, chopped

2 tablespoons tandoori masala paste (page 80)
1 tablespoon lemon juice
1 teaspoon garam masala
1 teaspoon paprika
1 teaspoon coriander seeds, roasted
1 tablespoon chopped fresh mint
1 teaspoon aromatic salt (page 30)

METHOD

1 De-vein and wash the prawns (see Chef's Tip on page 149). Dry them well.

2 Make the batter by mixing all the ingredients together. Add sufficient water to make a thick batter.

3 Put the prawns into the batter and stand whilst the oil heats up.

4 Heat the deep fryer to 375°F/190°C. One at a time, with 10 seconds between each (to prevent the oil temperature from dropping too low and the items from sticking), lower each prawn into the batter, until half the batch is in.

5 Cook for 8 minutes. Remove and drain on kitchen paper in a warm place.

6 Repeat stages 4 and 5 with the second batch of prawns. Serve hot.

Vegetable Dishes

❈

With a population exceeding one billion in the curry lands, many of whom do not eat meat for religious or financial reasons, it is not surprising that a very wide range of superb vegetable recipes exist.

India has a greater selection of vegetables than we do, and many of their exotic items, known at Covent Garden and other markets as 'queer gear', are not readily available at the British greengrocers. There are many types of gourd (also called marrows and squashes) ranging from bottle gourd *(loukey)* ridge gourd *(turia or tori)*, bitter gourd *(karela)*, snake gourd, pumpkin and all manner of marrows to the long thin 'drumstick'. Roots include aubery (a sweetish Pakistani root), white radish *(mooli)*, the bitter *kachair,* and turmeric *(huldi)*. There are many types of beans, as well as cooking bananas (plantain and *bulogoo*), sweet potatoes *(sakar kandhi)*, aubergine *(brinjal)*, mustard leaves *(rai)* and fenugreek leaves *(methi)*. Fruit such as mangoes, pineapple and cherries are sometimes used as vegetables. My particular favourites are okra and tindla (known respectively in India as 'ladies' fingers' and 'gentlemens' toes'), see pages 164 and 165.

If you come across 'queer gear', I heartily recommend that you try it. And substitute different vegetables in these recipes as the mood takes you. My recipes give as wide a selection of vegetables as possible, and the portions are for main course dishes. Used as an accompaniment, halve the quantities to serve the same number of people.

Facing page, left to right: Bhandakka Bhajee (page 164), *Pao Bhajee* (page 176) and *Gajaraloo Kabab* (page 168). Note the bitter gourd and the *tindla* on the top tray.

> **CHEF'S TIP**
>
> *Stir-Fry Vegetables*
> A little common-sense must prevail when one stir-fries vegetables. Starchy and pithy vegetables will need to be chopped or sliced into quite small pieces and will need longer than soft vegetables.
>
> Because it presents a larger surface area to the heat, a thinly sliced vegetable will stir-fry quicker than a cube-sized one. For example a mange-tout is a perfect subject for stir-frying. A 1 inch (2.5cm) cube of potato is not, whereas a sliced or small $1/3$ inch (6mm) cube will work well.
>
> Theoretically, items should all be approximately the same shape and size to ensure they cook evenly. In practice this does not have to be the case.
>
> You must control both the heat – too hot and the surface will burn, and the inside will remain uncooked – and the water content. Sprinklings of water will help to prevent burning by replacing evaporating moisture, preventing the vegetables from drying up.

Vegetable Bhajee

Serves 4

I start this chapter with one of the Indian restaurant's most popular recipes. *Bhajee* simply means cooked vegetables. This recipe uses fresh vegetables, but the method is a perfect way to use up leftovers. For example you could use 3oz (75g) each of fresh or leftover sweet potatoes, parsnips, carrots, courgettes and peas.

INGREDIENTS

1lb (450g) combination of fresh or pre-cooked leftover vegetables weighed after stage 1 (see above)
2 tablespoons ghee or vegetable oil

4oz (110g) onions, finely chopped
1 tablespoon mild curry paste (page 31)
salt to taste

METHOD

1 Prepare the vegetables, discard unwanted matter and cut, as needed, into smallish bite-sized pieces.

2 Heat the ghee or oil in a karahi or wok. Stir-fry the onion and the curry paste for 3-4 minutes.

3 Add the vegetables and stir-fry (see Chef's Tip above). With the combination suggested in the introduction, I would start with the potato and parsnip, then add the carrot after 3-4 minutes, the courgettes 2-3 minutes later, and the peas 2-3 minutes after that.

4 When cooked to your liking, salt to taste, and serve at once.

Chaunkgobhi Bhoona

· STIR-FRY BRUSSELS SPROUTS ·

Serves 4

I have never encountered Brussels sprouts in India – they are not traditional in the sub-continent. But that is no reason not to incorporate them into a spicy recipe. Brussels sprouts are tiny cabbages. They are classified into four sizes the smallest of which should be used for best appearance in this simple and tasty stir-fry.

INGREDIENTS

1lb (450g) miniature Brussels
*   sprouts, weighed after stage 1*
3 tablespoons butter
2 inch (5cm) cube ginger, thinly
*   sliced into matchsticks*
2 teaspoons panch phoran (page
*   29)*

1 tablespoon mild curry paste
*   (page 31)*
1 tablespoon green masala paste
*   (page 32)*
4oz (110g) onions, thinly sliced
salt to taste

METHOD

1   Discard the sprouts' outer leaves and cut off stalks as appropriate.

2   Steam, boil or microwave the sprouts to readiness (still crunchy), then drain.

3   Heat the butter in a karahi or wok. Stir-fry the ginger for 20 seconds. Add the panch phoran and stir-fry for a further 10 seconds. Add the two pastes and when simmering, add the onion. Stir-fry for around 5 minutes.

4   Add the drained hot sprouts and mix in well. Salt to taste, and serve.

Mushroom Balti Bhajee

Serves 4

Few things are nicer than this dish – but do serve the mushrooms as soon as they are cooked. They get soggy if they stand around.

INGREDIENTS

1lb (450g) button mushrooms
2 tablespoons ghee or vegetable
oil
4oz (110g) onions, very finely
chopped

1 tablespoon mild curry paste
(page 31)
salt to taste

METHOD

1 Wash and dry the mushrooms. Only peel them if the skins are 'tired'. Slice them or keep them whole, as you wish.

2 Heat the ghee or oil in a karahi or wok. Stir-fry the onion and the curry paste for 3-4 minutes.

3 Add the mushrooms and briskly stir-fry for about 5 minutes.

4 Salt to taste. Serve at once.

Foogath

· LIGHTLY COOKED VEGETABLES ·

Serves 4

I've come across a number of interpretations of *foogath* on my visits to India. However, none was better than this one which I encountered at the former British Raj hill station of Ooty, 7,000 feet up in the mountains. The faded and jaded Ooty Club (where the British invented snooker) has seen better days. On the occasion I was there it was lunchtime and the only diners at the celebrated club (jacket and tie essential) were a journalist and me. It took 1½ hours for lunch to come. This was one of the dishes, but was, however, worth the wait.

INGREDIENTS

4oz (110g) each of carrot, spinach, white radish (mooli) and parsnip, weighed after stage 1
3 tablespoons sesame oil
3oz (75g) desiccated coconut (fresh preferably)
½ teaspoon turmeric
2-4 fresh red chillies, cut in long slices

salt to taste
1 full recipe onion tarka (page 26)

Spices
1 teaspoon mustard seeds
1 teaspoon sesame seeds
⅓ teaspoon fenugreek seeds

METHOD

1 Wash and pare the vegetables, discarding unwanted matter. Run each one through a fine shredder, and mix together well.

2 Heat the oil in a karahi or wok. Stir-fry the **spices** for 30 seconds. Add the desiccated coconut, turmeric and chillies.

3 Add the shredded mixture in about six batches, about 20 seconds apart. This allows them to soften, bit by bit. When all are in the pan, lower the heat and stir-fry for between 3-5 minutes.

4 Salt to taste, and serve with the tarka garnish.

Facing page: Mushroom Balti Bhajee

Bhandakka Bhajee

· OKRA CURRY ·

Serves 4

Okra, or 'ladies' fingers', are rather pithy, ribbed, green, chilli-shaped, pointed vegetables with a stalk varying in size from 2-4 inches (5-10cm) and more.

They are rather difficult to cook. The first factor is careful selection. It is usually better to choose smaller ones – the large ones are often scaly. To prepare them, wash them carefully and dry them. Just before cooking, cut off the point and trim off the stalk, then cook at once. Do not cook them in water, otherwise they ooze sap while cooking. Even slight overcooking results in a soggy mush and again that sticky sap. It's most unpleasant, and unfortunately this is one of those dishes which many standard curry houses get wrong. It can only be successful if it is cooked fresh. A microwave is the best of all, giving lovely crisp results. Alternatively try this stir-fry method.

INGREDIENTS

1lb (450g) small okra, weighed after trimming (stage 4 of method)
2 tablespoons vegetable oil
2 teaspoons cummin seeds
4oz (110g) onions, very finely chopped
1 tablespoon mild curry paste (page 31)

2-3 tomatoes, finely chopped
1 tablespoon chopped fresh coriander
3-4 pieces each of red and green pepper, seeded
2-4 fresh red chillies
1 tablespoon brown sugar
salt to taste

METHOD

1 Carefully (so as not to damage them) wash the okra. Do not trim them yet.

2 Heat the oil in a karahi or wok. Stir-fry the cummin seeds for 30 seconds then add the onion and curry paste and stir-fry for 5 minutes.

3 Add the tomato, coriander, pepper, chillies and sugar, and continue to stir-fry for 5 more minutes.

4 During stage 3 trim the okra. Add them to the karahi and gently stir-fry until they are cooked to your liking.

5 Salt to taste, and serve at once.

Tindla

· GENTLEMEN'S TOES ·

A far less familiar exotic vegetable, that is at least as far as Britain is concerned, is *tindla*, also known in India as 'Gentlemen's Toes'! *Tindla* vaguely resemble gooseberries in colour – green with white stripes, though they are a little larger and they are oval. They are available from Asian food stores. You can see them in the photograph on page 158, in front of the red pepper.

Cook them whole or halved, substituting them for the okra in the previous recipe. Or for a cutely named dish – ladies' fingers and gentlemen's toes – cook half and half okra and *tindla*.

Niramish

· BENGALI STIR-FRY ·

Serves 4

A traditional recipe from the eastern part of the subcontinent. No oil is used, and its lightness and freshness make it a delight. The choice of vegetables to use is yours. I like to use root vegetables – 4oz (110g) each of potato, turnip, carrot and swede.

INGREDIENTS

1lb (450g) any single vegetable, or a combination
1 tablespoon chopped fresh coriander
salt to taste

1 teaspoon ground coriander
1 teaspoon yellow mustard powder
1 teaspoon sesame seeds
1/2 teaspoon turmeric

Spices
1 teaspoon ground cummin

METHOD

1 Pare the vegetables, trim as necessary, and dice into small cubes about 1/3 inch (8mm) in size.

2 Blanch for 5 minutes (or steam or microwave) until slightly softened. Strain.

3 Place straight into a karahi or wok. Stir-fry to the simmer then add the **spices** and coriander.

4 Stir-fry until the vegetables are to your liking. Salt to taste, and serve at once.

Subz-e-Bahar

· FRESH VEGETABLE FRY ·

Serves 4

The spinach and red pepper give the contrasting base colours to your choice of fresh vegetables. Here I use cauliflower, broccoli, beans, peas and mushrooms.

INGREDIENTS

3oz (75g) each of cauliflower, broccoli, French beans, spinach, mushrooms and peas
1oz (25g) fresh fenugreek leaves (if available)
1/2 red pepper, seeded
2 tablespoons vegetable oil

2 garlic cloves, chopped
4oz (110g) onions, finely chopped
1 tablespoon mild curry paste (page 31)
1 teaspoon tandoori paste (page 80)
salt to taste

METHOD

1 Cut the cauliflower and broccoli into minuscule florets. Slice the beans into 1/2 inch (1cm) pieces. Shred the spinach, and slice the mushrooms. Shred the fresh fenugreek leaves (if available) and slice the red pepper.

2 Heat the oil in a karahi or wok, and stir-fry the garlic for 30 seconds. Add the onion and the pastes and stir-fry for 3-4 minutes.

3 Add about 3-4 tablespoons of water and the spinach and fenugreek. Stir until they go soft then add the remaining vegetables. Stir-fry for about 8 more minutes. Salt to taste, and serve at once.

Sabzi Caldine

· GOAN VEGETABLE STIR-FRY ·

Serves 4

This quick and easy stir-fry uses coconut as its base.

INGREDIENTS

1¹/₂lb (675g) equal mixture of soft vegetables such as courgettes, celery, chokoes (chayotes or christophenes), custard marrows (patisson) and French beans
2 tablespoons vegetable oil
4oz (110g) onions, finely chopped
2-6 fresh red chillies, chopped
salt to taste

Purée
flesh and water from 1 fresh coconut, or 4 tablespoons coconut milk powder
1 teaspoon ground cummin
1/2 teaspoon turmeric
1 garlic clove, finely chopped
1/2 inch (1cm) cube ginger, finely chopped

METHOD

1 Wash, prepare and trim the vegetables. Cut into slices.

2 Make the **purée** in the blender, using either the fresh coconut or powder and water as required.

3 Heat the oil in a karahi or wok. Stir-fry the onion for 5-8 minutes.

4 Add the purée and stir-fry to the simmer.

5 Add the vegetables and chillies, and stir-fry until cooked to taste. Salt to taste, and add sprinklings of water if needed.

Tamako or Tushako

· BAMBOO SHOOT CURRY ·

Serves 4

The Nepalese adore bamboo shoots. They pickle them and they curry them in a number of recipe variations. This curry is one of them.

Fresh whole bamboo shoots are sometimes available, particularly from Chinese food shops, when this recipe comes into its own. Otherwise use canned whole shoots.

INGREDIENTS

1lb (450g) bamboo shoots, peeled
2 tablespoons mustard or light oil
4oz (110g) onions, thinly sliced
2 tablespoons mild curry paste
(page 31)

1 teaspoon garam masala (page 29)
1 tablespoon fresh coriander leaves
salt to taste

METHOD

1 Cut the peeled bamboo shoots into cubes about ³/₄ inch (2cm) in size.

2 Heat the oil in a karahi or wok. Stir-fry the onion for 5 minutes or so. Add the curry paste and when sizzling, add the bamboo shoots.

3 Stir-fry briskly, adding sprinklings of water to prevent sticking.

4 A few minutes is all you need. Season with the garam masala, coriander and salt to taste, and serve at once.

Gajaraloo Kabab

· VEGETABLE KEBAB ·

Makes 8

The vegetable kebab bears no resemblance to a meat kebab, except vaguely in its shape. Indeed it has no right to be called a kebab. It is in fact a rissole. Its flavouring is essentially South Indian, and whilst it is not to be found in that region, it is a good tasty non-meat dish. It requires careful handling whilst cooking to prevent it breaking up.

INGREDIENTS

vegetable oil
2 garlic cloves, finely chopped
1 inch (2.5cm) cube ginger, cut into thin strips
1 tablespoon chopped fresh coriander
1 tablespoon mild curry paste (page 31)
1 tablespoon ground almonds
1 tablespoon coconut powder
salt to taste
1lb (450g) mashed cooked potato

6oz (175g) carrots, scraped and finely shredded
1 egg, beaten
mixture of equal parts fresh breadcrumbs and semolina

Spices
2 teaspoons ground cummin
1 teaspoon garam masala
1 teaspoon paprika
¹/₂ teaspoon turmeric
¹/₂ teaspoon mango powder

METHOD

1 Heat 1 tablespoon of the oil in a karahi or wok. Stir-fry the **spices** for 1 minute, then the garlic for 1 minute, and the ginger for 2 minutes. Remove from the pan and cool.

2 In a mixing bowl mix together all the remaining ingredients except for the egg, breadcrumbs and semolina. The mixture should be quite dry. If it is not add a small quantity of gram flour (besan).

3 Divide the mixture into eight and carefully roll into sausage shapes.

4 Coat with the egg, then roll in the mixture of breadcrumbs and semolina.

5 Shallow-fry in minimal oil until the kebabs are hot and golden.

6 Serve with rice and, if liked, a gravy or sauce (choose from those on pages 32, 84, 85, 101, 122, 133, 142, 147, 149, 171, 193 and 194).

Loukey Masalam

· STUFFED BOTTLE GOURD CURRY ·

Serves 4

The bottle gourd or *loukey* resembles the ten pin bowling skittle in shape (but not in taste, I hasten to add!). It is popular in India where it is sometimes used as a water container, and it is available in the West. Substitute with a standard marrow if necessary.

INGREDIENTS

1 x 2-2¼lb (900g-1kg) loukey
(bottle gourd)
1 portion curry masala gravy
(page 32)
a sprinkling of fresh coriander
leaves

Filling
10oz (275g) yellow gram chana
2 tablespoons vegetable oil
2 garlic cloves, chopped
1 inch (2.5cm) cube ginger,
chopped

2oz (50g) cashew nuts, chopped
1oz (25g) sultanas
1 tablespoon chopped fresh
coriander
salt to taste

Spices (roasted and ground)
1 teaspoon coriander seeds
1 teaspoon cummin seeds
6-8 green cardamoms
6-8 cloves
2 inch (5cm) piece cassia bark

METHOD

1 For the **filling**, soak and cook the chana as described in stages 1-3 of the recipe for masala dhal on page 204.

2 Heat the oil in a karahi or wok. Stir-fry the garlic and ginger for 3 minutes. Add the cashews, sultanas, coriander and the **spices**, and simmer for 5 minutes. Add the chana and simmer gently to reduce to a fairly dry mixture. Slightly over-salt or to taste.

3 Peel the gourd. Cut off both ends and scrape the seeds out from the middle. Keep the gourd whole.

4 Boil up ample water in a large saucepan. Immerse the gourd and simmer for 5 minutes. Remove and drain until cool enough to handle.

5 Stuff the gourd with the mixture. There should be spare mixture: use this in the gravy at stage 7. Wrap the stuffed gourd loosely in a parcel of kitchen foil.

6 Preheat the oven to 375°F/190°C/Gas 5 and place the gourd on an oven rack above an oven tray. Bake for 15-20 minutes.

7 During stage 4 make up the gravy, incorporating any spare stuffing from stage 5.

8 To serve, cut the gourd into slices, pour the gravy over them, then garnish with the fresh coriander leaves.

Kurilo

· NEPALESE ASPARAGUS ·

Serves 4

Asparagus grows freely in the Nepalese summer, and the hardy mountain people look forward to the brief time when the crop can be picked and enjoyed. This simple creamy recipe is quick to make, and does great justice to succulent, fresh asparagus. Use the tastier green variety in preference to the white.

INGREDIENTS

2lb (900g) green asparagus
2 tablespoons sunflower or light
  oil
1 garlic clove, finely chopped
1 tablespoon green masala paste
  (page 32)
5 fl oz (150ml) double cream

3 fl oz (85ml) soured cream

Garnish
garam masala
fresh red chilli, chopped
salt
fresh coriander leaves

METHOD

1 Cut the asparagus into 2 inch (5cm) lengths, keeping the tip in one piece, and discarding the stalk where it becomes tough.

2 Do not boil asparagus – it becomes mushy and loses flavour. Steam for 15 minutes or, even better, microwave for about 3 minutes.

3 Heat the oil in a karahi or wok. Stir-fry the garlic for 30 seconds. Add the green paste and the creams and stir-fry until simmering.

4 To serve, place the asparagus into a serving dish and pour the sauce over it. This minimises the risk of breaking the fragile tips. **Garnish** with sprinklings of garam masala, chilli, salt and fresh coriander leaves.

Ravaiya

· STUFFED BABY AUBERGINE ·

Serves 4

This delightful Gujarati recipe requires care and a light hand to produce a fascinating dish, perfect for a special occasion like a dinner party. The preparation can be done in advance, and the dish finished off in the oven. Serve with a creamy curry, and a spicy rice.

INGREDIENTS

8 small aubergines, each about
  2-3oz (50-75g)
1 teaspoon garam masala

1 tablespoon chopped fresh mint
1 tablespoon sultanas, chopped
1 teaspoon brown sugar

Stuffing
2 tablespoons vegetable oil
2 garlic cloves, finely chopped
4oz (110g) onions, finely chopped
1 tablespoon mild curry paste
  (page 31)
5oz (150g) mashed cooked potato
2oz (50g) shredded carrot

Sauce
5 fl oz (150ml) akhni stock (page
  33) or water
1 tablespoon green masala paste
  (page 32)
1 large plantain, peeled and thinly
  sliced
salt to taste

METHOD

1 Make the **stuffing** first. Heat the oil in a karahi or wok, and stir-fry the garlic, onion and curry paste for 5 minutes.

2 Add the remaining stuffing ingredients and mix in well. Allow to cool at least enough to handle.

3 Wash, then blanch the aubergines for 3 minutes (steam or microwave) simply to soften them. You can cool them now if reheating later, or proceed immediately.

4 Using gloves (if they are hot), cut off the stalk and slit each aubergine to create a pocket. Carefully stuff the pocket with some filling. Put on an oven tray.

5 Preheat the oven to 325°F/160°C/Gas 3 and bake for about 15 minutes, or to your liking.

6 During stage 5 make the **sauce**. Simply heat the water or akhni stock in the karahi or wok. Add the green masala paste and, when simmering, add the spare stuffing and the plantain. Simmer until the aubergines are ready. Salt to taste. It should be quite fluid.

7 Serve over the aubergines. Sprinkle the garam masala over the top.

Makai Mutter Masala
· SWEETCORN WITH PEAS ·

Serves 4

Red, yellow and green colours make this dish attractive in appearance as well as taste.

INGREDIENTS

12oz (350g) sweetcorn
8oz (225g) peas
2 tablespoons butter
1 teaspoon black cummin seeds
1 teaspoon lovage seeds
1 tablespoon mild curry paste
(page 31)

4oz (110g) onions, finely chopped
3oz (75g) tomatoes, finely
chopped
salt to taste

METHOD

1 Steam, boil or microwave the sweetcorn and peas to readiness.

2 Heat the butter in a karahi or wok. Stir-fry the seeds for 10 seconds, then add the curry paste and stir-fry for another 30 seconds.

3 Add the onion and tomato and, once sizzling, the sweetcorn and peas.

4 Mix well, salt to taste, and serve at once.

Koora Uthapam Masala
· COCONUT PANCAKE STUFFING ·

Serves 4

On page 68 we saw how to make a South Indian pancake. Here is a typical stuffing recipe from the state of Andra Pradesh. It can, of course, be served on its own as a vegetable curry.

INGREDIENTS

12oz (350g) boiled potatoes, cut
into small cubes
2 tablespoons sesame oil
2 teaspoons mustard seeds
1 tablespoon yellow gram chana,
uncooked
1 tablespoon black urid lentils,
uncooked
1 teaspoon turmeric
1 inch (2.5cm) cube ginger,
chopped

4oz (110g) onions, chopped
2 tablespoons cashew nuts
4oz (110g) peas
4 tablespoons desiccated coconut
(fresh or dry)
1-4 fresh chillies, chopped
10-12 curry leaves
salt to taste

METHOD

1 Heat the oil in a karahi or wok. Stir-fry the mustard seeds and the chana and urid lentils for about 1 minute.

2 Add the turmeric, ginger, onion and nuts and stir-fry for 2-3 more minutes. Add a splash of water to keep things mobile.

3 Add the potatoes, peas, coconut, chillies and curry leaves. When sizzling, salt to taste.

Hari Mirchi Kari

· GREEN CHILLI CURRY ·

Serves 4

This curry is not for the faint-hearted – it should be very hot indeed. They adore hot food in South India where I collected this fiery recipe. The cabbage adds body.

INGREDIENTS

1lb (450g) fresh green chillies
2 tablespoons vegetable oil
8oz (225g) onions, finely chopped
1 portion curry masala gravy
  (page 32)
3 tablespoons green masala paste
  (page 32)

6oz (175g) green cabbage,
  shredded
salt, chilli powder and ground
  black pepper to taste

METHOD

1 Remove the stalks from the chillies, but keep them whole.

2 Heat the oil in a karahi or wok. Stir-fry the onion for about 5 minutes. Add the curry gravy and green paste and mix in well.

3 Add the chillies and the cabbage and slowly simmer on low heat for about 15 minutes, stirring from time to time. Add a little water if it starts sticking. Salt to taste. This curry is ideal for reheating or freezing.

Note: If the chillies are not hot enough for you, add extra hot chilli powder and ground black pepper at stage 2, to taste.

Porial Kadama

· FESTIVAL VEGETABLES ·

Serves 4

Porial is a Tamil coconut-based vegetable dish, made on special occasions such as weddings or the Pongal (harvest) Festival.

INGREDIENTS

1 fennel bulb
1 kohlrabi bulb
1 celeriac bulb
6 inch (15cm) piece white radish (mooli)
8oz (225g) red sweet potato
1 tablespoon vegetable oil
4oz (110g) onions, chopped
4 fl oz (120ml) coconut milk
1 large firm mango, skinned, stoned and chopped
a few fresh pineapple chunks
2-4 fresh red chillies, chopped
1 tablespoon chopped fresh coriander

salt to taste

Spices 1
1 teaspoon mustard seeds
1 teaspoon cummin seeds
1 teaspoon sesame seeds
1/2 teaspoon turmeric
10-15 curry leaves, fresh or dried

Spices 2 (roasted)
1 tablespoon black urid lentils, polished
1 teaspoon coriander seeds
1/2 teaspoon black cummin seeds

METHOD

1 Prepare the fennel, kohlrabi, celeriac and mooli, discarding unwanted matter, and dicing into small pieces.

2 Blanch, steam or microwave the potato until soft. Cut into small cubes.

3 Heat the oil in a karahi or wok. Stir-fry **spices 1** for 20 seconds, then the onion for 5 minutes.

4 Add the coconut milk and, when simmering, add **spices 2**, all the vegetables, the mango, pineapple, chillies and coriander. Stir-fry until cooked to your liking, adding a little water if needed, to keep things mobile.

5 Salt to taste and serve at once (see Chef's Tip below).

CHEF'S TIP

Pineapple
A pineapple makes a magnificent container for food. Remove the leafy top and cut and scoop out the flesh, taking care not to pierce the casing. Take a thick slice off the base so that it stands upright. When you have made a container, invert it so that excess juices run out. To use, simply fill with food, garnish with whole chillies and serve (see opposite).

Facing page:
Porial Kadama

Chugander

· SRI LANKAN BEETROOT ·

Serves 4

Here's a vegetable which does not come to mind immediately as being in the Indian repertoire. Beetroot not only grows in the sub-continent, it is used in sweet as well as savoury dishes. The leaves are used as well.

INGREDIENTS

1lb (450g) fresh beetroot
4oz (110g) beetroot leaves, or
    spinach

2 tablespoons sesame oil
1 tablespoon garam masala
salt to taste

METHOD

1 Peel and dice the beetroot into ³/₄ inch (2cm) cubes.

2 Wash the leaves, remove the tough stalks, then shred the leaves coarsely.

3 Heat the oil in a karahi or wok. Add the beetroot cubes and stir-fry for around 5 minutes. Add sprinklings of water and the leaves. Continue to stir-fry for 2-3 more minutes.

4 Add the garam masala and salt to taste. Serve hot.

Pao Bhajee

· CURRY IN A BUN ·

Serves 4

On one of my recent visits to Bombay I was with Atique Choudhury, the owner of Spices Restaurant, London N16. He suddenly went into ecstasies about an item on the menu at the Sheraton Searock Hotel's coffee shop. It was pao bhajee, a Bombay street snack available everywhere at colourful kiosks. Bombay snobs call it the 'poor man's meal'. In fact it's a delicious and totally acceptable light meal, eaten with a sesame burger bun (which you can make yourself, see page 248). Eat as a quick meal (as Bombay does), rather like we view baked beans on toast. Use canned vegetables for a particularly good flavour.

INGREDIENTS

1 x 14oz (400g) can mixed
    vegetables in brine
1 x 14 oz (400g) can sweetcorn
    kernels
1 portion curry masala gravy
    (page 32)

0-4 fresh green chillies, chopped
2 teaspoons garam masala
salt to taste

METHOD

1 Open the cans and strain the contents. Keep the resultant liquid for delicious stock, using some in this recipe.

2 Put the gravy, chillies and the canned items into a saucepan. Bring to the simmer.

3 Add the garam masala, salt to taste and serve piping hot with a halved sesame or pao bun (which may be optionally toasted).

Satrangi Korma
· CASHEW NUT CURRY ·

Serves 4

A mild and creamy korma, south Indian style. It uses cashew nuts and coconut milk in place of the north's dairy produce, and vegetables in place of meat, and is consequently totally vegan.

INGREDIENTS

9oz (250g) raw cashew nuts
4 tablespoons sesame oil
1 portion curry masala gravy
  (page 32)
2 canned tomatoes, chopped
1 tablespoon chopped fresh
  coriander
salt to taste

Paste
2 garlic cloves

1 inch (2.5cm) cube ginger
1 fresh coconut, flesh and water
  (page 23)

Spices
1 teaspoon mustard seeds
1 teaspoon sesame seeds
1 teaspoon white poppy seeds
1/2 teaspoon aniseed
1/3 teaspoon fenugreek seeds
10-12 curry leaves, fresh or dry

METHOD

1 Put the **paste** ingredients into the blender or food processor and mulch until smooth and pourable, using water as needed.

2 Heat the oil in a karahi or wok. Stir-fry the cashew nuts until they turn golden. Watch carefully – they burn easily. Remove from the oil and drain.

3 Using the same oil, stir-fry the **spices** for 30 seconds. Add the paste and stir-fry for a further 5 minutes.

4 Add the curry gravy, tomato and coriander and when simmering, mix in the cashews. Salt to taste. Serve at once.

Kari or Karikai

· EXOTIC VEGETABLE CURRY ·

Serves 4

The *Oxford English Dictionary* attributes the word 'curry' to the Tamil South Indian word *Kari* as far back as 1628, when the early English voyagers to India could well have been shown this dish when they asked what was being prepared. Whether or not this is true matters not – *kari* has remained unchanged for thousands of years.

INGREDIENTS

1lb (450g) mixture of 'exotic' vegetables of your choice (see below), weighed after stage 1
1 teaspoon turmeric
2 tablespoons mustard oil
1 teaspoon mustard seeds
1 teaspoon black urid lentils, polished

1 teaspoon dry red chillies, chopped
1 fresh coconut, flesh and water, shredded (page 23)
salt to taste
1 full recipe onion tarka (page 26)

METHOD

1 You could use, for example, some or all of, 1 plantain, some baby aubergine, Kenyan beans, sweet potato and pumpkin. Prepare the vegetables, discarding unwanted matter and cutting into suitable pieces.

2 In a large saucepan bring ample water to the boil. Add the turmeric and vegetables and simmer for 5 minutes. Strain, discarding the water.

3 Heat the oil in a karahi or wok. Stir-fry the mustard seeds, lentils and chillies for 30 seconds. Add the coconut and the vegetables and stir-fry until cooked to your liking. Salt to taste.

4 Serve hot garnished with the tarka.

Kaeng Galumbee Dom

· THAI CABBAGE CURRY ·

Serves 4

The Thai curry is a fearsome experience. It is fired up with handfuls of midget green or red chillies, each one of which has enough heat to power a space rocket. The colour of the curry sauce is determined by the initial curry paste which can be green, red or orange. In this case I have chosen the former, getting its colour from the use of the fresh herbs and its wonderful fragrance from the lime leaves and lemongrass. The midget chillies are hard to get but fun to use if you can find them. Use 4-6 standard chillies, chopped, as the alternative. I have treated their inclusion as an option for those who cannot stand the heat.

INGREDIENTS

1lb (450g) green cabbage, weighed after stage 1
8oz (225g) spring onions, with leaves
4 tablespoons vegetable oil
14 fl oz (400ml) thick coconut milk
3 tablespoons nam-pla (fish sauce)
2 tablespoons brown sugar
20-30 fresh green miniature chillies, whole (optional)
6-10 large fresh basil leaves, finely chopped
1 large fresh lime leaf, finely chopped
salt to taste

Curry paste
1 green pepper, seeded and coarsely chopped

1 inch (2.5cm) piece ginger
8 tablespoons onion purée (page 25), or finely chopped shallots
2 tablespoons garlic purée (page 24)
1 teaspoon ground coriander
1 tablespoon fresh lemongrass leaves, finely chopped, or 1 teaspoon powder
1 tablespoon nam pla (fish sauce)
1 teaspoon kapi (shrimp paste)
1 teaspoon chopped fresh coriander leaves
6-7 fresh or dried lime leaves

METHOD

1 Wash and chop the cabbage into strips, discarding unwanted matter.

2 Remove the spring onion root and any discoloured leaves, then chop the green leaves and white bulbs fairly finely.

3 Steam or microwave the cabbage and spring onion until soft.

4 Blend all the curry paste ingredients together in the blender or food processor, using enough water to obtain a thick paste.

5 Heat the oil in a large pan, and stir-fry the curry paste with a little of the coconut milk for about 5 minutes.

6 Add the remaining coconut milk, the fish sauce, sugar and the chillies, plus some water if necessary to enable the items to boil.

7 Simmer for 5 minutes then add the steamed greens, basil and lime leaf. Salt to your taste, stir and serve promptly.

Aloo Hari Ghobi

· SWEET POTATO AND BROCCOLI ·

Serves 4

This curry could be made with ordinary potato and cauliflower, and it is a very good traditional combination. However, change the potato to the wonderfully flavoured red sweet potato, and cauliflower to bright green broccoli for a colourful and very tasty change.

INGREDIENTS

8-12oz (225-350g) red sweet potatoes
8-12oz (225-350g) broccoli, weighed after stage 2
3 tablespoons light vegetable oil
2 teaspoons panch phoran (page 29)

2-4 garlic cloves, chopped
4oz (110g) onions, chopped
1 tablespoon mild curry paste (page 31)
1 tablespoon tomato purée
aromatic salt to taste (page 30)

METHOD

1 Scrub the potatoes but do not peel them. Dice them into 1½ inch (4cm) cubes.

2 Cut the broccoli into small florets, discarding leaves and stalks.

3 Blanch the potato and broccoli together in boiling water for 3 minutes (or steam or microwave until slightly soft).

4 During stage 3, heat the oil in a karahi or wok, and stir-fry the panch phoran for 30 seconds, then add the garlic and 30 seconds later the onion. Stir-fry for 5 minutes. Add the curry paste and tomato purée. Stir well then add the blanched vegetables.

5 Stir-fry for the few minutes it takes to cook the vegetables to your liking. Salt to taste. Serve at once.

Sag Aloo Bhaji

· SPINACH AND POTATO CURRY ·

Serves 4

This is an authentic recipe from the Pakistan Punjab. The area of the Punjab gained its name because five *(panch)* rivers *(ab)* join together to form the giant river Indus. In this fertile area grow plentiful spices and crops. The Punjab's food is savoury and spicy and its derivatives appear in nearly all curry houses worldwide. Here is a superb traditional version.

INGREDIENTS

12oz (350g) boiled peeled potato, diced into bite-sized pieces
10oz (275g) spinach leaves, preferably fresh, weighed after stage 1
3oz (75g) fenugreek leaf, preferably fresh
3 tablespoons ghee or vegetable oil
6 garlic cloves, finely chopped
1 inch (2.5cm) cube ginger, finely chopped
4oz (110g) onions, finely chopped
2-3 tomatoes, chopped

1 tablespoon chopped fresh coriander
salt to taste
1 full recipe onion tarka (page 26)

Spices
1 teaspoon white cummin seeds
1 teaspoon mustard seeds
1/2 teaspoon black cummin seeds
1/2 teaspoon fenugreek
1/2 teaspoon aniseed
2-3 bay leaves
3-4 dry red chillies

METHOD

1 Prepare the spinach and fenugreek leaves. Discard unwanted matter and wash, then chop coarsely.

2 Boil, or better, steam the leaves until soft (about 3 minutes). Take off the heat.

3 Heat the oil in a karahi or wok. Stir-fry the garlic for 30 seconds, then the ginger for a further 30 seconds. Then add the onion and stir-fry for 5 minutes.

4 Add the **spices** and the potato, and stir-fry for 2-3 minutes.

5 Add the steamed leaves, tomato and coriander, and salt to taste. Serve hot, garnished with the tarka.

Chota Aloo Baigan

· BABY POTATOES AND AUBERGINES ·

Serves 4

The trend towards miniature vegetables is growing. They cost a little more, but they look excellent. This recipe, incorporating cherry tomatoes and cherries, if in season, looks wonderful.

INGREDIENTS

16-20 baby new potatoes, each
  cherry sized
6-8 baby aubergines, as small as
  possible
2 tablespoons pistachio or light oil
1 teaspoon each of sesame,
  mustard and cumin seeds
4oz (110g) onions, finely chopped
1 tablespoon green masala paste
  (page 32)

6-8 cherry tomatoes
6-8 cherries, white or red
  (optional)
2 teaspoons char masala (page 29)
1 tablespoon fresh coriander
  leaves
salt to taste
2 tablespoons raw pistachio nuts

METHOD

1 Scrub the potatoes. Blanch them in boiling water for about 3-4 minutes.

2 Do the same to the aubergines. Then remove stalk and slice the flesh.

3 During this, heat the oil in a karahi or wok. Stir-fry the seeds then add the onion and stir-fry for 5-6 minutes.

4 Add the green paste, the potatoes and aubergines, and stir-fry for 3-4 minutes. Splash in a little water as required.

5 Add the tomatoes and cherries, char masala and coriander and gently stir-fry for a further 3-4 minutes, taking care not to break the softening ingredients. Salt to taste. Serve at once, garnished with the pistachio nuts.

Jeera Aloo
· CUMMIN-SPICED POTATO ·

Serves 4

There are few dishes nicer than this simple lightly spiced potato dish.

INGREDIENTS

*1lb (450g) King Edward or other
  large potatoes
2 teaspoons turmeric
1 teaspoon salt*

*3 tablespoons butter ghee
2 teaspoons cummin seeds
1 tablespoon mild curry paste
  (page 31)*

METHOD

1 Scrub the skins of the potatoes clean, only peeling them off if they are very scarred and wrinkled.

2 Chop the potatoes into wedges, about six per potato. Rinse well.

3 Boil an ample amount of water in a saucepan, and when it comes to the boil, add the turmeric, salt and the potatoes. Simmer until cooked (about 15 minutes). Strain off the water. The potato pieces will be a lovely golden yellow colour.

4 Heat the ghee in a karahi or wok. Add the cummin seeds and, almost at once, the curry paste. Add the hot potatoes, stir well and once they are coated, serve hot.

*Facing page, left to right: Ugavela Moong (page 218) and Chota Aloo
Baigan (opposite, above)*

Aloo Chutneywalla

· POTATOES IN CHUTNEY SAUCE ·

Serves 4

I encountered this dish at the Taj Mahal Hotel in Delhi, where one of India's master chefs, Arwind Saraswat, works. This recipe is my interpretation of his superb dish.

INGREDIENTS

1lb (450g) potatoes, preferably
  smallish new ones
4 tablespoons vegetable oil
1 tablespoon garam masala
salt to taste
green pepper slices for garnish

Paste
2 fl oz (50ml) vinegar (any type)
3 tablespoons sweet mango
  chutney
2-4 garlic cloves, chopped
1 tablespoon mild curry paste
  (page 31)

1 tablespoon chopped fresh
  coriander
1 tablespoon chopped fresh mint,
  or 1 teaspoon bottled mint
1 tablespoon ground almonds
1 tablespoon coconut milk
  powder
1 teaspoon ground coriander
1 teaspoon mango powder
0-4 fresh red chillies, chopped
  (optional)
milk

METHOD

1 Put the **paste** ingredients in the blender or food processor and mulch until smooth and pourable, using milk as required.

2 Scrub the potatoes. Peel them only if they need it.

3 Cut them into thick round slices, and simmer in boiling water for about 8-10 minutes until almost cooked.

4 Heat the oil in a karahi or wok. Carefully (to avoid spluttering) pour the paste into the oil and stir-fry on low heat for 10 minutes, keeping it thick but fluid by adding water as needed.

5 Add the potato slices and garam masala and simmer until cooked. Salt to taste, garnish with the slices of green pepper, and serve.

Aloo Barela Banarasi
· STUFFED POTATOES ·

Serves 4

Baked or jacket potatoes with a fine spicy stuffing served with a lovely golden sauce.

INGREDIENTS

4 large baking potatoes (Red Desirée or similar are best)
4 tablespoons mild curry paste (page 31)
a sprinkling of fresh coriander leaves

Stuffing
2oz (50g) cashew nuts
3 tablespoons ground almonds
1 tablespoon chopped fresh mint
1 tablespoon cut fresh chives

1 teaspoon brown sugar
½ teaspoon chilli powder (optional)

Sauce
4 tablespoons ghee
1 teaspoon turmeric
1 tablespoon mild curry paste (page 31)
2 tablespoons gram flour (besan)
salt to taste

METHOD

1 Wash the potatoes and dry them on kitchen paper.

2 Preheat the oven to 375°F/190°C/Gas 5. Coat the potatoes with the curry paste then wrap them in kitchen foil quite tightly. Bake for 1 hour.

3 Meanwhile, for the **stuffing**, put the ingredients into the blender or food processor, and mulch to a coarse paste.

4 After an hour's baking, open out the foil carefully, remove the potatoes and slit them lengthways. Literally put the stuffing in then re-cover them with the foil. Continue cooking for a further 30 minutes or more (overcooking will not harm them).

5 For the **sauce**, mix the remaining sauce ingredients with some water to make a thin paste. Add any spare stuffing to it. Heat the ghee in a karahi or wok. Carefully but quickly (to avoid spluttering) add the sauce to the ghee. Stir-fry continuously (to allow the flour to thicken without lumps), for 3-4 minutes. It should be thin enough to pour easily. Salt to taste.

6 Remove the potatoes from the oven and check they are cooked by piercing them with a skewer or small knife (no need to unwrap the foil). Then, if cooked, remove and discard the foil.

7 To serve, pour the sauce over the stuffed potatoes and garnish with fresh coriander.

Aloo Masala Mash

· SPICED MASHED POTATO ·

Serves 4

I'm sure you love mashed potato as much as I do. India, of course, can add an extra dimension to almost any dish. Try this one and see.

INGREDIENTS

1lb (450g) potatoes, peeled and halved
2 tablespoons butter
1 tablespoon single cream
1 tablespoon yoghurt

1 teaspoon tandoori masala paste (page 80)
1 teaspoon garam masala
1 tablespoon chopped fresh mint
1/2 teaspoon salt

METHOD

1 Put the peeled potatoes into ample boiling water and simmer until cooked, about 15 minutes. Check by piercing with a small knife or skewer.

2 Strain and put the potato into a large bowl. Mash it with a fork, masher or electric hand-whisk.

3 Once mashed, add the butter, cream and yoghurt, and work these in. Finally add the paste, garam masala, mint and salt. Serve hot.

Aloo Tiki Patish

· POTATO RISSOLE ·

Makes 8

A popular accompaniment which goes with any dish. Try with rice and dhal.

INGREDIENTS

1lb (450g) mashed cooked potato
2 tablespoons mild curry paste
  (page 31)
1 tablespoon chopped fresh
  coriander
1 teaspoon coriander seeds,
  roasted

1 teaspoon lovage seeds
1 teaspoon salt
about $^1/_2$ cup breadcrumbs
about $^1/_2$ cup semolina
vegetable oil for shallow frying

METHOD

1 Mix all the ingredients together (except for the breadcrumbs, semolina and oil) to create a mouldable mixture.

2 Divide the mixture into eight equal-sized portions, and mould them into round discs (the *tiki*).

3 Mix the breadcrumbs and the semolina together and dab each *tiki* into it, so that all are well coated.

4 Heat some oil in a flat frying pan.

5 Put four tikis into the pan and fry for 5 minutes. Turn them over and fry for 5 more minutes. Remove and keep warm.

6 Repeat stages 4 and 5 with the remaining *tiki*. Serve hot.

Facing page, above: A colourful Indian market stall with a tempting display of exotic fruits

Aloo Took

· FRIED POTATOES ·

Serves 4

This simple potato dish hails from Sindh in Pakistan, although I first met it at the excellent Chutney Mary's restaurant, in London's Chelsea. Boiled whole potato is pressed flat, then deep-fried. It is devoid of spice – unique in this book – and could grace any European meal.

INGREDIENTS

8 potatoes, each about 3oz (75g), peeled

METHOD

1 Cook the potatoes – the microwave is fastest – then let cool.

2 Preheat the deep-fryer to 375°F/190°C.

3 Press the potatoes flat with the palm of your hand.

4 Immerse one potato into the oil. 20 seconds later put the next in and so on until four are in. (This keeps the temperature of the oil up.)

5 Fry for about 3-4 minutes. Remove, repeat with the other four potatoes, and serve.

Savoury Fried Potatoes

Serves 4

Chips are becoming as popular in India as everywhere else on earth. However, India likes to add a little zest, and it's in the sprinkling. Incidentally I once had these at a café in Bombay Airport with a remarkable mayonnaise dip in which chilli powder had been mixed. Try them either way. Here is the way professional chefs get crisp chips.

INGREDIENTS

1lb (450g) King Edward (or other floury) potatoes
vegetable oil for frying

1 teaspoon salt
1 teaspoon chilli powder (optional)

Spices
1 tablespoon garam masala (page 29)

METHOD

1 Peel and cut the potatoes into chip shapes.

2 Soak them in salty water for about an hour. This removes the starch.

3 Drain them and dry them by placing on kitchen paper, whilst the deep-fryer heats up to 375°F/190°C.

4 Place half the chips into the fryer basket and lower into the fat carefully. Fry for 5 minutes. Remove and drain.

5 Repeat with the second batch.

6 Raise the deep-fryer temperature to 390°F/190°C. Re-fry the first batch of chips for just 1 minute. Drain and repeat with the second batch.

7 Coat with the **spices**. Serve hot.

Dairy and Egg Dishes

India adores dairy products. Milk, cream, yoghurt, a unique form of set curds called paneer (which for want of a better name, we call cheese) and whey, the by-product of paneer, are all used, as they have been since dairy farming was introduced to India by the Aryans some 4,000 years ago. To make paneer see page 22. Alternatively you could use tofu instead.

Eggs are popular too. They can be used hard-boiled as a garnish, or curried in omelette and scrambled dishes. When we think of eggs, we normally think of chicken's eggs, but for a change smaller eggs such as pheasant, partridge, guinea fowl or bantam look good. And for miniature eggs use quail eggs.

In Europe we now have seven grades of chicken eggs: Grade 1 is 70g (2^1/$_2$oz) or over; Grade 4 is 55-60g (2-2^1/$_4$oz); Grade 7 is 45g (1^1/$_2$oz) or under.

Facing page, from the top: Sag Paneer Charminar (page 196), *Nawabi Paneer Kofta* (page 192) and *Bharuchi Akari* (page 201)

Sag Paneer

· SPINACH WITH INDIAN CHEESE ·

Serves 4

Juicy chunks of paneer are tossed with spicy spinach to create one of North India's masterpieces. It looks good, tastes good and is easy to make.

INGREDIENTS

1lb (450g) frozen spinach (puréed leaves)
1 full recipe paneer, cubed (page 22)
2 tablespoons ghee
1 teaspoon cummin seeds
1 tablespoon garlic purée (page 24)
4 tablespoons onion purée (page 25)

1 tablespoon mild curry paste (page 31)
2 tablespoons green masala paste (page 32)

Garnish
yoghurt
garam masala (page 29)

METHOD

1 Thaw the spinach in a strainer, and retain the resultant liquid.

2 Heat the ghee in a karahi or wok. Stir-fry the seeds for 30 seconds. Add the garlic purée and 30 seconds later the onion purée. Stir-fry for a further 5 minutes. Add splashings of spinach liquid to keep things mobile.

3 Add the pastes and when simmering, the spinach. Add the paneer and stir-fry until it is hot. Salt to taste. Serve garnished with a curl of yoghurt and sprinkling of garam masala.

Nawabi Paneer Kofta

· CHEESE BALLS IN RICH RED SAUCE ·

Serves 4

Also known as Shahi Paneer Kofta, this is a recipe from the former royal kitchens of the Nawab of Lucknow. Here it is served in a rich red sauce.

INGREDIENTS

1 full recipe paneer (page 22), crumbled
2oz (50g) cornflour
2 garlic cloves, finely chopped
1 egg
1 teaspoon black cummin seeds
1 teaspoon aromatic salt (page 30)

sufficient vegetable oil for shallow frying
1 full recipe tikka masala sauce (page 133)

Garnish
chopped almonds
edible silver leaf (page 109)

METHOD

1 Mix the first six ingredients together to create a mouldable mass.

2 Divide into sixteen and roll into balls.

3 Heat the oil in a flat frying pan. Shallow-fry the balls until they are golden. Stir gently to prevent them breaking up.

4 Make the sauce as described on page 133, and when reduced a little, and mature in taste, add the koftas.

5 Serve hot, garnished with the nuts and silver leaf.

Navrattan Paneer Korma

· MILD CHEESE CURRY ·

Serves 4

This dish is steeped in history, originating from the court of Akbar, the Moghul emperor.

INGREDIENTS

Navrattan
1 full recipe paneer (page 22)
16-20 cherries, white or red
2 rings canned pineapple
9oz (250g) frozen mixed
* vegetables (containing peas,*
* sweetcorn, carrot and beans),*
* thawed*
1 tablespoon hazelnuts
1 tablespoon sultanas

Sauce
2 tablespoons ghee

1 teaspoon garlic purée (page 24)
3 tablespoons onion purée (page 25)
3 fl oz (85ml) double cream
3 fl oz (85ml) yoghurt
2 teaspoons garam masala (page 29)
salt to taste
edible silver leaf (page 109)
sprinkling of freshly chopped coriander

METHOD

1 Make the paneer, and dice it into ⅓ inch (8mm) cubes.

2 Remove the stones and stalks from the cherries. Dice the pineapple rings into ⅓ inch (8mm) cubes.

3 For the **sauce**, heat the ghee in a karahi or wok. Stir-fry the garlic for 20 seconds, then add the onion and continue for a further 5 minutes.

4 Lower the heat, then add the cream, yoghurt and garam masala, and stir-fry it to the simmer.

5 Add the **navrattan** ingredients. Simmer for 5 minutes. Salt to taste. Serve attractively garnished with silver leaf and coriander.

Kadai Balti Paneer

· SPICY PANEER 'CHIPS' ·

Serves 4

In this recipe, paneer is cut into chip shapes, which are fried or deep-fried then tossed in the kadai, balti style, with a light curry sauce. Delicious!

INGREDIENTS

1 full recipe paneer (page 22)
vegetable oil for frying
1 teaspoon char masala (page 29)
1 tablespoon chopped fresh
* coriander*
salt to taste
a squeeze of fresh lemon

Sauce
1 tablespoon ghee
1 teaspoon cummin seeds

1 teaspoon fennel seeds
1 teaspoon sesame seeds
8oz (225g) onions, finely chopped
2 tablespoons mild curry paste
* (page 31)*
1 tablespoon tandoori masala
* paste (page 80)*
1 tablespoon tomato purée
3-4 slices red and green pepper
1 teaspoon dried fenugreek

METHOD

1 Make the paneer and leave until solid.

2 For the sauce, heat the ghee in a karahi or wok. Stir-fry the seeds for 30 seconds then add the onions and stir-fry for a further 5 minutes.

3 Add the pastes, tomato purée, pepper and dried fenugreek. Stir-fry until stage 6. Keep things mobile using whey (page 22) or water.

4 During stage 3, cut the paneer into chip shapes and either deep-fry them at 350°F/180°C for about 4 minutes, or shallow-fry in a few tablespoons of oil in a karahi or wok. Either way they should be evenly coloured pale golden.

5 Add the hot cooked paneer 'chips', char masala and fresh coriander to the sauce. Salt to taste and stir well. Squeeze fresh lemon juice over the dish and serve at once.

Facing page, above: Kadai Balti Paneer

Chole Paneer

· CHICKPEA CHEESE ·

Serves 4

A splendid taste combination of chickpeas and paneer balls. They look good too.

INGREDIENTS

1 full recipe paneer (page 22)
1 portion curry masala gravy
(page 32)
9oz (250g) cooked chickpeas

2 teaspoons garam masala
1 tablespoon chopped fresh mint,
or 1 teaspoon dried mint
salt to taste

METHOD

1 Cut the paneer into ¼ inch (5mm) cubes or, better still, using a baby melon scoop, shape the paneer into balls.

2 Heat the gravy, and add the chickpeas and paneer.

3 When simmering, sprinkle with the garam masala and mint. Stir and salt to taste. Serve hot.

Sag Paneer Charminar

· SPINACH AND CHEESE PIE ·

Serves 4

I adore Hyderabad. It is in central south India and has some fabulous food. Its city centrepiece is the Charminar (meaning four towers), a 16th-century arch, perfect in its symmetry. Circled by roads full of honking buses and teeming people, it is the epitome of India.

This dish is my own, and is a tribute to this charismatic city. It is a filo pastry pie filled with layers of spicy paneer and spinach.

The fried egg is added as an idiosyncratic option – you'll have to see page 10 to find out why!

INGREDIENTS

18oz (500g) packet filo pastry
2-4 tablespoons melted ghee
1 egg (optional)

Filling
8oz (225g) fresh spinach
2 tablespoons ghee
1 teaspoon cummin seeds
2 garlic cloves, finely chopped
4oz (110g) onions, finely chopped

0-4 fresh red chillies, chopped
1 full recipe crumbled paneer
  (page 22)
1 tablespoon mild curry paste
  (page 31)
6oz (175g) humous (chickpea
  purée)
1 teaspoon salt
2 teaspoons garam masala

METHOD

1 Make the filling first. Wash and finely chop the spinach. Steam it for about 10 minutes.

2 Meanwhile heat 2 tablespoons of ghee in a karahi or wok. Stir-fry the cummin seeds and garlic for 30 seconds, then the onion and chillies for 5 minutes. Add the spinach.

3 Mix together the paneer, curry paste and humous. Add to the karahi with the salt and garam masala. Mix well, remove from the heat and allow to cool a little.

4 Preheat the oven to 350°F/180°C/Gas 4. Melt the ghee for the pastry in a small pan. Choose an oven tray about 12 x 10 inches (30 x 25cm) with sides at least 2 inches (5cm) high. Brush it with ghee.

5 Have a damp clean tea towel to hand. Open the filo packet. Cut the entire bunch of sheets to the size of the oven tray. Cover the sheets with the tea towel to stop the filo drying out (which it does fast).
   Note: if the packet size is standard 12 x 20 inches (30 x 50cm), halve it to 12 x 10 inches (30 x 25cm) and repack the spare half in a plastic bag for future use.

6 Take one sheet of filo (cover the rest), and put it into the oven tray. Brush it with ghee. Repeat with the next five sheets. Do not press the sheets together. Drop them lightly on top of each other. This results in lighter pastry. Spread about one-third of the filling lightly over the pastry.

7 Repeat stage 6 three more times using all the sheets in the packet (usually 24), so that you have four layers of pastry of six leaves each, interspersed with three layers of filling.

8 Cut through the top layers of filo once lengthwise and three times across, cutting about half way through.

9 Bake for 30 minutes, then inspect. It should now be pale gold. Increase the heat to 425°F/220°C/Gas 7. If you wish to use an egg, press the pastry down to create a concave dip. Break the egg into the dip and either way bake for 10-15 minutes more. Inspect during this time. Remove when golden in colour.

10 Serve hot with rice and gravy (see Index) or cold on a picnic.

Sabzi Nargissi Kofta

· VEGETABLE SCOTCH EGG ·

A minced vegetable mixture wrapped around a hard-boiled egg, rolled in breadcrumbs and shallow- or deep-fried.

INGREDIENTS

4 large eggs or 8 medium eggs, or 12 quails' eggs.
1/2 quantity vegetable kebab mixture (page 168)

1 egg, beaten
1/2 cup each semolina and breadcrumbs mixed
vegetable oil for frying

METHOD

1 Hard-boil the eggs. (Quails' eggs will only take 4 minutes.) When cool, shell and set aside.

2 Make up half the vegetable kebab mixture to stage 2 of the recipe on page 168.

3 Wrap sufficient mixture around each egg. Coat each one with raw egg. Roll in the semolina and breadcrumb mixture.

4 Shallow- or deep-fry in oil until each is golden and evenly cooked. Serve hot with dhal and rice.

Masala Poro
· SPICY OMELETTE ·

Serves 1

Only the sick eat un-spicy food in India. Even the omelette receives spicy treatment. This was my breakfast dish when I was last in the deep south of India at the wonderful Kovalum beach resort. I warn you, it is uncompromisingly hot!

INGREDIENTS

2 eggs
1 tablespoon vegetable oil
1 teaspoon mustard seeds

1-3 fresh green chillies, chopped
1 tablespoon chopped onion
salt to taste

METHOD

1 Heat the oil in a flat frying pan. Stir-fry the mustard seeds for 10 seconds. Add the chillies and onion, and stir-fry for about 2 minutes.

2 Meanwhile briskly beat the eggs with a fork or whisk.

3 Pour the eggs over the fried items. Deftly and swiftly twist the pan so that the egg rolls right round it.

4 Fry on medium heat until just firm. Optionally turn it, or slide it out of the pan. Salt to taste and serve flat not folded.

Karhi
· YOGHURT CURRY ·

Serves 4

This traditional Punjabi dish is thick and sour. Based on yoghurt, its name could well be one of the derivations for the word curry. Traditionally fresh pakoras or singhora are served in the sauce, and the curry is served with rice.

INGREDIENTS

1lb (450g) yoghurt
1 pint (600ml) whey (page 22) or water
2oz (50g) gram flour (besan)
16-20 singhara (page 62)
1 full recipe onion tarka (page 26)
aromatic salt to taste (page 30)

Spices
2 teaspoons garam masala
1 teaspoon turmeric
1/2 teaspoon ginger powder
0-2 teaspoons fresh chilli powder

METHOD

1 Put the yoghurt into a 5 pint (2.75 litre) saucepan. Stir in the whey or water, using a fork or whisk.

2 Bring to the boil, regularly whisking, then reduce to a rolling simmer.

3 In a bowl, mix together the gram flour, the **spices** and a little water to make a pourable paste.

4 Slowly add some of the yoghurt and whey from the pan until the paste is quite runny, whisking to prevent lumping.

5 Return this mixture to the saucepan and whisk until it stops thickening. Continue the rolling simmer for 20-25 minutes, whisking from time to time. Add water if it reduces too much.

6 Small round singhara go into this thin sauce, and these should be deep-fried during stage 5 (page 62). Put them piping hot into the sauce at the end of stage 5. Salt to taste.

7 Garnish with onion tarka, and serve at once with plain rice.

Turkari Malai

· CREAMY CURRY ·

Serves 4

The *turkari* has been described as a spicy seasoned stew, and in fact defines a method of cooking, using plentiful liquid and slow cooking. Another term for this is *kalia*. This is a cream-based vegetable stew.

INGREDIENTS

1lb (450g) mixed root vegetables (see below)
1 pint (600ml) akhni (page 33) or vegetable stock
2-4 garlic cloves, quartered
1 inch (2.5cm) cube ginger, finely chopped
0-4 red chillies, whole
2 fl oz (50ml) milk
20-30 saffron strands
3 fl oz (85ml) single cream

2 teaspoons char masala (page 29)
salt to taste
fresh herbs to garnish

Spices
3-4 bay leaves
6-8 cloves
2 inch (5cm) piece cassia bark
4-6 green cardamoms
2 star anise
1 teaspoon fennel seeds

METHOD

1 Prepare the vegetables of your choice, discarding all unwanted matter. Some of the following would be suitable: parsnip, swede, turnip, white radish, daikon, carrot, turnip, celeriac, sweet potato or potato.

2 Bring the akhni or vegetable stock and **spices** to the simmer from cold. Add the vegetables, garlic, ginger and chillies and simmer until soft.

3 During stage 2, heat the milk and saffron to warm, not hot, and let stand for a few minutes. Mash the saffron strands, so that they exude as much colour as possible, then add to the vegetables.

4 Add the cream, char masala and salt to taste. Serve at once with plain rice and/or Indian bread, garnished with the herbs.

Moglai Sabzi

· CREAMY VEGETABLES ·

Serves 4

This dish makes an interesting contrast with the preceding one. In true Moghul style it is much richer and is cooked in the korma or oil-based style.

INGREDIENTS

1lb (450g) soft vegetables (see below).
4 tablespoons ghee
2-4 garlic cloves, chopped
1 inch (2.5cm) cube ginger, chopped
5 fl oz (150ml) milk
20-30 saffron strands
3 fl oz (85ml) double cream
2 teaspoons char masala (page 29)
1 tablespoon chopped fresh coriander
salt to taste

Spices
4-6 green cardamoms
4-6 cloves
2-3 bay leaves

Garnish
fresh herbs
chopped pistachio nuts
edible silver leaf (optional, page 109)

METHOD

1 Prepare the vegetables, discarding unwanted matter. Choose from some or all of the following: mangetouts, leek, marrow, avocado, fennel bulb, celery, etc.

2 Heat the ghee in a karahi or wok. Stir-fry the **spices** for 30 seconds. Add the garlic and ginger and stir-fry for 1 minute. Add 3 fl oz (85ml) of the milk, and the vegetables, and stir-fry for about 4-5 minutes. Take off the heat.

3 During stage 2, heat the remaining milk and saffron from cold to warm, not hot, and let it stand for a few minutes. Mash the saffron strands so that they exude as much colour as possible.

4 Add the saffron milk, the cream, char masala and fresh coriander to the karahi and mix in well. Return to the heat and simmer until you are ready to serve. Salt to taste. Garnish with herbs, nuts and silver leaf, and serve at once.

Bharuchi Akari

· SPICY SCRAMBLED EGG ·

Serves 4

The Parsees are a tiny religious community of around 100,000 people. They have lived in the Bombay area since they fled from their home of Persia 1000 years ago. Their food is a unique combination of Persian and Indian. This scrambled egg dish is typical. From Persia comes sweet and sour (fruit, nuts sugar and yoghurt), from India the spicing. Serve with piping hot puffy puris.

INGREDIENTS

2 fresh or dried apricots or
  peaches
2 tablespoons vegetable oil or
  ghee
2 garlic cloves, finely chopped
1 inch (2.5cm) cube ginger, finely
  chopped
2oz (50g) onions, finely chopped
1 tablespoon mild curry paste
  (page 31)
1 teaspoon sultanas
1 tablespoon hazelnuts, chopped
1 tablespoon brown sugar

6 eggs, beaten
2 tablespoons yoghurt
aromatic salt (page 30)

Garnish
12 red or white cherries (when in
  season)
double cream
ground black pepper and/or
  garam masala (page 29)
chopped fresh coriander or
  parsley

METHOD

1 Wash, stone and cut up the fruit of your choice. If using dried fruit, soak it for a few minutes in a little water then strain it.

2 For the garnish, cherries not only taste good, but they give the dish an excellent appearance. They must be fresh though, so can only be used in season. Stone them but keep them whole.

3 Heat the oil in a karahi or wok. Stir-fry the garlic, ginger and onion for 2-3 minutes. Add the curry paste and continue to stir-fry for a couple more minutes.

4 Add the apricots or peaches, sultanas, nuts and sugar and, when sizzling, add the eggs.

5 Stir-fry briskly to scramble the eggs into the mixture. When the eggs have started to set, add the yoghurt and stir-fry until the eggs have set to your liking. Salt to taste.

6 Serve at once, garnishing with a curl of double cream, a sprinkling of black pepper and/or garam masala, the cherries and a topping of fresh coriander or parsley.

Legume Dishes

After rice, lentils form one of the major families of ingredients in the Indian culinary repertoire. Lentils are a legume, as are beans and peas. In some cases, such as mangetouts, the pod or case is consumed. Generally it is their seeds (called pulses) which are the main crop and are eaten fresh, or they are dried. Once the pulse is dry it will keep indefinitely. It is used whole or split, with its skin on or polished off. There are over 60 varieties of pulses. Fortunately you will not need that many in your store cupboard.

The lentil you will meet most here is the red lentil, *masoor dhal,* familiar as the small bright orange disc in its split and polished version. Its skin is an olive green colour. Other lentils used in my recipes are chickpeas *(kabli chana),* green *moong,* brown *moong,* black *urid,* yellow oily lentils *(toovar* or *toor),* and yellow lentils *(chana* or gram), which when ground become gram flour *(besan).*

Dried beans used in my recipes include red kidney beans *(rajma),* black-eye beans *(lobia),* lablab (from the hyacinth plant), fava, pigeon *(gunga)* and butter beans. Fresh legumes include peas, mangetouts, Kenyan, broad and runner beans.

Facing page, from the top: Kair Sangri (page 218), *Maharani Dhal* (page 208) and *Cochin Sambar Masaladar* (page 210)

Masala Dhal

· SPICED LENTILS ·

Serves 4

This dish is a kind of staple. It is cheap, it virtually cooks itself, it can be kept in a warmer, be cooled, frozen and reheated. It is indestructible. It makes a tasty accompaniment to any curry or, for an astonishingly good meal, try it on its own with plain rice.

INGREDIENTS

6-8oz (175-225g) red masoor
  lentils, split and polished
1-1¹/₂ tablespoons mild curry
  paste (page 31)

1¹/₂-2 teaspoons garam masala
salt to taste
1 full recipe onion tarka garnish
  (optional, page 26)

METHOD

1 Pick through the lentils to remove any grit or impurities. Rinse them several times, then drain and immerse in ample water for 4 hours.

2 To cook, drain and rinse, then measure an amount of water twice the volume of the drained lentils into a 4 pint (2.25 litre) saucepan. Bring to the boil.

3 Put in the lentils and simmer for about 30 minutes, stirring as the water is absorbed. The texture should be pourable, not too thick and not too thin.

4 When ready, add the paste, garam masala and salt to taste. Optionally garnish with the tarka.

Dhal Dhansak

· LENTIL AND VEGETABLE DHANSAK ·

Serves 4

Here is a quick version of the celebrated Parsee *lamb dhansak* (see page 96), which has a delicious lentil base with accompanying vegetables. Serve it as an accompaniment or main dish.

INGREDIENTS

4oz (110g) red masoor lentils,
  split and polished
2oz (50g) yellow gram chana,
  split and polished
1 x 14oz (400g) can ratatouille in oil
1oz (25g) butter
1 tablespoon mild curry paste
  (page 31)

1 tablespoon coconut powder
2 teaspoons garam masala
1 teaspoon dried mint
1 tablespoon chopped fresh
  coriander
salt to taste

METHOD

1 Mix the lentils, then pick through them, rinse, soak and cook as in stages 1-3 of the above recipe.

2 Add the remaining ingredients, simmer for 5 minutes or so, and serve.

Palaka-ka-Dala

· SPINACH DHAL ·

Serves 4

A robust and exceedingly good recipe from Rajasthan from where the most savoury dishes come.

INGREDIENTS

5oz (150g) red masoor lentils, split and polished
2oz (50g) yellow gram chana, split and polished
8oz (225g) spinach, washed and dried
2 teaspoons dry fenugreek leaves

1 tablespoon garam masala
2 tablespoons yoghurt
1 tablespoon chopped fresh coriander
1oz (25g) butter
salt to taste

METHOD

1 Mix the lentils, then pick through them, rinse, soak and cook as in stages 1-3 of Masala Dhal (opposite), but simmer for about 40 minutes.

2 Add the remaining ingredients. Mix well, simmer for 5 minutes, salt to taste, and serve.

Ragada

· SOUR CHANA ·

Serves 4

A tart-tasting recipe using yellow gram chana and tamarind purée. It is delicious served with plain rice and chutneys.

INGREDIENTS

8oz (225g) yellow gram chana, split and polished
6 fl oz (175ml) coconut milk
10-12 curry leaves, fresh or dry
1/2 teaspoon turmeric
1 teaspoon cummin seeds

1 tablespoon tamarind purée (page 24)
1/4 teaspoon asafoetida
0-2 fresh green chillies, chopped
salt to taste

METHOD

1 Pick through the lentils, then rinse, soak and cook as in stage 1-3 of Masala Dhal (opposite).

2 Add the remaining ingredients to the pan. It should be the consistency of thick soup, so add water if needed. Salt to taste, and serve.

Parangikkai Thoran

· PUMPKIN ·

Serves 4

The *thoran* or *thovaran* is a method of cooking to be found in Southern India. Vegetables, in this case a pumpkin, are shredded and wrapped around a ball of spicy purée. This is then steamed and served with a tarka (or garnish) of spices. Here is a simplified version.

INGREDIENTS

2oz (50g) yellow gram chana,
  split and polished
1lb (450g) pumpkin flesh, finely
  shredded
3-4 large lettuce leaves
2 tablespoons sesame oil
salt to taste

Paste
1 fresh coconut, flesh and water

6 fresh red chillies
4 garlic cloves
2oz (50g) red onion
1/2 teaspoon turmeric

Spices
12-15 curry leaves
1 teaspoon sesame seeds
1 teaspoon mustard seeds
1 teaspoon dry red chillies

METHOD

1 Pick through the lentils to remove any grit or impurities. Rinse them several times, then drain and immerse in ample water for 4 hours.

2 Drain and rinse the lentils then measure an amount of water twice the volume of the drained lentils. Put the water into a saucepan and bring it to the boil.

3 Put in the lentils and simmer for about 30 minutes, stirring as the water is absorbed.

4 Meanwhile grind the **paste** ingredients into a thick purée, using the coconut water.

5 Line the steamer with lettuce leaves. Place a layer of about half the pumpkin in the steamer, followed by the paste, then cover with the remaining pumpkin.

6 Cover and steam for about 10 minutes.

7 During stage 4 heat the oil in a karahi or wok, and stir-fry the **spices** for 30 seconds. Add the lentils and stir-fry briskly until they go crisp (a couple of minutes). Salt to taste.

8 Serve the pumpkin layers garnished with the stir-fry ingredients.

Dal Bhukara

· BROWN LENTILS ·

Serves 4

The city of Bhukara is in Russia, a couple of hundred miles north of Afghanistan. It was the ancestral home of the Moghul emperors. India's greatest tandoori restaurant, located at the Maurya Sheraton hotel in Delhi, is called the Bhukara. It has branches in the USA, so let's hope one day they may open in the UK. This dark creamy lentil dish goes wonderfully with tandoori dishes.

INGREDIENTS

6oz (175g) black urid lentils, whole, skin on
2oz (50g) red masoor lentils, split and polished
3 tablespoons ghee
3 garlic cloves, finely chopped
4 tablespoons onion purée (page 25)
salt to taste

Spices (roasted and ground)
2 teaspoons coriander

1 teaspoon cummin
1 teaspoon black cummin
2 brown cardamoms
2 inch (5cm) piece cassia bark
6 cloves

Garnish
2 teaspoons chopped fresh mint
single cream

METHOD

1 Mix and pick through the lentils, to remove any grit or impurities. Rinse them several times, then drain and immerse in ample water for 4 hours.

2 Drain and rinse the lentils, then measure an amount of water twice the volume of the drained lentils. Put the water into a 4 pint (2.25 litre) saucepan and bring to the boil.

3 Put in the lentils and simmer for about 45 minutes, stirring as the water is absorbed. The texture should be pourable, not too thick and not too thin.

4 Heat the ghee in a karahi or wok, and stir-fry the garlic and onion purée for about 10 minutes. Add the **spices** and continue stir-frying for 5 more minutes.

5 Mix the fried mixture in with the lentils, and add a little water. Lightly mash some of the lentils to create a creamy texture. Salt to taste.

6 Serve with a sprinkling of mint and a curl of cream.

Maharani Dhal

· THE QUEEN'S LENTILS ·

Serves 4

India's greatest queens lived in Jaipur, the Maharanis, and this lentil dish was their favourite.

INGREDIENTS

3¹/₂oz (100g) green moong lentils, split, skin on
3¹/₂oz (100g) black urid lentils, split, skin on
1 tablespoon mild curry paste (page 31)
2 fl oz (50ml) double cream

1 teaspoon mango powder
1 teaspoon cummin seeds, roasted
1 teaspoon garam masala
2oz (50g) butter
salt to taste
lemon

METHOD

1 Mix the lentils together, then pick through them to remove grit or impurities. Rinse them several times, then drain and immerse in ample water for 4 hours.

2 Drain and rinse the lentils, then measure an amount of water twice the volume of the drained lentils. Put the water into a 4 pint (2.25 litre) saucepan and bring to the boil.

3 Add the lentils and simmer for about 45 minutes.

4 When tender, mix in the remaining ingredients except for the lemon. Salt to taste.

5 Serve with parathas and chutney or accompanying curry and rice, with a twist of lemon.

Mogar

· DRY MOONG LENTILS ·

Serves 4

This dish will end up fairly dry with each grain separate, tender and tasty. You may need a little practice to get it exactly right. If there is insufficient water the dhal grains will not cook right through, if too much you'll get a sauce.

INGREDIENTS

8oz (225g) brown moong lentils, whole, skin on
2 tablespoons ghee
2-4 garlic cloves, finely chopped
14 fl oz (400ml) water
2-3 tomatoes, finely chopped
0-2 fresh green chillies, chopped
1 tablespoon chopped fresh coriander
salt to taste
lemon

Spices (whole)
1 teaspoon mustard seeds
1 teaspoon cummin seeds
12-16 curry leaves, fresh or dry

Spices (ground)
2 teaspoons coriander
1 teaspoon turmeric
1 teaspoon white sugar
$1/2$-2 teaspoons chilli powder
$1/4$ teaspoon asafoetida

METHOD

1 Pick through the lentils to remove any grit or impurities. Rinse them several times, then drain and immerse in ample water for 4 hours.

2 Make the **ground spices** into a paste using a little water.

3 Heat the ghee in a saucepan with a close-fitting lid. Stir-fry the **whole spices** for 20 seconds. Add the garlic and continue for 30 seconds. Lower the heat.

4 To cook the lentils, drain and rinse them, then add them to the karahi. Stir-fry until they look dry. Add the spice paste, plus the measured water and, when simmering, put the lid on.

5 It will take 30-40 minutes to cook by absorption. Inspect after about 15-20 minutes. Add the tomato, chillies and fresh coriander. Add a little water if it looks too dry.

6 When tender, salt to taste and serve. Keep in the warmer or let it cool and reheat the next day. Like rice, the longer it rests the more separate the grains. Serve with a twist of lemon.

Cochin Sambar Masaladar

· LENTIL AND VEGETABLE CURRY ·

Serves 4

In the south of India *sambar* is a way of life. It is eaten for breakfast, lunch and supper. It has a unique texture, being 75 per cent puréed lentils, the remainder mixed vegetables and tangy southern spices.

Choose a suitable combination from the following vegetables: aubergine, mooli (white radish), potato, green beans, sweet potato.

INGREDIENTS

12oz (350g) yellow oily toovar
lentils, split and polished
6 tablespoons mustard oil
4oz (110g) onions, thinly sliced
4oz (110g) vegetables (see above),
weighed after preparation
1-3 tablespoons tamarind purée
(page 24)
4 tablespoons grated coconut
flesh, or desiccated coconut
salt to taste

Spices (ground)
1 teaspoon coriander
1 teaspoon turmeric
1 teaspoon chilli
¼ teaspoon asafoetida

Spices (whole)
1 teaspoon mustard seeds
¼ teaspoon fenugreek seeds
6 curry leaves, dried or fresh

METHOD

1 Pick through the lentils to remove any grit or impurities, and rinse them several times then drain and soak in ample water for 24 hours.

2 Drain and rinse the lentils, then boil with the **ground spices** in twice their volume of water. Simmer until the lentils become soft (about 45 minutes). They may need a little mashing and a bit more water to keep the puréed texture not too dry.

3 Towards the end of stage 2, heat the oil and fry the **whole spices** for 1 minute, then add the onion and fry for 5 minutes or until brown.

4 Prepare the vegetables as appropriate, trimming, peeling, etc. Blanch in boiling water and cut into small cubes. If using potatoes, boil until cooked then cut into cubes.

5 Add the tamarind purée and coconut to the lentils, along with enough water to give a thick sauce consistency. When simmering, mix in the fried items and vegetables. Add salt to taste and when piping hot, serve.

Parippu Masoor
· TOOVAR AND RED LENTILS ·

Serves 4

A south Indian recipe combining hard oily nutty toovar (or toor) dhal with soft red (masoor) dhal. The texture provides a great combination of crunchy particles in a purée.

INGREDIENTS

5oz (150g) red masoor lentils,
  split and polished
3oz (75g) yellow oily toovar
  lentils, split and polished
2 tablespoons sesame oil
2 garlic cloves, finely chopped
1 inch (2.5cm) cube ginger,
  chopped
4oz (110g) onions, chopped
1 tablespoon brown sugar
2 tablespoons vinegar (any type)
1 tablespoon chopped fresh
  coriander
1 teaspoon garam masala
salt to taste

Spices 1
1 teaspoon coriander seeds
1 teaspoon cummin seeds
1 teaspoon black peppercorns
1 teaspoon sesame seeds

Spices 2
1 tablespoon mild curry powder
  (page 28)
1 teaspoon chilli powder
¹/₂ teaspoon turmeric
¹/₂ teaspoon fenugreek seeds
¹/₄ teaspoon asafoetida

METHOD

1 Keeping the lentils separate, pick through them to remove any grit or impurities. Rinse them several times, then drain and soak in ample water – 4 hours for the masoor, and 24 hours for the toovar.

2 Drain, rinse and combine the lentils, then measure an amount of water twice the volume of the drained lentils into a 4 pint (2.25 litre) saucepan. Bring to the boil.

3 Put in the lentils and simmer for about 45 minutes, stirring as the water is absorbed. The texture should be pourable, not too thick and not too thin.

4 Towards the end of stage 3, heat the oil in a karahi or wok. Add **spices 1** and stir-fry for 30 seconds. Add 2-3 tablespoons of the lentils. Stir-fry for a couple of minutes (until they crisp up), then add the garlic and stir-fry for a further minute, then the ginger for another minute. Add the onion and brown sugar. Reduce the heat and continue stir-frying for 5 minutes.

5 During this stage mix **spices 2** with enough vinegar to create a pourable paste. Add to the karahi.

6 When the lentils are tender, strain off excess water if necessary.

7 Put them into the karahi, then add the coriander, garam masala and salt to taste. Serve hot.

Dhal Ghobi Tikka

· LENTIL AND CABBAGE RISSOLES ·

Makes 24

On page 69 we met the *vadai,* a small deep-fried spicy rissole made from ground lentils, served cold in yoghurt. Here we meet other *vadai* which are served hot as part of the main course. There are three traditional shapes, all made from a lentil-flour 'dough' ball of about $1\frac{1}{2}$ inches (4cm) diameter. The first is a sphere, the second a disc and the third a ring with a hole in the middle, resembling a small doughnut.

Vadai, whatever shape, are made from ground urid dhal flour. The *amavadai* is made from a mixture of ground toovar and gram flour. The *pogoda* is made from ground moong dhal. All are from south India and are served with a coconut-based curry, rice and chutneys.

INGREDIENTS

1 full recipe vadai 'dough'
  (page 69)
8oz (225g) white cabbage,
  spinach or carrot, or a
  combination, all finely shredded

1 tablespoon chopped fresh
  coriander
2 teaspoons garam masala
gram flour (besan)
vegetable oil for deep-frying

METHOD

1 Make the vadai dough, following the recipe on page 69 until the end of stage 4, using the lentils of your choice.

2 Steam or microwave the shredded vegetables. Cool them and mix them into the dough, along with the coriander and garam masala.

3 Sprinkle some flour on to your work surface, then roll out 24 small balls about $1\frac{1}{2}$ inch (4cm) diameter. Shape them to discs or rings as you wish.

4 Heat the deep-fryer or oil in a pan to 375°F/190°C.

5 Place the balls in one by one about 10 seconds apart (so that the oil temperature is maintained), until you have eight in the pan. Cook for 8-10 minutes. Remove and set aside, keeping warm.

6 Repeat twice more to cook the remaining balls.

Moringar Dhal Kadhi

· DRUMSTICK AND LENTIL CURRY ·

Serves 4

Drumsticks are a curious member of the gourd family. They grow on the moringa tree and are especially popular in south India. The drumstick or *moringai kai* as it is known in Tamil *(seeng* in Hindi) is a rather hard, scaly and ribbed gourd which grows to between 15 and 18 inches (38-45cm) in length. To eat it you have to hold the drumstick in your hand and suck or chew the pulp out, discarding the husky stick. The flesh is really delicious in this tangy lentil base curry.

INGREDIENTS

8 drumstick gourds
4oz (110g) yellow oily toovar
  lentils, split and polished
4 tablespoons coconut milk
  powder
1-4 fresh green chillies, chopped

15-20 curry leaves
1 tablespoon mild curry paste
  (page 31)
whey (page 22) or water
salt to taste

METHOD

1 Pick through the lentils, then rinse, soak and cook as in stages 1-3 of Masala Dhal on page 204.

2 Scrape the drumsticks to remove the outer skin. Cut off the tops and bottoms, then cut them into equal lengths of about 4-6 inches (10-15cm).

3 Blanch in boiling water for 4 minutes (or steam or microwave) until soft.

4 When the lentils are soft and the water absorbed, add the coconut, chillies, curry leaves and paste, and enough whey or water to make it thinnish. When simmering add the drumstick pieces. Salt to taste. Serve hot.

CHEF'S TIP

Making flour
To make lentil or rice flour of any type, including gram flour (besan) from chana dhal, simply place the dry lentils or rice on a flat oven tray to a depth of no more than $1/2$ inch (1cm). Put in the oven preheated to 350°F/180°C/Gas 4 for 10 minutes. Remove and cool down completely. In small batches in the coffee grinder or spice mill (or even the mortar and pestle), grind to a fine powder.

Kirima

· LENTILS WITH PEAS AND BEANS ·

Serves 4

This Kashmiri black, green and red combination is really delightful, and you must cook it in such a way as to retain each colour. This peppery gingery dish is quite amazing served just with plain rice.

INGREDIENTS

6oz (175g) black urid lentils, whole, skin on
3oz (75g) red kidney beans
2 tablespoons ghee
1 inch (2.5cm) cube fresh ginger, chopped
0-2 fresh red chillies, chopped
1 tablespoon mild curry paste (page 31)
1 tablespoon tandoori masala paste (page 80)

1 tablespoon green masala paste (page 32)
3oz (75g) peas
salt to taste

Garnish
1 full recipe onion tarka (page 26)
garam masala (page 29)

METHOD

1 Pick through the lentils to remove any grit or impurities. Rinse them several times, then drain and immerse in ample water overnight.

2 Soak the red kidney beans overnight as well. Rinse several times next day, and drain.

3 Boil the kidney beans in ample water for about 1 hour or until soft.

4 At the same time boil the lentils with ample water in a separate pan, then simmer for about 45 minutes or until soft.

5 Strain both well and mix them in one large pan. Mix in the ghee, ginger, chillies and pastes then add the peas. Salt to taste. Serve garnished with the tarka and garam masala.

Facing page: Charu (page 55), plain rice and Kirima (above)

Ras Khaman

· BABY DUMPLING CURRY ·

Serves 4

Baby lentil dumplings served in a light whey-based spicy sauce. This recipe uses the whey that is left after making paneer (page 22).

INGREDIENTS

*1 full recipe vadai 'dough', made
  to stage 4 of the recipe on
  page 69*
vegetable oil for shallow-frying
1¼ pints (750ml) whey (page 22)
4 tablespoons gram flour (besan)

*2 tablespoons mild curry paste
  (page 31)*
salt to taste
fresh coriander leaves
chilli powder

METHOD

1 Sprinkle some extra flour on to your work surface and roll the dough into marbles about ¾ inch (2cm) in diameter.

2 Heat the oil in a karahi or wok and shallow-fry the marbles in several batches until golden, setting them aside. It doesn't matter that they go cold.

3 Heat the whey in a large 4-5 pint (2.25-2.75 litre) saucepan.

4 Mix the measured gram flour with enough water to make a thin purée. Heat this in the oil remaining in the karahi, stir-frying until it thickens.

5 Add it to the whey with the curry paste. Salt to taste. You should now have a gently simmering soup consistency. Add the marbles.

6 When hot, serve with the garnish of leaves and chilli powder.

Rajma Do-Piaza

· KIDNEY BEANS WITH ONION ·

Serves 4

The technique of do-piaza is generally referred to as using two *(do)* lots of onions *(piaza)* in different stages of the cooking process. This nutritious recipe uses spring onions, red onions and an onion tarka to achieve maximum flavour.

INGREDIENTS

8oz (225g) red kidney beans
4-6 bay leaves
3 tablespoons mustard oil
2-4 garlic cloves, chopped
8oz (225g) red onions, chopped
2 tablespoons brown sugar
1 tablespoon tandoori masala
*   paste (page 80)*
1/2 red pepper, seeded and
*   chopped*
0-4 fresh red chillies, chopped
6-8 spring onions, leaves and
*   bulbs chopped*

2 teaspoons garam masala
4 tablespoons yoghurt
salt to taste
1 full recipe onion tarka (page 26)

Spices
1 teaspoon cummin seeds
1 teaspoon coriander seeds
4-6 green cardamoms
2 inch (5cm) piece cassia bark

METHOD

1 Soak the red kidney beans overnight. Rinse several times next day and drain.

2 Boil the kidney beans with the bay leaves in ample water for about 1 hour or until soft.

3 During stage 2, heat the oil in a karahi or wok. Stir-fry the **spices** for 30 seconds. Add the garlic and stir-fry for 30 more seconds. Add the red onions and the brown sugar, lower the heat and stir-fry for 10 minutes.

4 Add the tandoori paste, red pepper, chillies and the beans, and gently simmer for a further 5 minutes.

5 Add the spring onions, garam masala, yoghurt, salt to taste and serve when hot, garnished with onion tarka.

Kair Sangri
· RUNNER BEANS WITH TINDLA ·

Serves 4

This very traditional recipe from Rajasthan uses *sangri,* a type of string beans and *kair,* small sour green seeds. I am using runner beans and *tindla* (see page 165) which is available from Asian shops occasionally, or gooseberries, fresh when in season.

INGREDIENTS

1lb (450g) runner beans, weighed
*   after stage 1*
3oz (75g) tindla or gooseberries
2 tablespoons light vegetable oil
1 teaspoon mustard seeds
1 teaspoon cummin seeds
1/4 teaspoon asafoetida
1 tablespoon sweet mango
*   chutney, chopped*

1-2 fresh red chillies, chopped
salt to taste

Garnish
1 full recipe onion tarka (page 26)
some fresh coriander leaves

METHOD

1 Prepare the beans. Wash, string and trim them, and cut diagonally into bite-sized pieces. Wash the gooseberries and top and tail.

2 Steam or microwave to soften them.

3 Heat the oil in a karahi or wok, and stir-fry the seeds and asafoetida for 20 seconds. Add the soft beans and gooseberries and gently stir-fry to mix in. Add the mango chutney and the chillies. Salt to taste. Serve garnished with the tarka and leaves.

Ugavela Moong
· CURRIED BEANSPROUTS ·

Serves 4

A lovely light and fresh dish using newly sprouted beansprouts or shoots. Most greengrocers sell sprouted moong dhal, but it is really easy to sprout them yourself. And any whole lentil will work (see Chef's Tip opposite). Try chickpeas as well. Serve hot as an accompaniment with curry and rice.

INGREDIENTS

1lb (450g) beansprouts
4 tablespoons water
1 tablespoon mild curry paste
*   (page 31)*

1 full recipe onion tarka (page 26)
1/2 teaspoon mango powder
salt to taste
fresh coriander leaves

Right is one of India's architectural masterpieces – the Hawa Mahal (Palace of the Winds), which is part of the Jaipur Royal Palace. Made from pink sandstone it stands five storeys high and overlooks the city. Behind the stone filigree windows the women of the harem were able to people-watch without themselves being observed. See page 154 for a recipe named after the Hawa Mahal.

METHOD

1 Heat the water in a karahi or wok. Mix in the curry paste.

2 Add the sprouts and stir-fry for 3-4 minutes.

3 Shake in the tarka and mango powder, and salt to taste. Serve at once, hot and crisp, garnished with leaves.

CHEF'S TIP

Beansprouts
These are made by allowing green moong dhal and other lentils to germinate, which requires water and the correct temperature.

To sprout dry lentils, soak them overnight, rinse in warm water, strain then spread out on kitchen paper on a tray. Put them in a dark, warm place for 24 hours. Inspect, rinse in warm water, strain and place on new kitchen paper. Return to the dark warmth. Repeat the process until they sprout, then leave in a light place until about an inch in length.

Do Phalee Bhaji

· TWO-BEAN CURRY ·

Serves 4

A combination of beans (seeds) and bean pods make a visually interesting dish. You could use broad beans and runners. Here I've used the colourful lablab beans. These come in a mixture of colours – creamy, red brown and black and they all have a tiny white 'tail'. I also use fresh green Kenyan beans for colour contrast.

INGREDIENTS

6oz (175g) lablab beans, dry
14oz (400g) Kenyan beans, fresh
2 tablespoons vegetable oil
1 teaspoon panch phoran (page 29)
2-3 garlic cloves, chopped
1 inch (2.5cm) cube ginger, chopped

0-2 fresh red chillies, chopped
2-3 tomatoes, chopped
1 tablespoon mild curry paste (page 31)
1 full recipe onion tarka (page 26)
salt to taste
garam masala (page 29) to taste

METHOD

1 Pick through the lablab beans to remove any grit or impurities. Rinse them several times, then drain and immerse in ample water for 12 hours.

2 Drain and rinse them, then pinch their skins off. Bring an ample amount of water to the boil in a 4 pint (2.25 litre) saucepan. Add the lablab beans and simmer for about 45 minutes.

3 Prepare the Kenyan beans: top and tail and chop them.

4 Towards the end of stage 2 heat the oil in a karahi or wok. Stir-fry the panch phoran for 20 seconds, then add the garlic and ginger and continue for another minute.

5 Now add the chillies, tomatoes and Kenyan beans and stir-fry for about 5 minutes. Drain the lablab beans and add them to the karahi with the curry paste and onion tarka. Stir-fry until all is cooked to your liking. Add salt and garam masala to taste.

Chhai Sem Bhajee

· SIX-BEAN CURRY ·

Serves 4

There are so many kinds of beans – some dried, some fresh – and the idea of combining several came to me one day when I was stock-taking the kitchen store cupboard. I found several packets of beans there. It was midsummer and fresh runner, broad and Kenyan beans were available to cook. I also had black-eye beans *(lobia*, small white round beans with a black comma in the tail), and *valor* beans (small cream-coloured round beans). If these are not to hand you can use other beans such as red kidney beans *(rajma)*, small brown fava beans, or *gunga* (pigeon) beans which are small and pink. Fresh alternatives include mangetouts. If you do not have all six beans use less types and adjust quantities.

INGREDIENTS

2oz (50g) black-eye beans, dry
2oz (50g) butter beans, dry
2oz (50g) valor white beans, dry
4oz (110g) broad beans, fresh or frozen
4oz (110g) Kenyan beans, fresh or frozen
4oz (110g) runner beans, fresh or frozen
2 tablespoons sunflower or sesame oil

4 garlic cloves, finely chopped
6oz (175g) onions, peeled and thinly sliced
1 tablespoon mild curry paste (page 31)
salt to taste

Spices
2 teaspoons sesame seeds
1 teaspoon cummin seeds
1 teaspoon black mustard seeds

METHOD

1 Pick through the dry beans to ensure there is no grit. Combine and soak them overnight in plenty of water.

2 To cook, bring a pan of ample water to the boil. Rinse the beans a few times, then simmer for 40 minutes or so.

3 Prepare the fresh or frozen beans and simmer to a crunchy texture in another pan of water (about 3-5 minutes)

4 Heat the oil and fry the **spices** for a minute, then the garlic for 1 minute, and the onion for 5 minutes. Finally add the curry paste. This will give the whites and greens of the beans a wonderful golden appearance. The amount of runniness is up to you. Simply add water (or better, vegetable stock) to taste. If you've got it right the texture should be crispy and crunchy, enhanced by the spices.

5 Combine everything, mixing well. Salt to taste and serve.

Rice Dishes

✺

The Romans called rice *oryza sativa*. This name derived from the ancient Greek *orusa*, which in turn came from the Arabic *alruzz* (or *arruzz*). Tracing the word back further still, it came from the ancient Persians, who called rice *w'rijza'h*. The Persians were influenced by the northern Indian Sanskrit word, *vrihi* or *brisi,* which derived from south India, where, in Tamil it was and still is called *arisi*. In modern Persian it is *birinj* and in Armenian, *brinz,* hence biriani. In modern Spain, it is *arroz*, in Italy *riso* and in France *riz*. We know it, of course, as rice.

But frankly we are beginners at rice eating. The grass plant whose grain is rice, originated in southern India and was cultivated in heavily irrigated 'paddy' fields 9,000 years ago. That Tamil word *arisi,* derived from the word *ari,* 'to separate', describes the process of separating the husk from the grain to produce 'brown rice'. Further milling removes the brown bran to produce the more familiar white polished grain. Rice is the indisputable major staple of over half the world's population, and there are about 7,000 varieties. It comes in short (round), medium and long grains, and some types cook to a glutinous mass, whilst others go dry and fluffy. Indians prefer it the latter way, and the best rice for the purpose is Basmati.

Facing page, clockwise from the top: Bisi Bela Bhaat (page 237), Hyderabadi Special Biriani (page 232) and Murghi Ruti (page 236)

Plain Rice by Boiling

Serves 4

This is the quickest way to cook rice, and it can be ready to serve in just 15 minutes from the water boiling. Two factors are crucial for this method to work perfectly. Firstly, the rice must be Basmati rice. Patna or long-grained, quick-cook, or other rices will require different timings and will have neither the texture nor the fragrance of Basmati. Secondly, it is one of the few recipes in this book which require *precision timing*. It is essential that for its few minutes on the boil you concentrate on it or else it may overcook and become stodgy.

A 3oz (75g) portion of dry rice provides an ample helping per person; 2oz (50g) will be a smaller but adequate portion.

INGREDIENTS

8-12oz (225-350g) Basmati rice
2-3 pints (1.2-1.75 litres) water

METHOD

1 Pick through the rice to remove grit and impurities.

2 Boil the water. It is not necessary to salt it.

3 While it is heating up, rinse the rice briskly with fresh cold water until most of the starch is washed out. Run hot tap water through the rice at the final rinse. This minimises the temperature reduction of the boiling water when you put the rice into it.

4 When the water is boiling properly, put the rice into the pan. Start timing. Put the lid on the pan until the water comes back to the boil, then remove the lid. It takes 8-10 minutes from the start. Stir frequently.

5 After about 6 minutes, taste a few grains. As soon as the centre is no longer brittle but still has a good *al dente* bite to it, drain off the water. The rice should seem slightly *under*cooked.

6 Shake off all the excess water, then place the strainer on to a dry tea towel which will help remove the last of the water.

7 After a minute place the rice in a warmed serving dish. You can serve it now or, preferably, put it into a very low oven or warming drawer for at least half an hour. As it dries, the grains will separate and become fluffy. It can be held in the warmer for several hours if needed.

Plain Rice by Absorption

Serves 4

Cooking rice in a pre-measured ratio of water which is all absorbed into the rice is undoubtedly the best way to do it. Provided that you use Basmati rice, the finished grains are longer, thinner and much more fragrant and flavourful than they are after boiling.

The method is easy, but many cookbooks make it sound far too complicated. Instructions invariably state that you must use a tightly lidded pot and precise water quantity and heat levels, and never lift the lid during the boiling process, etc., etc. However, I lift the lid, I might stir the rice, and I've even cooked rice by absorption without a lid. Also, if I've erred on the side of too little water, I've added a bit during 'the boil'. (Too much water is an unresolvable problem, however.) It's all naughty, rule-breaking stuff, but it still seems to work.

It's useful to know that 10oz (300g) is 2 tea cups dry rice, and 20 fl oz (1 pint/570ml) is about 1^1/$_3$ volume of water to 1 of rice. This 10:20 (or 2 teacups:1 pint) combination is easy to remember, but do step up or step down the quantities as required in proportion. For small appetites, for instance, use 8oz (225g) rice:16 fl oz (450ml) water to serve four people. For large appetites use 12oz (350g) rice:24 fl oz (685ml).

Cooking rice does need some practice, but after a few goes at this you'll do it without thinking. Here is my foolproof method.

INGREDIENTS

10oz (300g) Basmati rice
20 fl oz or 1 pint (570ml) water

METHOD

1 Soak the rice in water to cover for about half an hour.

2 Rinse it until the rinse water runs more or less clear, then drain.

3 Bring the measured water to the boil in a saucepan (as heavy as possible, and with a lid) or casserole dish with a capacity at least twice the volume of the drained rice.

4 As soon as it is boiling add the rice and stir in well.

5 As soon as it starts bubbling put the lid on the pan and reduce the heat to under half. Leave well alone for 8 minutes.

6 Inspect. Has the liquid on top been absorbed? If not, replace the lid and leave for 2 minutes. If and when it has, stir the rice well, ensuring that it is not sticking to the bottom. Now taste. It should not be brittle in the middle. If it is, add a little more water and return to the heat.

7 Place the saucepan or casserole into a warming drawer or oven preheated to its very lowest setting. This should be no lower than 175°F/80°C and no higher than 210°F/100°C (about Gas ^{1}/$_8$). You can serve the rice at once, but the longer you leave it, the more separate the grains will be. Thirty minutes is fine, but it will be quite safe and happy left for up to 90 minutes.

Aromatic Rice

Serves 4

There is no finer and more fragrant dish than Basmati rice spiked with aromatic spices. This combination is my favourite, but you can adjust spices to your liking. Saffron can be added optionally, for yellow colouring and additional fragrance.

The full complement of spices listed below gives a really tasty rice. You can omit some if you don't have them to hand. Some restaurants just use the fennel and black cummin seeds, and these are fragrant. If you don't like chewy spices, omit or remove the cloves, bay, cassia, etc.

INGREDIENTS

10oz (300g) Basmati rice
1 tablespoon butter ghee

Spices
2-3 bay leaves
4-6 green cardamoms

4-6 cloves
2 inch (5cm) piece cassia bark
1 teaspoon fennel seeds
1/2 teaspoon black cummin seeds
1 brown cardamom
2 star anise

METHOD

BY BOILING

1 Cook the rice to the end of stage 6 of the recipe on page 224.

2 Heat the ghee in a karahi or wok, and stir-fry the **spices** for 30 seconds.

3 Add the drained rice to the karahi. It can be hot straight from boiling or it can be cold.

4 Mix well and go to stage 7 on page 224. And see Chef's Tip 2 on page 229 for colouring.

BY ABSORPTION

1 Follow to the end of stage 2 of the recipe on page 225.

2 Measure and pre-boil the water or, for tastier results, use 10 fl oz (285ml) each of milk and water.

3 Heat the ghee in a karahi or wok. Stir-fry the **spices** for 30 seconds. Add to the drained uncooked rice and very gently (so as not to break the grains) stir in well.

4 Add the boiling water to the rice and continue with the recipe on page 225 from stage 5. And see Chef's Tip 2 on page 229 for colouring.

Jeera Mattar Pullao

· CUMMIN-SPICED PEA-FRIED RICE ·

Serves 4

Basmati rice spiced with cummin seeds and saffron, and punctuated with green peas. It tastes as good as it looks.

INGREDIENTS

8-12oz (225-350g) Basmati rice
2 tablespoons milk
20-25 saffron strands
2 tablespoons butter ghee
1 tablespoon onion in long thin
* strips*

2 teaspoons cummin seeds
1 tablespoon mild curry paste
* (optional, page 31)*
3oz (75g) cooked peas
salt to taste

METHOD

1 Prepare and cook the rice by either of the methods explained on pages 224-225.

2 Warm but don't boil the milk, and put the saffron into it. After 10 minutes press the saffron to help it exude its colour.

3 As soon as the rice has begun to boil, heat the ghee in a karahi or wok. Stir-fry the onion until it crisps up (about 5 minutes). Add the seeds and the curry paste as an optional extra.

4 When the rice is cooked place it in a warming pan. Add the stir-fry and the peas carefully so as not to break the rice grains.

5 Pour the saffron milk over the rice. Do not stir the rice.

6 Put the lid on the pan and place it into a warmer, or the lowest your oven will go. Leave there for a minimum of 30 minutes, stirring after that time. Salt to taste. It can be held in the warmer for longer if you wish.

CHEF'S TIP

A bacteria called *Bacilleusereus* can be present in rice. Most spores are destroyed by cooking for a minimum of 2 minutes at temperatures in excess of 158°F/70°C. All my rice methods involve a boiling temperature of 212°F/100°C for at least 8 minutes, so there should be no problem. However, a few spores may survive and these will multiply if the rice is kept at a temperature of less than 145°F/63°C. I recommend drying your rice in the warmer at a minimum of 175°F/80°C until you serve. About 30 minutes minimum and 90 minutes maximum will dry your rice safely to fluffy grains.

Pullao Rice

The Iranian dish *pollou* or *pillau* (from the Persian *pollo,* cooked rice) is a combination of Basmati rice cooked by absorption with spices and meat or poultry or vegetables. This dish was taken east to India, where pullao rice and pullao rice dishes are some of the most important dishes of the sub-continent. Westwards, the most famous Persian dish became the basis of *pilau* or *pilaf* in Turkey and Armenia, the *pilafi* dishes of Greece and the *paellas* of Spain.

Any main ingredient can accompany pullao, and, at the restaurant it is quickly knocked up, not being cooked in the traditional manner.

Here are eight superb variations. Begin by preparing 1 full recipe of Aromatic Rice (page 226), adjusting the **spices** as you like. Adding saffron or colouring is also optional (see Chef's Tip 2 on page 229).

EGG PULLAO

Hard-boil 4 eggs. Quarter or slice them and mix them hot or cold into the cooked rice. Serve after 30 minutes or more in the warmer when the eggs will be warm.

MIXED VEGETABLE PULLAO

Use about 3oz (75g) cooked mixed vegetables of your choice, diced into ¼ inch (5mm) cubes. Good colour contrast is important – use carrots, French beans, sweet potatoes, sweetcorn, peas, etc.

MUSHROOM PULLAO

Chop about 3oz (75g) raw mushrooms. Add them raw to the rice. Left for 30 minutes or more in the warmer they will warm, soften and absorb flavours.

PRAWN PULLAO

Use about 5oz (150g) of peeled cooked prawns. They can be cold (but not frozen). Half an hour or more in the warm rice will warm them up.

SEAFOOD PULLAO

You can substitute any seafood – crab, lobster or scampi etc. – or a combination for the prawn recipe.

FISH PULLAO

Any cooked fish can be used, but it must be skinned and filleted. Use about 4oz (110g) cooked fish, cut into 1 inch (2.5cm) pieces. As with the prawn recipe, the fish can be cold when added to the rice, providing it has 30 minutes or more in the warmer.

MEAT OR POULTRY PULLAO

The trick here is to keep back a few pieces of curried or tandoori-baked meat or poultry. (It is not worth starting from scratch with them for this particular recipe.) It is, of course ideal for using up leftovers. Fully heat up the meat (and especially poultry) before adding it to the rice. Use at least four pieces per person.

KEEMA PULLAO

Again keep back about half a cupful of curried mince or shak-shu-ka (see page 100) or use leftovers. Fully heat it up before adding to the rice.

CHEF'S TIP 1

Flavouring Rice

The two basic methods of cooking rice described on pages 224-225 produce 'plain' or unflavoured rice. Plain rice is perfectly acceptable to eat just as it is. Sometimes it is preferable, when the accompanying dishes are particularly rich. However, plain rice can be considerably enhanced by adding flavourings, which can consist of spices, herbs, onion, garlic, nuts, vegetables, fruit and even flowers.

In the case of boiled rice you can only add pre-cooked flavourings to the rice after it has been cooked. In the case of rice cooked by absorption the spicings are best cooked into the rice before the water is added. Many recipes in this chapter give you various options.

CHEF'S TIP 2

Colouring Rice

There is no doubt that colouring your rice adds greatly to its appearance. There are two very ancient traditional methods, using the natural colourings, turmeric and saffron.

Turmeric can only be boiled in. All your grains will be evenly coloured ranging from orange to pale yellow – the less you use the paler the colour. Add between $^1/_8$-$^3/_4$ teaspoon of turmeric at stage 2 of the recipe on page 224.

Saffron must be added after cooking or else its fragrance will be destroyed. Warm 3 tablespoons or 2 fl oz (50ml) milk. Do not boil it. Take it off the heat and add the saffron. After a few minutes, press the strands to let them exude their colour.

When the rice is cooked by either method and (optionally) flavoured, and in its warming dish, pour the saffron milk over it and leave the rice unstirred for 30 minutes or more. Mix it well just before serving.

Choricos Pullao

· SAUSAGE RICE ·

Serves 4

A surprise on my last trip to Goa was my introduction to the Goan sausage, a fabulous inheritance of its Portuguese ancestry. The Portuguese called it the *choricos de reine*, the 'sausage of the king'. It consists of chopped salted smoked pork, chilli, garlic and spices, stuffed into narrow casings, twisted into a number of sausages about 2 inches (5cm) long.

The nearest substitute available in the UK is the Spanish *chorizo* (or Portuguese *longaniza*). They are not so spicy, so we can make up the spicing in the cooking.

INGREDIENTS

8-12oz (225-350g) uncooked
  Basmati rice
3-4oz (75-110g) chorizo meat,
  chopped into small pieces,
  casing discarded
2 tablespoons light oil
2-4 garlic cloves, chopped
4oz (110g) onions, chopped
2-4 fresh green chillies, chopped

3-4 tomatoes, chopped
1/2 teaspoon salt
1/2 teaspoon garam masala

Spices
1 teaspoon cumin seeds
1 teaspoon mustard seeds
6-8 green cardamom seeds

METHOD

1 If cooking the rice by boiling, do this first (see page 224).

2 Heat the oil in a karahi or wok. Stir-fry the garlic and onion for 10 minutes.

3 Add the chorizo, **spices**, chillies and tomato and, when soft, add the pre-boiled rice and mix well. Or add the uncooked (rinsed, soaked and strained) rice and cook by absorption (see page 225).

4 Add salt and garam masala just before serving.

Chicken Tikka Biriani

Serves 4

For the record the biriani, like the pullao (see page 228), also originated from ancient Persia. The traditional Persian biriani would include meat and dried fruit slowly cooked to produce a mild, sweet and savoury dish. India made it spicier and more aromatic.

The Indian restaurant's interpretation of pullao is served with a garnish from the greengrocer (tomato, cucumber, lettuce, onion, etc) with sliced boiled egg and/or omelette, sultanas and nuts, all served with a curry gravy. They call it biriani. This following recipe is for restaurant-style chicken tikka biriani. It is followed by a number of variants. For more authentic birianis, see pages 232 and 234.

INGREDIENTS

1lb (450g) cooked aromatic rice
  (see page 226)
8oz (225g) cooked chicken tikka
  (page 82)
1 tablespoon mild curry paste
  (page 31)

1 tablespoon flaked almonds
2 teaspoons sultanas (optional)
1 teaspoon brown sugar
0-2 teaspoons chilli powder
salt to taste

METHOD

1 Put the rice and chicken into a karahi or wok and stir-fry until hot.

2 Add the curry paste and nuts, sultanas (if using), sugar and chilli powder, and mix well. Salt to taste.

3 Garnish as described above. Serve with a gravy (see Index).

In place of the chicken tikka use:

VEGETABLE BIRIANI 8oz (225g) mixed vegetables

MEAT BIRIANI 8oz (225g) meat bhoona (page 98)

KEEMA BIRIANI 8oz (225g) curried mince (shak-shu-ka) (page 100)

KING PRAWN or PRAWN 8oz (225g) cooked prawns (page 149)

Opposite: Choricos Pullao. The actual choricos (sausages) referred to on page 9 appear on the right of the picture.

Hyderabadi Special Biriani
· SPECIAL CHICKEN BIRIANI ·

Serves 4

This traditional Hyderabadi-style biriani cannot be bettered, and is worth the effort it takes to make it. Part-cooked rice lines a shallow, lidded oven dish. A layer of the main ingredient, in this case quail drumsticks (but you could use 4 chicken drumsticks), goes next and a final layer of rice covers it. Milk infused with saffron is added, the lid goes on and it gently bakes in the oven. The result is a pretty yellow rice punctuated with meat, peas and spices.

INGREDIENTS

10oz (275g) uncooked Basmati rice
1 tablespoon butter ghee
8 quail drumsticks, stir-fried in a little curry or tandoori paste
30 strands saffron infused in 2 fl oz (50ml) warm milk
2-3 tablespoons freshly cooked peas
some onion tarka (page 26)
salt to taste

Spices
1/2 teaspoon turmeric
2-3 bay leaves
4-6 green cardamoms
4-6 cloves
2 inch (5cm) piece cassia bark
1 teaspoon fennel seeds
1 brown cardamom
2 star anise

METHOD

1 Par-cook the rice by absorption, following the recipe on page 225, but cooking the rice for 6 minutes only.

2 Heat the ghee in a kahari or wok and stir-fry the **spices** for 30 seconds. Add the spices to the rice and any cooking liquid, and mix well.

3 Preheat the oven to 350°F/180°C/Gas 4. Layer half of the rice in a shallow, lidded dish. Add the quail drumsticks and top with the remaining rice. Add the saffron milk. Put the lid on and place the dish into the oven.

4 Cook for 30 minutes, then turn off the heat, leaving the rice undisturbed for a minimum of 30 further minutes, and a maximum of 1 hour.

5 Fluff up before serving, adding the peas and salt to taste. Sprinkle onion tarka over it.

Lobster Palala

Serves 4

I encountered this absolutely delicious dish at the home of an Indian air-force officer in Goa. Close inspection revealed that it was a cross between a pullao and a paella. The recipe, it appeared, had been passed by word of mouth to the Goan house cook via her grandmother. Between 1492 and 1962, Goa was a Portuguese colony, and the paella had reached Iberia via the Arab Moors by the 11th century.

INGREDIENTS

1 lobster or crawfish, weighing about 1³/₄lb (800g)
4 tablespoons sesame oil
4oz (110g) chicken breast, skinned and cubed
6oz (175g) onions, chopped
2-4 garlic cloves, chopped
4 cherry tomatoes
1 red pepper, seeded and diced
¹/₂ teaspoon salt
20 fl oz or 1 pint (600ml) stock or water
8-12oz (225-350g) uncooked Basmati rice
2 tablespoons lemon juice
about 1 cupful peas, cooked
3oz (75g) prawns (about 50 small, shelled)

6 mussels
6 clams
3 inch (7.5cm) smoked sausage (chorizo) cubed
20 saffron strands
sprigs of fresh parsley
lemon

Spices
1 teaspoon aniseed
1 teaspoon paprika
¹/₂ teaspoon garam masala (page 29)
¹/₂ teaspoon turmeric
¹/₄ teaspoon black cummin seeds
¹/₄ teaspoon freshly ground black pepper

METHOD

1 Remove lobster meat from shell and cut into 1 inch (2.5cm) pieces (see Chef's Tip on page 155).

2 Heat the oil in a karahi or wok, add the chicken pieces and fry for 5 minutes until the chicken is evenly golden. Remove it and keep aside. Stir-fry the onion and garlic in the pan, then add the tomatoes, red pepper, salt, a little of the stock or water and the **spices**. Cook, stirring occasionally, for 10-12 minutes, until the mixture is thick.

3 Rinse and drain the rice, add it to the pan, and fry for 3-4 minutes. Add the remaining stock or water and the lemon juice and bring to the boil. Reduce the heat and stir in the peas. Return the chicken to the pan and cook for 15 minutes. Add the lobster meat, prawns, mussels, clams and sausage. Add the saffron and cook for a further 5 minutes till the chicken is cooked through, and all the cooking liquid has been absorbed.

4 Remove the karahi from the heat, sprinkle with parsley, and serve immediately with a twist of lemon and chutneys.

Gosht Biriani-e-Dum Pukht

· LAMB AND RICE PIE ·

Serves 4

*D*um pukht means 'containing the steam', and it applies to a dish which is nearly cooked. The technique originated in ancient Persia. A close-fitting lid was sealed with pastry dough. Then the sealed pot was surrounded with hot coals, buried in the sand for a few hours and left undisturbed to finish off for an hour or more.

This pie is a perfect vehicle for finishing off biriani. It takes no short cuts, and therefore requires some effort. But the magical moment when the pastry is cut and the fragrant steam escapes, makes it well worthwhile.

INGREDIENTS

8oz (225g) ready-made puff pastry, thawed if frozen
8oz (225g) lean lamb or beef
2-4 garlic cloves, finely chopped
2 inch (5cm) cube ginger, finely chopped
2 tablespoons ghee
4oz (110g) onions, chopped
3oz (75g) yoghurt
2 fl oz (50ml) single cream
salt to taste
8oz (225g) Basmati rice
20-25 fresh whole mint leaves
30-35 fresh whole coriander leaves

Spices 1 (roasted and ground)
1 tablespoon coriander seeds
1 teaspoon cummin seeds
6-8 cloves
3-4 brown cardamoms
1 teaspoon garam masala

Spices 2
4 bay leaves
2 x 2 inch (5cm) pieces cassia bark
1 teaspoon fennel seeds
6 cloves
6 green cardamoms
2 star anise

METHOD

1 Cut the meat into cubes about 1¼ inch (3cm) in size.

2 Grind the garlic and ginger in the food processor, with enough water to create a pourable purée. Leave standing for 15 minutes until the end of stage 4.

3 Heat the ghee in a karahi or wok, and stir-fry the onion until brown (about 10 minutes).

4 Add the meat cubes and seal them by stir-frying for 5 minutes. Reduce the heat. Stir in **spices 1**.

5 Put the garlic and ginger purée into a strainer and extract as much juice as you can. Pour this over the meat.

6 Add the yoghurt, cream and salt to taste, and simmer for about 45 minutes. Sprinkle in a little water as required. The meat should now be quite dry, but tender.

Above: Gosht Biriani-e-Dum Pukht. For a change I added mixed cooked vegetables to the cooked rice in stage 7.

7 Meanwhile, cook the rice, preferably by absorption (page 225) with **spices 2**. As soon as the water has been absorbed, mix the rice into the meat karahi. Salt to taste.

8 Following the recipe on page 125, line a round 2 pint (1.2 litre) pie dish with a layer of rolled-out puff pastry. Place the biriani into the pie dish, and top with the mint and coriander leaves. Put the pastry lid in place, and seal well.

9 Put the dish into the oven preheated to 425°F/220°C/Gas 7, and bake for 25-30 minutes.

10 Serve at once or, better, let it stand in a warm place for up to 30 minutes.

Tengai Sadam
· COCONUT RICE ·

Serves 4

This rice, cooked in the South Indian style, is really scrumptious.

INGREDIENTS

8-12oz (225-350g) Basmati rice
flesh of 1 coconut
2 tablespoons coconut or light
   vegetable oil

1 tablespoon black urid lentils
1 teaspoon mustard seeds
1 teaspoon dry red chilli, chopped
salt to taste

METHOD

1 Prepare and cook the rice by either of the methods explained on pages 224 and 225, and cook to the end of stage 5 (boiled) or stage 6 (absorption).

2 Chop the coconut flesh into small 1/4 inch (5mm) pieces.

3 Heat the oil in a karahi or wok. Stir-fry the lentils, mustard seeds and chilli for 2-3 minutes. Add the coconut and stir-fry for about 5 more minutes.

4 Add the rice to the fried ingredients, stirring carefully (so as not to break the grains). Then put it into a casserole and into a warmer or oven at the very lowest heat possible.

5 Leave it there for a minimum of half an hour, stirring after that time. It can be held in the warmer for longer, if you wish.

Murghi Ruti
· CHICKEN WITH RICE CAKE ·

Serves 4

Here's a way to use up leftover roast chicken, from South India. Ruti is a 'cake' made from ground cooked rice. Serve on its own or with a curry dish.

INGREDIENTS

8oz (225g) boiled and cooled rice,
   any type
6oz (175g) pre-cooked chicken
   pieces, off the bone
2 tablespoons vegetable oil
2-4 garlic cloves, finely chopped
2 inch (5cm) cube ginger, chopped
4oz (110g) onions, chopped
flesh of 1 fresh coconut, coarsely
   chopped or shredded

1-4 fresh red and/or green chillies,
   chopped
a squeeze of lemon

Spices
2 teaspoons coriander seeds
1 teaspoon cummin seeds
1/2 teaspoon fenugreek seeds
1/2 teaspoon turmeric

METHOD

1 Put the rice in a blender or food processor, using enough water to make a creamy paste.

2 Heat the oil in a karahi or wok. Stir-fry the **spices** for 20 seconds, then the garlic and ginger for a minute. Add the onion and stir-fry for 5 minutes. Add the chicken, coconut and chilli and mix well.

3 Mix half of the chicken mixture with the rice paste.

4 Spread the resultant paste over a large flat pan such as an omelette pan, to a depth of about 1½ inches (4cm). Cook on gentle heat until firm and hot right through.

5 Spoon the remaining chicken mixture over the rice cake and flash under a hot grill to brown the top. Serve with a squeeze of lemon.

Bisi Bela Bhaat

· RICE, LENTILS AND VEGETABLES ·

Serves 4

A sumptuous South Indian mixture of rice, lentils, nuts and vegetables – a meal in itself. Simply add a curry gravy. We met yellow oily toovar lentils in the previous chapter. They need soaking for 24 hours, and cooking for about 45 minutes.

INGREDIENTS

flesh and water from 1 fresh
  coconut
11oz (300g) boiled Basmati rice
  (page 224)
7oz (200g) cooked yellow oily
  toovar lentils
4oz (110g) mixed frozen
  vegetables, thawed
salt to taste

Spices
2 teaspoons coriander seeds
6-8 cloves

2 inch (5cm) piece cassia bark
4-6 green cardamoms
2 brown cardamoms
12-15 curry leaves
½ teaspoon fenugreek seeds

Garnish
6-8 cherry tomatoes, halved
2oz (50g) cashew nuts, fried until
  golden
1 full recipe onion tarka (page 26)

METHOD

1 Grind the coconut to a pourable paste, using water as required.

2 Combine the rice, lentils and vegetables in a karahi. Stir-fry until hot. No oil is needed. Add the coconut paste and the **spices**. Salt to taste.

3 Garnish with the tomatoes, cashews and onion tarka. Serve with a light curry gravy and coconut chutney.

Breads and Chutneys

❋

The Egyptians were making leavened flatbreads in bakeries over 3,500 years ago. The technique spread from there eastwards. The Iranian word for bread is *'nane'* from which is derived the celebrated Indian *naan* bread. Unleavened breads are simply made from grain flour and water dough. All traditional Indian breads *(roti)* are flat and dry-griddled, fried, deep-fried or baked in the clay oven. The flour can be millet *(bajra)*, gram *(besan)*, rice *(chaval)*, cornflour *(makkhi)*, barley *(koda)*, refined white wheat flour *(maida)* and wholemeal brown wheat flour *(ata)*. Ata, also called chupatti flour, is made from 'hard' wheat grains, finely milled. It is high in gluten and therefore ideal for dough making. Ata flour is available in the natural brown form and a more refined 'white' form (which is in fact a pale buff colour).

This chapter also includes an interesting selection of chutneys. *'Chatnee'* is an ancient Hindustani word, which passed into English shortly after the East Indian Company began trading in Madras. Chutneys became associated with sweet and sour fruits – with the celebrated mango chutney still at the top of the popularity list after three centuries. In India many chutneys (or pickles) involve meat, poultry, fish and seafood. But most are sour and vegetable based. My selection here is easy to make and one or more should be served with any meal or snack.

Facing page: Breads, from the top are *Ata Naan* (page 241), *Pao* (page 248), and *Podina Dhania Paratha* (page 247). The chutneys are *Tamartar Murumba* (page 251) on the left, and *Burrhani Raita* (page 249) on the right.

Breads

Basic Dough Making

Before we get down to the individual breads, it is important to study basic dough-making techniques. Once you have mastered the method you will confidently produce perfect bread. The principal secret to success lies in the first kneading, or mixing, of the basic ingredients – flour and water. This requires patient and steady mixing either by hand or by machine, transforming the tacky mass of flour and water into a dough. It should be elastic without being sticky and should feel satisfying to handle. It should also be pliable, springy and soft.

Below are the basic methods for making unleavened and leavened dough.

UNLEAVENED DOUGH

flour types and quantities as given in specific recipes

1 Choose a large ceramic or glass bowl and put in the flour.
2 Add hot water little by little and work it into the flour with your fingers. Soon it will become a lump.
3 Then remove it from the bowl and knead it with your hands on a floured board or work top until the lump is cohesive and well combined.
4 Return it to the bowl and leave it for 10-15 minutes, then briefly knead it once more. It will then be ready to use in the recipes.

LEAVENED DOUGH

flour types and quantities as given in specific recipes
fresh yeast or natural yoghurt

1 Dissolve the fresh yeast in a little lukewarm water.
2 Put the flour in a *warmed* bowl, make a well in the centre and pour in the yeast. Yoghurt can be used in the absence of yeast by non-vegans.
3 Gently mix into the flour and add enough water to make a firm dough.

4 Remove from the bowl and knead on a floured board until well combined. Return to the bowl and leave in a warm place for a couple of hours to rise.

5 Your dough, when risen, should have doubled in size. It should be bubbly, stringy and elastic.

6 Knock back the dough by kneading it down to its original size.

Ata Naan

· BROWN FLOUR LEAVENED BREAD ·

Makes 4

Naan is the celebrated leavened bread. It is huge, light, fluffy and chewy. Its traditional tear-drop shape comes from being cooked by hanging at the top of the tandoor. Naans are normally made from self-raising or plain white flour, leavened with yeast or yoghurt. It makes a very pleasant change to use brown ata flour.

INGREDIENTS

2oz (50g) fresh yeast, or 3 tablespoons yoghurt
1½lb (675g) brown ata or wholemeal flour

lukewarm water
1 teaspoon wild onion seeds
melted butter ghee

METHOD

1 Using the yeast, water and brown flour, follow the recipe for leavened dough opposite. Add the seeds.

2 Divide the dough into four equal parts.

3 Roll each part into a tear-drop shape at least ¼ inch (5mm) thick.

4 Preheat the grill to three-quarters heat, cover the rack pan with foil, and set it in the midway position.

5 Put the naan on to the foil and grill it. Watch it cook (it can easily burn). As soon as the first side develops brown patches, remove it from the grill.

6 Turn it over and brush the uncooked side with a little melted ghee.

7 Return it to the grill and cook until it is sizzling. Remove.

8 Repeat stages 5-8 with the other three naan. Serve at once.

Kochuri (Dhal Puri)

· DEEP-FRIED LENTIL BREAD ·

Makes 16

Puri are 3-4 inch (7.5-10cm) diameter unleavened discs which, when deep-fried, balloon up into delightfully light tasty bread. This Bengali recipe adds cooked red masoor lentils to the ata flour dough. Red masoor lentils should be soaked for 4 hours then cooked for about 45 minutes before using in this recipe.

INGREDIENTS

8oz (225g) brown ata or
*   wholemeal flour*
4oz (110g) red masoor lentils,
*   cooked*

vegetable oil for deep-frying

METHOD

1   Follow the recipe for unleavened bread on page 240, adding the cooked lentils to the dough at the final stage.

2   Divide the dough into four equal lumps and divide each of these into four. (It's the easiest way of getting sixteen similar-sized pieces.) Shape each lump into a ball, then on a floured work surface roll each ball into a small thin disc about 3½ inches (9cm) in diameter.

3   Heat the deep-fryer to 375°F/190°C, and immerse one disc in the oil. It will sink initially, then rise and, hopefully, puff up like a balloon. Turn it when it does this, and remove after 30 seconds or so, then it should be golden. Shake off excess oil and keep the puri in a warming drawer or very low oven. Repeat with the remaining puris. Serve as hot and fresh as possible.

MINI WHITE FLOUR PURI

Follow the above recipe, but omit the lentils and add 1 tablespoon butter ghee when working the water into the dough. Make mini puri by dividing the dough into 32 equal-sized pieces instead of 16.

Facing page: Skilled hands knock back the puffy, risen dough

Bhare Naan

· STUFFED LEAVENED BREAD ·

Makes 4

Any Indian bread may be stuffed. Usual fillings are spicy mashed potato and/or vegetables, egg, keema, tandoori, kebab etc.

INGREDIENTS

2oz (50g) fresh yeast, or 3
*   tablespoons yoghurt*
lukewarm water
1¹/₂lb (675g) self-raising white
*   flour*
a sprinkling of wild onion seeds
melted ghee

Stuffing
4oz (110g) cooked mixed
*   vegetables, mashed*
1 tablespoon mild curry paste
*   (page 31)*
salt to taste

METHOD

1 Mix the stuffing ingredients together, and salt to taste.

2 Using the yeast or yoghurt, and the water and flour, follow the recipe for leavened dough on page 240. Add the seeds.

3 Divide the dough into eight equal parts, and roll two parts into a tear-drop shape at least ¹/₈ inch (3mm) thick.

4 Spread one quarter of the stuffing over one tear-drop shape and cover it with the other, pressing the edges firmly together. Repeat with the remaining three naans.

5 Cook each naan as from stage 4 of the recipe on page 241.

Bhare Chupatti

· STUFFED DRY UNLEAVENED BREAD ·

Makes 4

The chupatti is the ubiquitous staple bread of India. It is a thin flat disc, dry griddle cooked. We don't normally think of it as stuffed, but a thin layer of spiced potato transforms it.

INGREDIENTS

1lb (450g) brown ata or wholemeal flour
about ¹/₂-1 cup water

Stuffing
3oz (75g) mashed cooked potato

1 tablespoon chopped fresh coriander
1 teaspoon cummin seeds, roasted
¹/₂ teaspoon mango powder

METHOD

1 Mix the **stuffing** ingredients together.

2 Using the flour, follow the recipe for unleavened bread on page 240 to make a dough.

3 Divide the dough into eight equal lumps, and shape each lump into a ball. On a floured work surface, roll each ball into a thin disc about 6 inches (15cm) in diameter.

4 Spread a quarter of the filling on to one disc. Place the other disc on top and press the edges together. Repeat with the other three chupattis.

5 Heat a tava or frying pan to very hot. Test it by touching a tiny bit of flour on the bottom of the pan. If it turns brown at once the pan is ready.

6 Using no oil, cook the chupatti on one side only.

7 Using a spatula or fish slice, take the chupatti out of the pan and place, uncooked side up, under a preheated grill. The top side will now cook and should puff up. Repeat with the other three chupattis. Serve as hot as possible.

Maida Paratha

· LAYERED FRIED BREAD ·

Makes 4

The paratha is unleavened bread, a flat disc about 7 inches (18cm) in diameter, whose dough is rolled to create layers as in puff pastry, using the rope-dough or snake method. When shallow-fried, it should end up crispy on the outside yet still soft and 'melt-in-the-mouth'.

INGREDIENTS

1lb (450g) strong white flour
about ¹/₂-1 cup melted butter ghee

METHOD

1 Follow the recipe for unleavened bread on page 240.

2 Add 4 tablespoons of melted ghee, and mix well into the dough.

3 Divide the dough into four equal lumps. Shape the first lump into a long sausage, then flatten it into a strip about 12 x 3 inches (30 x 7.5cm).

4 Apply further melted ghee to the strip, then roll it from the long side to make a 'snake'. Gently flatten the snake with a rolling pin back into a strip of the same dimensions as above. You now have layered dough.

5 Cut the strip into two long strips about 12 x 1¹/₂ inches (30 x 4cm).

6 Now coil one strip around itself into a shape like a three-dimensional ice-cream cone. Lightly press it down with your hand, brush it with ghee and coil the second strip on top in the same shape.

7 Sprinkle extra flour on to the cone and again lightly press it down, then very lightly roll it out to a disc about 7 inches (17.5cm) in diameter. It should be obviously flaky and layered.

8 Heat a further 2 tablespoons of ghee on a tava (griddle pan) or large frying pan and fry the paratha until it is hot. Lift it out with tongs. Add more ghee and repeat on the other side. Keep in a warming drawer or very low oven. Repeat to make the remaining three parathas. Serve as hot and fresh as possible.

Bhare Lachadar Paratha
· STUFFED LAYERED FRIED BREAD ·

Makes 4

Using conventional ata flour here is a rope-dough paratha with stuffing. In this case, the stuffing is dry keema (mince) curry. Serve it with tikka or just raita for a satisfying meal.

INGREDIENTS

*1lb (450g) brown ata or
  wholemeal four
ample melted butter ghee*

Stuffing
*3oz (75g) Shak-Shu-Ka (page
  100), strained of excess gravy*

METHOD

Follow the previous recipe exactly, adding the keema during stage 2.

Khasta Roti
· PAN-FRIED BREAD ·

Makes 6

A white unleavened flour bread disc of 5 inch (13cm) diameter, spiced with lovage seeds, and pan-fried.

INGREDIENTS

*1lb (450g) strong white flour
about 1/2-1 cup water*

*2 teaspoons lovage seeds
2 tablespoons melted butter ghee*

METHOD

1 Follow the recipe for unleavened bread on page 240, adding the lovage seeds in stage 3.

2 Divide the dough into six equal lumps. Shape each lump into a ball, then on a floured work surface roll each ball into a disc about 5 inches (13cm) in diameter.

3 Heat the ghee in a tava or frying pan on medium high heat, then add a disc.

4 Cook it for a minute or so until it starts to fleck with brown. Turn it over and cook the other side. Place it in a warm drawer or very low oven. Repeat with the other five discs. Serve as hot as possible.

Podina Dhania Paratha
· HERBAL LAYERED BREAD ·

Makes 4

This paratha is made from a mixture of ata flour and gram (besan) flour, and it is crammed full of fresh herbs. Mint and coriander are traditional, but you can add any fresh herb such as basil, dill, parsley, etc.

INGREDIENTS

8oz (225g) brown ata or wholemeal flour
8oz (225g) gram flour (besan)
ample melted butter ghee

1 tablespoon chopped fresh coriander
1 tablespoon chopped fresh mint
1 teaspoon dried mint

METHOD

1 Follow the recipe on page 245 exactly, adding the coriander and mint at the beginning of stage 4.

Masala Kulcha
· SPICED LEAVENED BREAD ·

Serves 4

Onions and spices are kneaded into a leavened white dough which is rolled into 6 inch (15cm) discs for an exceptionally tasty grilled bread.

INGREDIENTS

2oz (50g) fresh yeast, or 3 tablespoons yoghurt
lukewarm water
1lb (450g) self-raising white flour
1 full recipe onion tarka (page 26)

1 teaspoon white sugar
1 teaspoon masala (page 28)
1/2 teaspoon aromatic salt (page 30)

METHOD

1 Following the recipe for leavened bread on page 240, mix the flour with yeast and water to make the dough, adding the tarka, sugar, masala and salt during stage 6.

2 Divide the dough into four equal lumps. Shape each lump into a ball, then on a floured work surface roll each ball into a disc about 6 inches (15cm) in diameter.

4 Preheat the grill to medium. Place the rack at the mid-height position. Grill each disc until blackened spots appear. Turn over and repeat.

Sheermal Roti
· PERFUMED LEAVENED BREAD ·

Makes 4

A flat round white flour leavened dough kneaded with milk and ghee, perfumed with saffron in milk and rosewater. It is rolled into a 6 inch (15cm) disc then grilled.

INGREDIENTS

2oz (50g) fresh yeast, or 3 tablespoons yoghurt
1lb (450g) self-raising white flour
lukewarm milk
2 fl oz (50ml) rosewater

1 tablespoon granulated sugar
30 saffron strands
1 teaspoon aromatic salt (page 30)
melted butter ghee

METHOD

1 Using the yeast, flour and milk instead of water, follow the recipe on page 240 for leavened bread. Use the rosewater and sugar at stage 3 as well and add the saffron strands and salt at stage 6.

2 Divide the dough into four equal parts, and roll each part into a disc of around 6 inches (15cm) in diameter.

3 Grill as for naan (see page 241) then repeat for the remaining three discs. Serve at once.

Pao
· BANGLE-SHAPED BUN (BAGEL) ·

Makes 4

We have met a few traditional Indian flat breads in the last few recipes. What is not widely known is that India also has conventional white bread and rolls, an inheritance from the British. This bagel-shaped bun, however, is of Portuguese origins and is popular in Bombay served with vegetable curry (page 176).

INGREDIENTS

6 fl oz (175ml) milk
1 teaspoon brown sugar
1oz (25g) fresh yeast
10oz (275g) strong white flour

1 egg, beaten
sesame, roasted cummin and mustard seeds (optional)

METHOD

1 Heat the milk to touch temperature (around 104°F/40°C). Mix in the sugar and yeast and let it stand for about 15 minutes to ferment.

2 Put the flour in a warmed bowl, make a well in the centre, pour in the milk and mix to a firm dough.

3 Remove from the bowl and knead on a floured board until well combined. Return to the bowl and leave in a warm place for a couple of hours to rise.

4 When risen, it should have doubled in size, and be bubbly, stringy and elastic. Knock it back by kneading it down to its original size.

5 Divide the dough into eight equal lumps. Roll one lump into a sausage about 8 inches (20cm) in length. Curl it into a ring. Put the ring on to a buttered baking sheet. Repeat with the other seven dough lumps. Leave them to prove in a warm place for around 15 minutes.

6 Preheat the oven to 375°F/190°C/Gas 5. Glaze each ring with the beaten egg and sprinkle on the seeds (if using).

7 Bake for 20 minutes, by which time they should be a nice golden colour. Serve hot or cold but fresh.

Chutneys

Burrhani Raita

· GARLIC IN YOGHURT ·

Enough for 4

This tasty combination is from Lucknow.

INGREDIENTS

1 tablespoon vegetable oil
$^1/_2$ teaspoon cummin seeds

4-6 garlic cloves, finely chopped
1 cupful yoghurt

METHOD

1 Heat the oil in a karahi or wok. Stir-fry the seeds for 10 seconds then add the garlic and stir-fry for 30 seconds.

2 Add to the yoghurt when cold. Mix well, chill and serve.

Mirchi Sil Batta

· FRESH GROUND CHILLI CHUTNEY ·

Ample for 4

For heat lovers only! This finely ground green purée will keep in the refrigerator for many days. For a really smooth purée seed the chillies, but you will need to use twice as many chillies.

INGREDIENTS

2oz (50g) fresh green chillies
1 tablespoon finely ground black pepper
¹/₂ teaspoon mango powder
¹/₃ teaspoon turmeric
distilled white vinegar

METHOD

Mulch everything down in the food processor into a fine lump-free purée, using vinegar as required.

Tamartar Murumba

· SWEET RED TOMATO CHUTNEY ·

Makes 1lb (450g)

This is a wonderful tasty sweet chutney, lightly spiced with black onion seeds. Not only is it superb with Indian food, but it actually goes with anything. Larger batches, say up to a maximum of 4lb (1.8kg), can be made by upping both quantities and timings. The cooked chutney will keep indefinitely.

INGREDIENTS

1lb (450g) tomatoes, quartered
5 fl oz (150ml) water
8oz (225g) sugar
1 garlic clove, chopped
2-3 bay leaves

5 fl oz (150ml) distilled white
  vinegar
1^1/$_2$ teaspoons nigella (black
  onion) seeds
1 teaspoon chilli powder

METHOD

1 Place the water and sugar in a 2^1/$_4$ pint (1.4 litre) saucepan, and dissolve completely on a low heat.

2 Raise the heat, add all the remaining ingredients, and bring to the boil.

3 Immediately lower the heat to achieve a gentle rolling simmer. At first it seems very watery as the tomatoes go to pulp but it quickly reduces and begins to caramelise. It is cooked after about 20 minutes, when it will have set to a syrupy texture. During the 20 minutes, inspect and stir three or four times.

4 Remove the pan from the heat and let it cool sufficiently to bottle in sterilised jars.

Sweet Green Tomato Chutney

Gardeners might ask what to do with all those tart green tomatoes that seem never to ripen. Here's the answer.

Follow the previous recipe, using green tomatoes in place of red. Unfortunately green tomatoes go a muddy sludge colour when cooked, so although it tastes good, it is infinitely more appetising to add a pinch of green food colouring at the beginning of stage 4.

Sweet Mango Chutney

Facing page, above: A wonderful display of chillies enhance the bowl of Mirchi Sil Batta (opposite) and the two glasses of Am Ras Khatta (page 266)

To make a wonderfully quick mango chutney, follow the recipe for Tamartar Murumba (above), omitting the tomatoes and substituting 1lb (450g) ripe chopped mango flesh, weighed after discarding the stones and skins.

Kaanji

· PUNJABI CARROT CHUTNEY ·

Makes enough for 4

Indian carrots are blood red in colour. Here, beetroot is incorporated to dye the carrot.

INGREDIENTS

6oz (175g) carrots, scraped and shredded
2oz (50g) fresh beetroot, peeled and shredded

2 fl oz (50ml) vinegar (any type)
1 teaspoon mustard seeds
1 teaspoon garam masala
0-1 teaspoon chilli powder

METHOD

Combine the ingredients and keep in the refrigerator for up to 24 hours. Serve chilled.

Dhania Chatni

· FRESH CORIANDER CHUTNEY ·

Makes ample chutney

Fresh coriander can be a little bitter when puréed, but with this combination of ingredients it is well balanced in taste – delicious in fact.

INGREDIENTS

4oz (100g) fresh coriander leaves
1 teaspoon garlic purée (page 24)
2oz (50g) fresh coconut flesh
a little coconut water (page 23)
20 raw cashew nuts

2-4 fresh green chillies, chopped
1 tablespoon lemon juice
1 tablespoon sugar
1 teaspoon salt

METHOD

1 Place everything into the blender or food processor and mulch down into a coarse but smooth purée, using coconut water as required.

2 Chill and serve. It will keep for 2-3 days in the refrigerator, and can be frozen.

Koprai Tuvaiyal

· COCONUT CHUTNEY ·

Makes sufficient for 4

Indispensible with all South Indian dishes – indeed any savoury recipe. Only fresh coconut will do. Keep any surplus in the freezer.

INGREDIENTS

*flesh and water of 1 fresh coconut
   (page 23)
1 tablespoon vegetable oil
2oz (50g) raw cashew nuts
2-3 fresh green chillies, chopped
1 inch (2.5cm) cube ginger,
   chopped
2 tablespoons freshly squeezed
   lemon juice*

1/2 teaspoon salt

Spices
*1 teaspoon mustard seeds
1 tablespoon black urid lentils,
   split and polished
10-12 curry leaves*

METHOD

1 Put the coconut flesh into the food processor and, using its water plus additional cold water, make a creamy purée.

2 Heat the oil in a karahi or wok. Stir-fry the **spices** for 30 seconds, then add the nuts, chillies and ginger, and continue to stir-fry for 3 minutes or so.

3 Cool a little then add to the purée in the food processor. Pulse into the purée. Add the lemon juice and salt, and enough water to keep it mobile. Chill and serve.

Tandoori Chutney

Makes an ample serving

The indispensable tangy accomaniment to all tandoori and tikka dishes.

INGREDIENTS

*6 tablespoons yoghurt
milk (see method)
1 tablespoon fresh lemon juice
1 teaspoon granulated sugar*

*1 teaspoon dried mint
1 teaspoon bottled mint in vinegar
1/4 teaspoon mango powder
1/4 teaspoon aromatic salt (page 30)*

METHOD

1 Mix everything together.

2 Use milk to thin the mixture if you wish it to be thinner.

Desserts and Beverages

✳

I have combined desserts and beverages in this chapter, for convenience rather than to make a point. Some of my selection of beverages are savoury, and some sweet. Some can be taken at any stage of the meal.

Most Indian desserts are heavy on sugar and calories and, as curry is rich and filling, many of us simply do not have room for more rich food. They are an acquired taste, but once you've acquired it they are delicious. In many parts of India the concept of a sweet course to finish the meal does not exist, in any case. Sweet dishes are served at any stage of the meal – or even at the beginning of it. Indeed most Indian-published cookbooks begin with desserts and sweets.

To suit western tastes, my selection of dessert recipes *is* designed to come at the end of the curry meal, and includes a wide variety of themes.

Facing page: Raj Bogh (page 260) and *Kurbani ka Mitha* (page 257) in the stemmed dishes. Below is a selection of paan mixtures with paan leaves, betel nut and betel nut cutter at the front (see Après Curry chapter, pages 270-75).

Desserts

Fresh Mango Hedgehog

Serves 2

There are dozens of species of mango. Some are small, sour and green and are perfect for pickling: others are large and lush and a beautiful orangey-golden colour. The juiciest and lushest of these is the Alphonso mango. With a tough outer skin and large stone, preparing a mango can be a messy business. This stylish preparation, called the hedgehog, not only looks good, but is a great talking point.

INGREDIENTS

1 fresh ripe mango

METHOD

1 Decide where the stone is. Stand the mango on its base. Using a sharp knife, cut from top to bottom, on one side running along the stone so that the cut is slightly off-centre.

2 Repeat with the other side of the mango and you will now have two halves (with the stone separate which you discard).

3 Work with one half of the mango, flesh upwards. Score the flesh with a paring knife in a wide criss-cross pattern. Don't cut through the skin.

4 Taking the mango in both hands and using your finger tips, press the skin in the centre of the mango upwards, holding the case with your thumbs.

5 The inverted flesh now gives you a 'hedgehog' effect. Repeat with the other half.

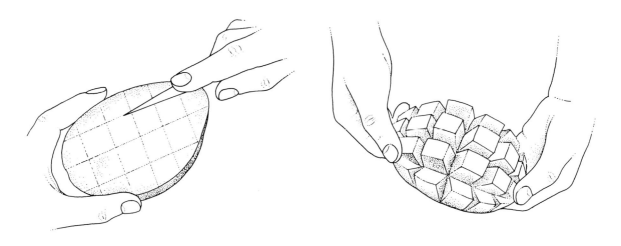

Kurbani ka Mitha

· APRICOT SYLLABUB ·

Serves 4

This light pudding is from Satish Arora, the master chef of the Taj Group. Served cold, it is neither too sweet nor too rich, and the crunchy nuts and praline give it a nice surprise taste.

INGREDIENTS

14oz (400g) dried apricots
2 tablespoons custard powder
1 pint (600ml) milk
1 tablespoon granulated white
  sugar
10 fl oz (300ml) double cream
3-4 drops vanilla essence
3-4 tablespoons brandy (optional)

Praline
2oz (50g) caster sugar
2oz (50g) raw almonds, chopped

Garnish
edible silver leaf (page 109)

METHOD

1 For the **praline**, put the caster sugar and chopped almonds into a heavy pan over a low heat.

2 When the sugar has caramelised (turned into a brown liquid), thinly spread it on to a cold oven tray. Leave to set.

3 When it is cold, break it into a crumbly crunchy mixture.

4 Put the apricots into a pan and cover with water. Simmer until the apricots are soft and the water is reduced.

5 Purée together in the food processor.

6 Mix the custard powder with enough of the milk to make a thin paste. Bring the remaining milk and the granulated sugar to the simmer. Add the custard paste and stir until it thickens. Then let it go cold.

7 Mix the custard, apricot purée, cream, vanilla, three-quarters of the praline and the optional brandy together.

8 Beat well. Carefully put into stemmed glasses. Garnish with edible silver leaf and the remaining praline. Chill in the refrigerator but serve within 2 hours to maintain the crunchiness.

Seb Bhargari

· APPLE FRITTERS ·

Serves 4

One of the few dishes to have come to India from Britain. I had these in Kashmir, but the Indian chef had added a little taste of India to the batter. Sliced apple is dipped in spicy batter and fried. It must be cooked and served at once.

INGREDIENTS

4 large apples
vegetable oil for deep-frying
caster sugar for dusting

Batter
5oz (150g) plain white flour
2 tablespoons coconut milk
* powder*
4 fl oz (120ml) milk

3-4 drops vanilla essence

Spices (ground)
1 teaspoon cinnamon or cassia
¹⁄₂ teaspoon mace
¹⁄₂ teaspoon ground cloves
¹⁄₂ teaspoon green cardamom
* seeds*

METHOD

1 For the **batter**, mix the flour and coconut milk powder with the milk to a thick consistency. Mix in the essence and **spices**.

2 Peel, core and cut the apples into thin slices.

3 Immediately coat one slice with the spicy batter. Lower into the oil preheated to 375°F/190°C. Follow with the next slice and so on until all the slices are frying (or as many as you can fry at one time).

4 Remove them preferably in the order they went in. Drain on kitchen paper. Dust with caster sugar and serve piping hot.

Singhara Halva

· CHESTNUT PUDDING ·

Serves 4

The emperor Jahangir described Kashmir as 'heaven on earth'. Its climate not only gave the royal court a cool retreat in the Indian summer, it gave them scenery and ingredients more akin to England than India: chestnuts, for example.

INGREDIENTS

1lb (450g) whole chestnuts, weighed after cooking and shelling
8-9oz (225-250g) canned chestnut purée
2 tablespoons brown sugar
1 fl oz (25ml) rosewater
2oz (50g) soft butter
1 teaspoon green cardamom seeds, ground

1 tablespoon charoli or sunflower seeds
2 fl oz (50ml) double cream

Garnish
double cream
edible silver or gold leaf (page 109)
chopped pistachio nuts

METHOD

1 Chop the whole chestnuts and mix them with the chestnut purée, the sugar, rosewater, butter, cardamom and charoli seeds.

2 Place in a pan on low heat and gently cook for 10-15 minutes. It should be quite thick but not too dry. Control this by adding the cream bit by bit.

3 Serve garnished with a curl of cream, edible silver leaf and pistachio nuts.

Mithai Pakora
· SWEET FRITTERS ·

Makes 8

This splendid pudding comes from Rajasthan, arguably the most exotic state in the world's most exotic country.

INGREDIENTS

3oz (75g) plain white flour
3oz (75g) gram flour (besan)
1¹/₂oz (40g) coconut milk powder
1 egg, beaten
milk
vegetable oil for deep-frying

2oz (50g) caster sugar
10-12 hazelnuts
10-12 walnuts, quartered
1 teaspoon green cardamom seeds
icing sugar for dusting
lemon wedges

METHOD

1 Mix the flours, coconut and egg with sufficient milk to make a batter, stiff enough to drop eventually off the spoon. Let it stand for 10 minutes whilst the deep-fryer heats to 375°F/190°C.

2 Add the sugar, nuts and cardamom seeds to the batter.

3 Place about one-eighth of the mixture into the hot oil and leave it for 15 seconds, when it will rise. Add the next one and carry on until all eight are in.

4 Cook for about 8 minutes, then remove them, preferably in the order they went in, and drain on kitchen paper. Dust with icing sugar and serve piping hot with lemon wedges.

Raj Bogh

SWEET PANEER BALLS ·

Serves 4

Saffron and cardamom flavour 'condensed' milk with golden fried cheese balls. Typically Indian tastes, except they would use a lot more sugar.

INGREDIENTS

1 full recipe paneer (page 22)
2oz (50g) unsalted butter
1 pint (600ml) milk
10 fl oz (300ml) water

2oz (50g) white granulated sugar
seeds of 12 green cardamoms
30 saffron strands
flaked almonds, lightly grilled

METHOD

1 Make the paneer, allowing it to go solid enough to cut (rather than crumbly)

2 Using a small melon scooper, shape the paneer into small balls (or cut them into small cubes).

3 Heat the butter in a flat pan and fry the balls until they are evenly pale gold.

4 In a large saucepan (at least 4 pints/2.25 litres), combine the milk, water and sugar, and bring to the simmer. Put the seeds into the pan.

5 Simmer to achieve a partial reduction, not too thick but not too thin. This will probably take about 45 minutes, but it depends on the thickness of your pan and the exact temperature of the heat. Stir frequently.

6 When it has reduced to your liking add the fried paneer balls and saffron and serve hot, garnished with the nuts.

Kulfi

· PISTACHIO ICE CREAM ·

Serves 4

Kulfi is the traditional Indian ice cream, which is quite different in texture to British ice cream. Adding spices and that very Indian ingredient, the pistachio nut, makes it very special.

INGREDIENTS

2 eggs, separated
1 oz (25g) icing sugar
5 fl oz (150ml) double cream
few drops vanilla essence
2 tablespoons chopped pistachio
   nuts

$^1/_2$ teaspoon ground cardamom
   seeds
few drops green food colouring
   (optional)
freshly grated nutmeg

METHOD

1 Whisk the egg whites until they thicken.

2 Add a teaspoon of sugar and whisk in. Repeat until all the sugar has been combined.

3 Separately whisk the egg yolks, then whisk them into the whites.

4 Separately whisk the cream until it peaks then add it, the vanilla, most of the nuts, the cardamom and the optional colouring into the egg, whisking slowly until well mixed.

5 Place in a chilled polythene tub and into the freezer for 3 hours or so. Remove it and whisk slowly to break up the water crystals.

6 Repeat this whisking after another 2 hours freezing, then leave to freeze solid for 24 hours or more.

7 Freshly grate some nutmeg and scatter the remaining pistachio nuts over the ice cream when serving.

Sevian

· SWEET VERMICELLI ·

Serves 4

Vermicelli is the thinnest of pasta threads. Although neither pasta nor noodles are used much in traditional Indian cuisine, they are very ancient and were well-known to early Arab traders, who were responsible for bringing this recipe via Persia to India.

INGREDIENTS

15 fl oz (450ml) milk
4 tablespoons ghee
3¹/₂oz (100g) cut vermicelli
1¹/₂ teaspoons green cardamom seeds

1 tablespoon sultanas
2 tablespoons brown sugar
sugared almonds (see Chef's Tip below)

METHOD

1 Heat the milk to the simmer.

2 Heat the ghee in a karahi or wok. Add the vermicelli and stir-fry until it browns a little (about 2-3 minutes). Lower the heat. Add the milk, cardamom, sultanas and sugar and stir-fry until the vermicelli goes quite soft (about 10-12 minutes).

3 Serve at once, garnishing with whole sugared almonds.

CHEF'S TIP

Sugared Almonds
These are delicious on their own or as a garnish for sweet dishes.

7oz (200g) whole almonds, shelled
6 tablespoons butter ghee
icing sugar

1. Heat the ghee in a karahi or wok, and stir-fry the nuts for 5 minutes.

2. Drain and when cool, dust with the sugar. Store in an airtight container until needed.

Bebinca

· GOAN LAYER CAKE ·

Serves 4

A 6 inch (15cm) diameter cake with ten layers. The traditional way to cook this Goan recipe (also called *bibique*) involves a 15-20 minute oven bake for each layer. It could take over 6 hours to prepare, and it was not unknown for the cake to measure 2 feet (60cm) in diameter and require 50 eggs! This method cuts both the time and the eggs!

INGREDIENTS

10oz (275g) granulated sugar
9oz (250g) plain white flour
2oz (50g) coconut milk powder
3-4 drops vanilla essence

10 egg yolks
melted butter
ground mace

METHOD

1 Heat sufficient water with the sugar to make a thin syrup. Let it cool enough to add the flour, coconut, vanilla, and egg yolks. Electric whisk it to create a pourable batter.

2 Preheat the grill to medium heat, and grease a 6 inch (15cm) cake tin.

3 Ladle into the tin a layer of batter about ¼ inch (5mm) thick and grill for about 3 minutes until golden and firm. Brush some melted butter on the first layer.

4 Whisk up the batter and repeat stage 3 until all the batter is layered into the tin. You should have about ten layers.

5 Cover the cake tin with foil and place it into the oven preheated to 375°F/190°C/Gas 5. Bake for 35 minutes.

6 Remove and allow to cool, then turn the cake out. Serve cold with ice cream, and sprinkle with mace.

Mango Fool

Serves 4

I remember as a child being given apple fool by my granny. She had a recipe for mango fool which her mother had given her in Agra in 1892, a century ago. When granny lived with us in London, she used to rue the fact that mangoes were unavailable in England. That was 40 years ago. Now they are as 'available' as apples, so here is her recipe. She'd have been pleased to know it is in this book.

INGREDIENTS

1lb (450g) fresh or canned mango flesh
4 tablespoons caster sugar

10 fl oz (300ml) whipping cream
ground mace

METHOD

1 Using an electric whisk, mash the mango and sugar into a purée.

2 In a separate bowl whisk the cream until it peaks.

3 Just before serving, fold the purée into the cream, lightly whisking to maintain an airy texture. Serve in stemmed glasses, garnished with ground mace.

Beverages

Dehati Chaach or Chaas
· SWEET YOGHURT DRINK ·

Serves 2

A sweet thirst-quencher for hot days from the Punjab and Delhi. In Gujarat it is called *chaas*.

INGREDIENTS

10 oz (275g) yoghurt
5 fl oz (150ml) water
1/2 teaspoon green cardamom seeds, ground

1 fl oz (25ml) rosewater
2 teaspoons sugar
crushed ice
nutmeg

METHOD

1 Whisk together the yoghurt, water, seeds, rosewater and sugar.

2 Serve with crushed ice in two tall glasses. Garnish with freshly grated nutmeg.

Thandai

· SWEET MILK DRINK ·

Serves 2

A milk-based thirst-quencher from the Moslem areas of Lucknow and Hyderabad. In some parts of India, thandai contains marijuana *(bhang)*, but it's not in this recipe!

INGREDIENTS

1 pint (600ml) milk
1 tablespoon ground almonds
10-12 saffron strands
6 peppercorns (optional)

¹/₂ teaspoon aniseed
2 teaspoons caster sugar
2-3 drops red food colouring
 (optional)

METHOD

1 Mix the ingredients together.

2 Serve with crushed ice in two tall glasses.

Masala Chaach or Chaas

· YOGHURT WITH MINT ·

Serves 2

Traditionally black salt *(kala nimak)* would be used in this drink. It is an acquired taste, reminding me of dehydrated sea water, so I have specified aromatic salt for my version of this thick savoury yoghurt drink.

INGREDIENTS

10oz (275g) yoghurt
5 fl oz (150ml) water
1 teaspoon chopped fresh mint
¹/₂ teaspoon ground cummin
¹/₂ teaspoon ground black pepper

¹/₂ teaspoon aromatic salt (page
 30)
crushed ice
chilli powder or paprika

METHOD

1 Whisk together the yoghurt, water, mint, cummin, pepper and salt.

2 Serve with crushed ice in two tall glasses. Garnish with chilli powder or paprika.

Matha

· YOGHURT WITH CORIANDER ·

Serves 2

This thick savoury yoghurt drink is from Rajasthan. Drink it, as the Rajasthanis do, after your meal as a digestive.

INGREDIENTS

10oz (275g) yoghurt
5 fl oz (150ml) water
1 teaspoon chopped coriander
  leaves

1/2 teaspoon aromatic salt (page 30)
1/2 teaspoon cummin seeds
1/2 teaspoon mustard seeds
crushed ice

METHOD

1 Whisk together the yoghurt, water, coriander and salt.

2 Roast the seeds, grind and add to the yoghurt.

3 Serve with crushed ice in two tall glasses.

Am Ras Khatta

· MANGO REFRESHER ·

Serves 2

This appetising drink can be sweet or savoury.

INGREDIENTS

1 large mango, skinned and
  stoned
15 fl oz (450ml) water
1 teaspoon dried mint

caster sugar to taste
crushed ice
1 fresh lime, halved

METHOD

1 Put the mango flesh into the blender with the water to make a smooth thin paste. Add the mint and sugar to taste.

2 Quarter fill two tall glasses with crushed ice. Top up with the purée. Squeeze a few drops of lime juice in, and put a piece of cut lime on the rim of the glass.

3 Use salt instead of sugar for the savoury alternative.

Tak

· THIN SAVOURY YOGHURT DRINK ·

Serves 2

This appetiser comes from the state of Maharashtra.

INGREDIENTS

5oz (150g) yoghurt
10 fl oz (300ml) whey if available
(page 22) or water

1 teaspoon aromatic salt (page 30)
crushed ice

METHOD

1 Using the electric whisk mix the yoghurt, whey or water and salt.

2 Serve with crushed ice in two tall tumblers.

Masala Chai

· INDIAN TEA ·

Serves 1

Every visitor to India will have encountered the ubiquitous *masala chai*. It is offered by traders when one enters their shops, by officials in Government offices, and at tea stalls everywhere. The first time you have it will shock you – it is in fact an all-milk spicy brew-up and very sweet – but it grows on you. Often evaporated milk is involved.

INGREDIENTS

5 fl oz (150ml) milk
1 teaspoon tea leaves or 1 tea bag
1 teaspoon sugar
2 green cardamoms

1 bay leaf
1 clove
1 inch (2.5cm) cube ginger

METHOD

1 Put all the ingredients into a saucepan, and simmer for 3-4 minutes.

2 Strain the infusion into a cup and serve piping hot.

Irish Mysore Coffee

Serves 1

This is the glamorous serving of a cream-topped liqueur coffee which, served in a stemmed glass, resembles an Irish stout, hence the name. I use Scotch whisky here, but any spirit or liqueur will work.

INGREDIENTS

brewed coffee
2 teaspoons dark brown sugar

2-3 tablespoons Scotch whisky
3-4 tablespoons double cream

METHOD

1 Make a pot of strong black coffee. Instant will do, but real coffee – from Mysore in India if you can get it – tastes best.

2 Using a pretty stemmed glass of 6 fl oz (175ml) capacity, put the sugar into the bottom.

3 Pour in the coffee, to two-thirds full. Stir to dissolve the sugar thoroughly. Add the whisky and stir well.

4 Invert a teaspoon over the glass with its tip touching the glass and the top of the coffee, slowly pour the cream on to the spoon. It will float on top of the coffee.

5 If it sinks, either there is insufficient sugar, the cream is too thin, or you are pouring too fast.

Khus Sharbat

· ROSE-PETAL SHERBERT ·

Serves 2

Sherberts originated in Persia and were introduced to India by the wife of the emperor Jehangir, Noorjehan. It was said that the first time she smelt rose petals in Kashmir's Shalimar gardens, it reminded her of her youth in Persia and a long-forgotten drink.

INGREDIENTS

30 rose petals
10 fl oz (300ml) water

1 tablespoon caster sugar
1 fresh lime, halved

METHOD

1 Soak the rose petals in the water overnight (12 hours maximum), then bring to the boil. As soon as it boils add the sugar and allow it to cool. Then strain it.

2 Put some crushed ice into two tumblers. Add the rosewater. Squeeze a few drops of lime juice in, and put a piece of cut lime on the rim of the glasses.

Après Curry

✳

In India and the surrounding countries there is a phenomenon which has no parallel in the West. It is a complete and massive industry, called simply *'paan'*. It involves an army of *'paan wallahs'* – traders – who prepare *'paan masalas'* or mixtures, dispensing their wares in smart restaurants, or street kiosks, or even door-to-door. Their customers include just everyone – a billion consumers, from the humblest street sweeper to the grandest ex-maharajah.

The observant visitor to India will have noticed these street kiosks with their bright dark green paan leaves and dozens of silver pots containing all sorts of weird and wonderful ingredients. The kiosks are invariably busy with individuals pointing here and there and then disappearing with a mystery green package which is popped into the mouth. Morning, noon and night, at home, at restaurants and in the street people are forever chewing. Smiling mouths and even teeth are bright red, and the less couth individual occasionally and deftly spits a copious red mouthful into a corner.

They are eating paan. This is best defined as a collection of edible ingredients, ranging from very bitter to very sweet. Some are dry seeds, and some are acidic and alkaline wet pastes.

Some paan ingredients have found their way to the Indian restaurant in the West, in the form of a colourful and fragrant mixture called supari (see page 273). Supari has rightly become accepted and popular as a mandatory conclusion to the curry meal, a kind of Après Curry!

It is just one of a number of ingredients which are available to paan fans. I examine them in this chapter, giving an assortment of paan ingredients which should be acceptable to everyone and which will bring an additional dimension to 'Après Curry' at home.

PAAN LEAVES

We met peppercorns, India's king of spices, on page 40 and it is not an exaggeration to say that pepper is the most widely used spice in the world. As well as the peppercorn, though, there is another item which grows on the pepper creeper, and which is harvested and eaten in immense tonnages all over the sub-continent. Unlike pepper this part is virtually unknown in the West – it is the leaf.

Called *Paan* (or *Pan*) in Hindi (and *Vethilai* in Tamil), it is not only a fundamental ingredient of paan, it has given its name to the paan industry. The leaf is darkish green and heart-shaped, with an average size of 5-6 inches (13-15cm) in length. They appear in the photograph on page 255. The leaf itself is rather bitter in taste, and it is quite tough, although not scaly. It serves as the wrapping for a number of ingredients, which are then consumed as a breath freshener, digestive aid and tooth cleaner.

BETEL NUT

A major ingredient of paan, the areca or betel nut grows on a very tall palm which is slimmer than the coconut tree. The nuts grow all over the sub-continent in clusters of several dozens. Each nut has an outer casing, rather like the horse chestnut or nutmeg which is discarded revealing the nut inside. This resembles a nutmeg in colour, shape and size. When dried it is cut with a purpose-made cutter (a two-handled guillotine, a cross between a secateur and a nut cracker), revealing mottled buff and brown colours inside. (The nuts and their cutter can be seen at the foot of the photo on page 255.)

Called *supari* in Hindi, *supadi* in Nepalese and *pakku* in Tamil, it is cut in chunks, finely sliced or shredded and is consumed voraciously on its own or in combination with other ingredients.

It is said to be an aphrodisiac and a digestive. It also is used ceremonially. It is rather bitter and is an acquired taste.

SOME INDIVIDUAL PAAN INGREDIENTS

Some aromatic spices can be chewed on their own at any time. Board an Indian Airlines flight and you'll be offered some as soon as you are seated. The choice is quite wide.

Spices

The following spices we have met already (see pages 36-38): aniseeds, green cardamom seeds, cloves and fennel seeds.

Seeds

Other seeds which we have not encountered in detail are seeds from the squash or gourd family. *Magaz* is a melon seed and *charmagaz* is a combination of four *(char)* squash seeds – cucumber, marrow, watermelon and pumpkin. All are oval creamy coloured discs with a tasty nutty flavour.

Nuts

Pine nuts *(chilgoza)* are also good in this context. As is the cuddapah almond or in Hindi, the *chirongi* or *charauli*. They are small, round pale brown and quite aromatic, almost minty in flavour.

Tobacco

The bitter taste so beloved by many paan eaters is enhanced by tobacco shreds.

Sweeteners

To counter the bitter tastes, sugar crystals or sugar balls are used. Factory-made sugar-coated fennel seeds or the smaller sugar-coated aniseeds come in white plus bright food colouring colours – red, pink, orange, yellow and green.

PRESENTATION

As you will now have gathered, paan eating is not only taken for granted in the sub-continent, it is also a perfect subject for ritual presentation.

There are some beautiful and elaborate paan boxes *(paana bata)*. Traditionally they are made of silver, and they usually incorporate heart shapes – large ones to house the leaves and a number of smaller ones to house the owners' choice of ingredients – seeds, pastes, betel, etc. There is seemingly no limit to the intricacies of design of the paan presenter. Even on the road, the middle class have a portable kit – perhaps a shallow silver leaf box with an accompanying embroidered pouch with enough pockets to hold the owner's favourite additives.

Après Curry, at home, we can use our ingenuity to serve a combination of acceptable delights – I recommend six to eight items in tiny bowls, for example:

> supari mix
> green cardamoms
> fennel seeds
> sugar-coated seeds
> sugared almonds (page 262)
> lime paste and/or rose-petal jam (page 274)
> pink coconut (page 275)

To serve, give the diners a small plate and cake fork and let them pick out their own choice of items. Serve with liqueur coffee (see page 268).

Supari Mix

Makes ample quantity

There are numerous combinations of mixtures of ingredients based on the betel nut, which can be purchased from specialist stores. This mixture combines bitter, savoury and sweet tastes.

INGREDIENTS

2oz (50g) shredded betel nuts
1oz (25g) sugar-coated aniseed or brown sugar crystals
1oz (25g) fennel seeds, roasted

1 tablespoon sunflower (charonji) seeds
1 teaspoon cummin seeds, roasted

METHOD

Mix all the ingredients together and store in an airtight jar, where it will keep well for months.

Lime Paste

This smooth white paste is one of the traditional options spread on to paan leaves.

In India it is actually made from quicklime, a white caustic alkaline powder (calcium oxide) made by grinding limestone. Water is added to make a paste. Alone, it is tasteless, and its appearance in paan is to supply calcium. Paan wallahs add freshly squeezed lime juice and even pink food colouring.

This recipe creates a tart paste using cornflour in place of quicklime.

INGREDIENTS

1 teaspoon cornflour   *freshly squeezed lime juice*
1 teaspoon icing sugar (optional)

METHOD

Mix together the flour and sugar and sufficient lime juice to make a spreadable paste.

Rose-Petal Jam

Serves 4

Many devotees of paan prefer a sweet rather than an acidic or bitter taste. I obtained this fragrant recipe from Delhi's favourite paan shop, Prince Pan Centre near the Red Fort.

INGREDIENTS

20 rose petals   *3 tablespoons caster sugar*
4 fl oz (120ml) water   *1 tablespoon semolina*

METHOD

1 Soak the rose petals in the water overnight (12 hours maximum).

2 Strain the water into a saucepan, add the sugar and bring to the simmer, reducing it to a syrup.

3 Chop up the rose petals. Take the syrup off the heat, add the semolina and the petals and mix in well.

4 When cold spread it on the paan leaves as required.

Pink Coconut

Serves 4

Attractive in appearance and very tasty in a paan leaf or with supari mix.

INGREDIENTS

3 tablespoons desiccated coconut
1 tablespoon caster sugar
1 teaspoon strawberry jam,
   puréed

2-3 teaspoons cream (any type)

METHOD

Mix the ingredients together to create a sticky pink mass.

A Home-made Paan

Here is a typical combination of ingredients for filling a paan leaf.

INGREDIENTS

1 paan leaf
¼ teaspoon lime paste
½ teaspoon rosepetal jam

supari mix
1 clove
edible silver or gold leaf (page
   109)

METHOD

1 Wash the paan leaf and dry it.

2 Spread the lime paste over the inside of the leaf. Put the jam and the supari mix into the middle. Fold one-third of the leaf over the filling then the other third over.

3 Close down the top, if it will, and peg with a clove (see the photograph on page 255).

4 Optionally cover the case with edible silver or gold leaf.

5 The correct and only practical way to eat paan.is to pop the whole thing into your mouth and chew it for ages.

Glossary

This glossary is very extensive, including some items not specifically mentioned in the recipes. It is intended to be used as a general reference work. If you do not find a particular word here it is worth checking to see whether it is in the index and can be found elsewhere in the book.

The 'Indian' words are mostly Hindi and some Urdu. The English spelling is 'standard' but can vary as words are translated phonetically.

A

Achar – Pickle

Adrak – Ginger

Ajwain or Ajowain – Lovage seeds

Akhni – Spicy consommé-like stock. Also called *yakni*

Aloo – Potato

Am – Mango

Am chur – Mango powder

Anardana – Pomegranate

Aniseed – *Saunf*. Small deliciously flavoured seeds resembling fennel seeds

Areca – Betel nut

Asafoetida – *Hing*. A rather smelly spice

Aserio – Small red-brown seeds with a slight aniseed flavour used medicinally

Ata or Atta – *Chupatti* flour. Fine wholemeal flour used in most Indian breads. English wholemeal is a suitable alternative.

B

Badain – Star anise

Badam – Almond

Balti – Balti dishes first appeared in the UK in the Midlands. Cubes of meat or chicken are marinated, then charcoal-grilled, then simmered in a sauce and usually served in a karahi or Balti pan

Bargar – The process of frying whole spices in hot oil

Basil – Used only in religious applications in Indian cooking, but widely in Thai cooking

Basmati – The best type of long-grain rice

Bay leaf – *Tej Pattia*. Aromatic spice

Besan – See *Gram flour*

Bhajee or Bhaji – Dryish mild vegetable curry

Bhajia – Deep-fried fritter, usually onion

Bhare – Stuffed

Bhoona or Bhuna – The process of cooking the spice paste in hot oil. A *bhoona* curry is usually dry and cooked in coconut

Bhunana – Roast

Bindi – Okra or ladies' fingers

Biriani – Traditionally rice baked with meat or vegetable filling with saffron, served with edible silver foil. The restaurant interpretation is a fried rice artificially coloured, with filling added

Blachan – see Shrimp Paste

Black salt – *Kala namak*. A type of salt, dark grey in colour. Its taste, of sea water, is relished in India but not, I find, in the West

Bombay Duck – A crispy deep fried fish starter or accompaniment to a curry. See page 46.

Bombay Potato – Small whole potatoes in curry and tomato sauce

Boti Kebab – Marinated cubes of lamb cooked in a tandoor oven

Brinjal – Aubergine

Burfi or Barfi – An Indian fudge-like sweetmeat made from reduced condensed milk, in various flavours

C

Cardamom – *Elaichi*. One of the most aromatic and expensive spices

Cashew nuts – *Kaju*

Cassia bark – Aromatic spice, related to cinnamon

Cayenne pepper – A blend of chilli powder from Latin America

Ceylon Curry – Usually cooked with coconut, lemon and chilli

Chana – Type of lentil. See *Dhal*

Charoli – Sweetish pink-coloured, irregularly shaped seeds with no English translation. Ideal in desserts. Sunflower seeds are a good alternative

Chawal – Rice

Chilgoze or Nioze – Small long creamy nuts with brown shells used in cooking or eaten raw

Chilli – *Mirch*. The hottest spice.

Chirongi or Charauli – Small rounded nuts resembling Egyptian lentils. Used in puddings or pullaos

Chor magaz – Melon seeds. Used as a thickener

Chupatti – A dry 6 inch (15cm) disc of unleavened bread. Normally griddle-cooked, it should be served piping hot. Spelling varies eg *Chuppati, Chapati* etc

Chutneys – The common ones are onion, mango and tandoori. There are dozens of others which rarely appear on the standard menu. See *Sambals*

Cinnamon – *Dalchini*. One of the most aromatic spices

Cloves – *Lavang*. Expensive and fragrant spice

Coriander – *Dhania*. One of the most important spices in Indian cookery. The leaves of the plant can be used fresh and the seeds whole or ground

Cummin or Cumin – *Jeera*. There are two types of seeds: *white* and *black*. The white seeds are a very important spice in Indian cookery. The black seeds (*kala jeera*) are nice in pullao rice and certain vegetable dishes. Both can be used whole or ground

Curry – The only word in this glossary to have no direct translation into any of the sub-continent's fifteen or so languages. The word was coined by the British in India centuries ago. Possible contenders for the origin of the word are, *korahi* or *karai* (Hindi), a wok-like frying-pan used all over India to prepare masalas (spice mixtures); *kurhi*, a soup-like dish made with spices, gram flour dumplings and buttermilk; *kari*, a spicy Tamil sauce; *turkuri*, a seasoned sauce or stew; *kari phulia*, *neem* or curry leaves; *kudhi* or *kadhi*, a yoghurt soup; or *koresh*, an aromatic Iranian stew

Curry lands – India is the main curry land with 800 million, mainly Hindu, people. Other curry lands are her Moslem neighbours to the west – Pakistan, Afghanistan, and, to a lesser extent, Iran which is the root of some Indian food. To the north lie Nepal and Bhutan whilst Moslem Bangladesh lies to the east. India's south-eastern curry-land neighbours include the predominantly Buddhist Burma and Thailand, whilst multinational Malaysia and Singapore, with huge, mainly Moslem Indian populations, are also curry lands. The tiny island of Sri Lanka has a very distinctive curry style and one must not forget significant pockets of curry-eating Asians in Africa and the Caribbean. The total number of people whose 'staple' diet is curry exceeds 1 billion people – 25 per cent of the world's population.

Curry leaves – *Neem* leaves or *kari phulia*. Small leaves a bit like bay leaves, used for flavouring

Cus cus – See poppy seed

D

Dahi – Yoghurt

Dalchini or Darchim – Cinnamon

Degchi, Dekhchi or Degh – Brass or metal saucepan without handles also called *Pateeli* or *batloi*

Dhal – Lentils. There are over 60 types of lentil in the sub-continent, some of which are very obscure. Like peas, they grow into a hard sphere measuring between 1/2 inch (1cm) (chickpeas) and 1/8 inch (3mm) (urid). They are cooked whole or split with skin, or split with the skin polished off. Lentils are a rich source of protein and when cooked with spices are extremely tasty. The common types are *chana* (resembling yellow split peas, used to make gram flour/

besan); *kabli chana* (chickpeas); *masoor* (the most familiar orangey-red lentil which has a green skin); *moong* (green-skinned lentil, used also to make bean sprouts); *toor*, or *toovar* (dark yellow and very oily); and *urid* (black skin, white lentil)

Dhania – Coriander

Dhansak – Traditional Parsee dish cooked in a purée of lentils, aubergine, tomato and spinach. Some restaurants also add pineapple pieces

Dill – Heart.

Do Piaza – Traditional meat dish. *Do* means two and *Piaza* means onion. It gets its name because onions appear twice in the cooking process

Doroo – Celery

Dosa or Dosai – A South Indian pancake made from rice and lentil flour. Usually served with a filling

Dum – Steam cooking. Long before the West invented the pressure cooker, India had her own method which lasts to this day. A pot with a close-fitting lid is sealed with a ring of dough. The ingredients are then cooked in their own steam under some pressure

E

Ekuri – Spiced scrambled eggs

Elaichi – Cardamom

F

Fennel – *Sunf* or *soonf*. A small green seed which is very aromatic, with aniseed taste.

Fenugreek – *Methi*. This important spice is used as seeds and in fresh or dried leaf form. It is very savoury and is used in many Northern Indian dishes

Fish sauce – Nam-pla (Thai), Nga-pya (Burmese), Patis (Philippine). It is the runny liquid strained from fermented anchovies, and is a very important flavouring agent

Five-Spice powder – Combination of five sweet and aromatic spices used in Chinese and Malay cooking. Usually ground. A typical combination would be equal parts of cinnamon, cloves, fennel seeds, star anise and Szechuan pepper

Foogath – Lightly cooked vegetable dish

G

Gajar – Carrot

Galingale or Galangel – A tuber related to ginger which comes in varieties called greater or lesser. It has a more peppery taste than ginger (which can be substituted for it). It is used in Thai cooking where it is called *kha*, and in Indonesian (*laos*) and Malay (*ken-*

kur). It is available in the UK in fresh form (rare), dried or powdered

Garam masala – Literally hot mixture. This refers to a blend of spices much loved in northern Indian cookery. The Curry Club garam masala contains nine spices

Garlic – *Lasan*

Ghee – Clarified butter or margarine much used in northern Indian cookery

Ginger – *Adrak* (fresh), *sont* (dried), a rhizome which can be used fresh, dried or powdered

Gobi or Phoolgobi – Cauliflower

Goor or Gur – Jaggery (palm sugar) or molasses

Gosht – Lamb, mutton or goat

Gram flour – *Besan.* Finely ground flour, pale blonde in colour, made from chana (see *Dhal*). Used to make *pakoras* and to thicken curries

Gulab jaman – An Indian dessert. Small 1 inch (2.5cm) diameter balls of flour and milk powder, deep-fried to golden and served cold in syrup. Cake-like texture

Gurda – Kidney. Gurda kebab is marinated kidneys skewered and cooked in the tandoor

H

Halva – Sweets made from syrup and vegetables or fruit. Served cold in small squares. It is translucent and comes in bright colours depending on ingredient used, eg orange (carrot), green (pistachio), red (mango), etc. Has texture thicker than Turkish delight. Sometimes garnished with edible silver foil

Handi – Earthenware cooking pot

Hasina kebab – Pieces of chicken breast, lamb or beef marinated in spices and then skewered and barbecued with onion, capsicum pepper, and tomato. Of Turkish origin

Hindi – Hindi is the official language of India. Although there are fourteen or so other languages in India, only Hindi translations have been used in this glossary. Spelling of Hindi words can vary in English because they are translated phonetically from many Hindi dialects

Hing – Asafoetida

Hopper – Kind of rice noodle found in Sri Lanka

Huldi – Turmeric

I

Idli – Rice and lentil flour cake served with light curry sauce. South Indian

Imli – Tamarind

Isgubul – Vegetable seed

J

Jaifal or Taifal – Nutmeg

Jaggery – see *Goor*

Jal Frezi – Sautéed or stir-fried meat or chicken dish, often with lightly cooked onion, garlic, ginger, green capsicum pepper and chilli

Jalebi – An Indian dessert. A flour, milk powder and yoghurt batter pushed through a narrow funnel into deep-frying oil to produce golden curly crispy rings. Served cold or hot in syrup

Javatri – Mace

Jeera or Zeera – Cummin

Jinga – Prawns

K

Kabli chana – Chickpeas. See *Dhal*

Kadhi – Yoghurt soup

Kaju – Cashew nut

Kala jeera – Black cummin seeds

Kala namak – Black salt

Kaleji – Liver

Kalongi – See Wild onion seeds

Karahi – *Karai, korai* etc. The Indian equivalent of the wok. The *karahi* is a circular two-handled round all-purpose cooking pan used for stir-frying, simmering, frying and deep-frying – in fact it is highly efficient for all types of cooking. Some restaurants cook in small *karahis* and serve them straight to the table with the food sizzling inside

Karela – Small, dark green, knobbly vegetable of the gourd family

Kashmir chicken – Whole chicken stuffed with minced meat

Kashmir curry – Restaurateurs' creation. A sweetish curry often using lychees or similar ingredient

Katori – Small serving bowls which go on a *thali* (tray)

Kebab – Skewered food cooked over charcoal. A process over 4,000 years old which probably originated in Turkey where 'kebab' means 'cooked meat'. It was imported to India by the Moslems centuries ago. (See Boti, Shami and Sheek kebabs)

Kecap manis – Indonesian version of soy sauce. It is sweeter and slightly sticky. Soy sauce is a good, though more salty, substitute

Keema – Minced meat curry

Kewra – Screwpine water. An extract of the flower of the tropical screwpine tree. It is a fragrant clear liquid used to flavour sweets. It is a cheap substitute for rosewater

Khir – Technique of making a sort of cream. Milk is cooked with cucumber and puréed

Khurzi – Lamb or chicken, whole with spicy stuffing and/or coating, also called *Kashi*

Kish mish – Sultanas

Kofta – Minced meat or vegetable balls in batter, deep-fried, and then cooked in a curry sauce

Kokum or Cocum – A variety of plum, pitted and dried. Prune-like and very sour. Also known in Malayan as mangosteen

Korma – To most restaurants this just means a mild curry. Traditionally it is very rich. Meat, chicken or vegetables are cooked in cream, yoghurt and nuts, and are fragrantly spiced with saffron and aromatic spices. Actually *korma* is a frying method and it is possible to find very hot *kormas*

Koya – Reducing milk to a thick sticky solid. Used for sweet making

Kulcha – Small leavened bread. It can be stuffed with mildly spiced mashed potato and baked in the tandoor

Kulfi – Indian ice cream. Traditionally it comes in vanilla, pistachio or mango flavours

Kus Kus – See poppy seed

L

Lasan – Garlic

Lassi or Lhassi – A refreshing drink made from yoghurt and crushed ice. The savoury version is *lhassi namkeen* and the sweet version is *lhassi meethi*

Lavang – Cloves

Lemongrass – *Takrai* (Thai), *serai* (Malay). A fragrant-leafed plant which imparts a subtle lemony flavour to cooking. Use ground powder (made from the bulb) as a substitute

Lentils – See *Dhal*

Lilva – A small oval-shaped bean which grows in a pod like the European pea

Lime Leaves – *Markrut* or citrus leaves. Used in Thai cooking, fresh or dried, to give a distinctive aromatic flavour

Loochees – A type of bread made in Bengal using white flour

Lovage – *Ajwain* or *ajowain*. Slightly bitter round seeds

M

Mace – *Javitri*. The outer part of the nutmeg

Macchi or Macchli – Fish

Madras – You will not find a traditional recipe for Madras curry. It is another restaurateurs' invention. But the people of South India *do* eat hot curries; some original chef must have christened his hot curry 'Madras' and the name stuck

Makhani – A traditional dish. Tandoori chicken is cooked in a ghee and tomato sauce

Makke – Cornflour

Makrut or Markrut – Citrus or lime leaf

Malai – Cream

Malaya – The curries of Malaya are traditionally cooked with plenty of coconut, chilli and ginger. In the Indian restaurant, however, they are usually mild and contain pineapple and other fruit

Mamra – Puffed *basmati* rice

Mango Powder – *Am chur*. A very sour flavouring agent

Masala – A mixture of spices which are cooked with a particular dish. Any curry powder is therefore a masala. It can be spelt a remarkable number of ways – massala, massalla, musala, mosola, massalam etc

Masoor – Red lentils. See *Dhal*

Mattar – Green peas

Meethi – Sweet

Melon seeds – *Chor magaz*

Methi – Fenugreek

Mirch – Pepper or chilli

Moglai or Moghlai – Cooking in the style of the Moghul emperors whose chefs took Indian cookery to the heights of gourmet cuisine three centuries ago. Few restaurateurs who offer Moglai dishes come anywhere near this excellence.

Mollee – Fish dishes cooked in coconut and chilli

Mooli – Large white radish

Moong – Type of lentil. See *Dhal*

Mulligatawny – A Tamil sauce (*molegoo* – pepper, *tunny* – water) which has become well known as a British soup

Murgh – Chicken

Murgh Masala(m) – A speciality dish of whole chicken, marinated in yoghurt and spices for 24 hours then stuffed and roasted. See also *Khurzi*

Mustard seeds – Small black seeds which become sweetish when fried

N

Namak – Salt

Nam Pla – Fish sauce

Naan or Nan – Leavened bread baked in the tandoor. It is teardrop shaped and about 8-10 inches (20-25cm) long. It must be served fresh and hot

Naan, Keema – Naan bread stuffed with a thin layer of minced meat curry then baked in the tandoor

Naan, Peshwari – Naan bread stuffed with almonds and/or cashew and/or raisins. Baked in tandoor

Nargis Kebab – Indian scotch eggs. Spiced minced meat around a hard-boiled egg, then deep fried

Naryal – Coconut

Neem – Curry leaf

Nga-Pi – Shrimp paste

Nga-Pya – Fish sauce

Nigella – Wild onion seeds

Nimboo – Lime (lemon)

Nutmeg – *Jaifal*

O

Okra – *Bindi*. A pulpy vegetable also known as ladies' fingers

P

Pan or Paan – Betel leaf folded around a stuffing – lime paste or various spices (see Supari) and eaten after a meal as a digestive

Pakoras – To all intents and purposes the same as the *bhajia*

Palak or Sag – Spinach

Panch Phoran – Five seeds (see page 29)

Paneer – Cheese made from cows' or buffaloes' milk which can be fried and curried

Papadom – Thin lentil flour wafers. When cooked (deep fried or baked) they expand to about 8 inches (20cm). They must be crackling crisp and warm when served. They come plain or spiced with lentils, pepper, garlic or chilli. Many spelling variations include popadom, pappodom etc

Paprika – Mild red ground pepper made from red capsicum peppers. Its main use is to give red colour to a dish

Paratha – A deep-fried bread

Pasanda – Meat, usually lamb, beaten and cooked in one piece

Patia – Parsee curry with a thick, dark brown, sweet and sour sauce

Patna – A long-grained rice

Pepper – *Mirch*. Has for centuries been India's most important spice. Peppercorns are a heat agent and can be used whole or ground

Phal or Phall – A very hot curry (the hottest), invented by restaurateurs

Piaz, Peeaz or Pyaz – Onion

Pickles – Pungent, hot pickled vegetables or meat essential to an Indian meal. Most common are lime, mango and chilli

Pistachio nut – *Pista magaz*. A fleshy, tasty nut which can be used fresh (the greener the better) or salted. It is expensive and goes well in savoury or sweet dishes such as biriani or pista kulfi (ice cream)

Poppy seed – Cus cus or Kus Kus. White seeds used in chicken curries, blue seeds used to decorate bread. (Not to be confused with the Moroccan national dish cous-cous, made from steamed semolina)

Prawn butterfly – Jinga prai patia. Prawn marinated in spices and fried in batter

Prawn puri – Prawns in a hot sauce served on puri bread

Pullao – Rice and meat or vegetables cooked together in a pan until tender. (see also Biriani)

Pullao rice – The restaurant name for rice fried with spices and coloured yellow

Pulses – Dried peas and beans, including lentils

Puri – A deep-fried unleavened bread about 4 inches (10cm) in diameter. It puffs up when cooked and should be served at once

Q

Quas chawal or Kesar chaval – rice fried in ghee, flavoured and coloured with saffron

R

Rai – Mustard seeds

Raita – A cooling chutney of yoghurt and vegetable which accompanies the main meal

Rajma – Red kidney beans

Rasgulla – Walnut-sized balls of semolina and cream cheese cooked in syrup (literal meaning 'juicy balls')

Rashmi kebab – Kebab minced meat inside a net-like omelette casing

Rasmalai – Rasgullas cooked in cream and served cold

Ratin jot – Alkanet root. It is used as a deep red dye for make-up, clothing and food

Rhogan Josh or Gosht – Literally it means red juice meat, or lamb in red gravy. It is a traditional northern Indian dish. Lamb is marinated in yoghurt, then cooked with ghee, spices and tomato. It should be creamy and spicy but not too hot. There are many ways of spelling it: rogon, roghan, rugon, rugin, etc; jush, joosh, jesh, etc; goosht, goose, gost, etc.

Rosewater – *Ruh gulab*. A clear essence extracted from rose petals to give fragrance to sweets. See Kewra

Roti – Bread

Ruh gulab – Rosewater essence

S

Sabzi – A generic term for vegetables

Saffron – *Kesar* or *zafron*. The world's most expensive spice, used to give a recipe a delicate yellow colouring and aroma

Sag or Saag – Spinach

Salt – *Namak*

Sambals – A Malayan term describing the side dishes accompanying the meal. Sometimes referred to on the Indian menu

Sambar – A South Indian vegetable curry made largely from lentils

Samosa – The celebrated triangular deep-fried meat or vegetable patties served as starters or snacks

Sarson ka sag – Mustard leaves (spinach-like)

Saunf or Souf – Aniseed

Seeng – Drumstick. A bean-like variety of gourd which looks exactly like a drumstick

Seenl – Allspice

Sesame seed – *Til*. Widely used in Indian cooking

Shami kebab – Round minced meat rissoles

Shashlik – Cubes of skewered lamb

Sheek or Seekh kebab – Spiced minced meat shaped on a skewer and grilled or barbecued. Also called shish kebab, shish meaning skewer in Turkish. See Kebab

Shrimp paste – *Blachan* (Malay), *Nga-Pi* (Burmese), *Kapi* (Thai). Very concentrated block of compressed shrimps. A vital flavouring for the cooking of those countries

Sonf – Fennel seed

Sont or Sonth – Dry ginger

Sub-continent – Term to describe India, Pakistan, Bangladesh, Nepal, Burma, and Sri Lanka as a group

Supari – Mixture of seeds and sweeteners for chewing after a meal. Usually includes aniseed or fennel, shredded betel nut, sugar balls, marrow seeds etc

T

Taipal or Jaiphal – Nutmeg

Tamarind – *Imli*. A date-like fruit used as a chutney, and in cooking as a souring agent

Tandoori – A style of charcoal cooking originating in north-west India (what is now Pakistan and the Punjab). Originally it was confined to chicken and lamb (see boti kebab) and naan bread. More recently it is applied to lobster etc. The meat is marinated in a reddened yoghurt sauce and placed in the tandoor

Tarka – Garnish of spices/onion

Tarka dhal – Lentils garnished with fried spices

Tava or Tawa – A heavy, almost flat, circular wooden-handled griddle pan used to cook Indian breads and

to 'roast' spices. Also ideal for many cooking functions from frying eggs and omelettes to making pancakes, etc

Tej patia – The leaf of the cassia bark tree. Resembles bay leaf which can be used in its place

Thali sets – To serve your meal in truly authentic Indian fashion use *thali* sets. A great and stylish talking point. Each diner is served a *thali* tray on which is a number of *katori* dishes in which different curry dishes, rice, chutneys, etc. are placed. Breads and papadoms go on the tray itself

Tikka – Skewered meat, chicken or seafood, marinated then barbecued or tandoori baked

Til – Sesame seed

Tindla – A vegetable of the cucumber family

Tindaloo – See Vindaloo

Toor or Toovar – A type of lentil. See Dhal.

Tukmeria or Tulsi – Black seeds of a basil family plant. Look like poppy seeds. Used in drinks

Turmeric – *Haldi* or *huldi*. A very important Indian spice, used to give the familiar yellow colour to curries. Use sparingly or it can cause bitterness

U

Udrak – Ginger

Urid – A type of lentil. See Dhal

V

Vark or Varak – Edible silver or gold foil

Vindaloo – A fiery hot dish from Goa. Traditionally it was pork marinated in vinegar with garlic. In the restaurant it has now come to mean just a very hot dish. Also sometimes called *bindaloo* or *tindaloo* (even hotter)

Z

Zafron – Saffron

Zeera – Cummin

The Store Cupboard

Here is a workable list of items you need to make the recipes in this book, subdivided into essential and non-essential. The essential items appear again and again in the recipes, the non-essential appear only in one or two. This list may look a bit formidable but remember, once you have the items in stock they will last for some time. I have listed in metric only as most of the packaging these days *is* metric only.

All items listed are available in the quantities stated, by post from The Curry Club, PO Box 7, Haslemere, Surrey GU27 1EP.

ESSENTIAL WHOLE SPICES

Bay leaves	3 g
Cardamom, black or brown	30 g
Cardamom, green or white	30 g
Cassia bark	30 g
Chillies	11 g
Cloves	20 g
Coriander seeds	60 g
Cummin seeds, white	25 g
Curry leaves, dry	2 g
Fennel seeds	27 g
Fenugreek leaves, dry	18 g
Mustard seeds	65 g
Peppercorns, black	47 g
Sesame seeds, white	57 g
Wild onion seeds	47 g

NON-ESSENTIAL GROUND SPICES

Asafoetida	50 g
Cardamom, green	25 g
Cassia bark	25 g
Cloves	25 g
Galangale (Laos)	20 g
Lemon Grass (Scrai)	20 g
Mango Powder	100 g

ESSENTIAL GROUND SPICES

Black pepper	100 g
Chilli powder	100 g
Coriander	100 g
Cummin	100 g
Garam masala	50 g
Garlic powder and/or flakes	100 g
Ginger	100 g
Paprika	100 g
Turmeric	100 g

ESSENTIAL DRY FOODS

Basmati rice	2 kg
Coconut Powder	100 g
Gram flour	1 kg
Masoor (red) lentils	500 g

NON-ESSENTIAL WHOLE SPICES

Alkenet root	3 g
Cinnamon quill	6 pieces
Cummin seeds, black	25 g
Dill seeds	25 g
Fenugreek seeds	47 g
Ginger, dried	6 pieces
Lovage seeds	27 g
Mace	8 g
Nutmeg, whole	6 nuts
Panch phoran	30 g

Pomegranate seeds	30 g
Poppy seeds	52 g
Saffron stamens	1/2 g

NON-ESSENTIAL DRY FOODS

Food colouring powder, red (beetroot powder)	25 g
Food colouring powder, yellow (annatto)	25 g
Lentils –	
Channa, split	500 g
Moong green, whole	500 g
Toor or tovar, split	500 g
Urid, whole black	500 g
Nuts –	
Almond, whole	50 g
Almond, ground	100 g
Cashew	100 g
Peanuts, raw	100 g
Pistachio	100 g
Papadoms, spiced and plain (pack)	300 g
Puffed rice (mamra)	100 g
Red kidney beans	500 g
Rice flour	500 g
Rose water, bottle	7 fl oz
Sev (gram flour snack)	200 g
Silver leaf (edible)	6 sheets
Supari mixture	100 g
Tamarind block	300 g

Index

Curry Club Books

The Curry Club Indian Restaurant Cookbook
Hints, tips and methods and approximately 150 recipes, incorporating all your restaurant favourites.

The Curry Club Favourite Restaurant Curries
The Club's favourite restaurants give their favourite curry recipes plus many new tips and secrets.

The Curry Club Indian Vegetarian Cookbook
150 totally new recipes, all vegetarian, all authentic to the Curry Lands, plus helpful background information.

The Curry Club Favourite Middle Eastern Recipes
150 spicy, tasty and delicious recipes from the 25 countries of the Middle East plus plentiful background information.

The Curry Club Chinese Restaurant Cookbook
Over 150 excellent recipes from top Chinese chefs and restaurants around the world.

The Curry Club Balti Curry Cookbook
The first ever cookbook on this exciting new curry technique.

Curry Club Tandoori and Tikka Dishes
60 recipes for all your favourite tandoori and tikka dishes, plus accompaniments.

Curry Club Vindaloo and Other Hot Curries
60 of the hottest and spiciest recipes in the world.

The Little Curry Book
A perfect small gift, this book contains anecdotes, fables and historical facts about curry, plus 16 popular recipes.

The Good Curry Guide
A guide to the 1000 best curry restaurants in Britain.

The above books are all available through your local bookshop. For further information on these and other Piatkus publications, please write to:

Piatkus Books
Freepost 7 (WD 4505)
London W1E 4EZ

PIATKUS